Alcatraz

The Last Escape

Ken Widner and Mike Lynch

Essex, Connecticut

LYONS
PRESS

An imprint of Globe Pequot, the trade division of
The Rowman & Littlefield Publishing Group, Inc.
4501 Forbes Blvd., Ste. 200
Lanham, MD 20706
www.rowman.com

Distributed by NATIONAL BOOK NETWORK

British Library Cataloguing in Publication Information available

Library of Congress Cataloging-in-Publication Data

Names: Widner, Ken, author. | Lynch, Mike, 1962- author.
Title: Alcatraz : the last escape / Ken Widner, Mike Lynch.
Description: Essex, Connecticut : Lyons Press, 2024. | Includes
  bibliographical references.
Identifiers: LCCN 2023048112 (print) | LCCN 2023048113 (ebook) | ISBN
  9781493081233 (paperback) | ISBN 9781493081240 (epub)
Subjects: LCSH: Anglin, Clarence. | Anglin, John. | United States
  Penitentiary, Alcatraz Island, California. | Escaped prisoners—United
  States—Biography. | Escapes—United States—History—20th century.
Classification: LCC HV8658.A54 W54 2024 (print) | LCC HV8658.A54 (ebook)
  | DDC 365/.641—dc23/eng/20240131
LC record available at https://lccn.loc.gov/2023048112
LC ebook record available at https://lccn.loc.gov/2023048113

♾™ The paper used in this publication meets the minimum requirements of American National
Standard for Information Sciences—Permanence of Paper for Printed Library Materials, ANSI/
NISO Z39.48-1992.

Contents

Contents

PREFACE

On those occasions when I look back on my life, I can't remember a time when I haven't been aware of my uncles' famous escape from Alcatraz Federal Penitentiary. Though I have no personal memories of John and Clarence Anglin, having been one and a half years old when they broke out on June 11, 1962, everything about them and what they did has made an impact on me as deep and significant as any person I've ever known. In many ways, my family's privacy has been ripped from us since that fateful day when we were thrust onto the world's stage. And this continued fascination with John and Clarence has intruded into our lives countless times since.

From that day forward my family has done its best to preserve their memories, reminding everyone they were uncles, brothers, sons, and friends before becoming notorious escapees. But when gaps exist regarding what we know about a person, we have a tendency to fill in those gaps. More often than not, this "filling process" is based on our own assumptions and interpretations of the truth rather than on the truth itself. Sadly, this has been the unfortunate outcome regarding my uncles. Many books have been written about them and the Alcatraz escape over the years, along with a host of television documentaries, which usually repeat the same inaccuracies and omissions. And since the people who write these books and are interviewed on these programs are lauded as experts, what they've purported to be "the truth" has become accepted as canon over time.

The same can be said for the 1979 film *Escape from Alcatraz*, starring Clint Eastwood. Though we as a family applauded the filmmakers' efforts to bring the escapees' story to the screen, which has had the effect of keeping this important historic event in the public's eye, the movie has also caused my family anger and frustration. Never once did Mr. Eastwood or the makers of the movie sit down with us and find out just who John and Clarence were, where they grew up, or what they wanted for their lives. Yes, they were criminals who repeatedly went to prison for a multitude of crimes, including robbing a bank, but they were also poor farmers who wanted better lives for themselves. Rather than spend the time to find out the truth, the film's decision-makers perpetuated the accepted narrative that Frank Morris, the third member of the escape, came up with the plan, and his uneducated compatriots, John and Clarence, pretty much went along with what he said and did. In actuality, the truth is very much different.

Rightly or wrongly, my family has been fiercely protective of what happened to John and Clarence after the escape, though the FBI and other government agencies have done everything in their power to pry the truth from us, some of it bordering on the illegal. Though many may disagree, my uncles were part of a family that still believes in sheltering them from those who'd do them harm. No one is disputing the fact both brothers deserved to go to prison after the 1958 bank robbery in Columbia, Alabama, but not many people know that their public defender was good friends with the judge, and that they were assured if they pled guilty to the crime, per his recommendation, they'd most likely get out of a federal prison in five years or less. The judge instead opted for harsher sentences. John was given ten years for the robbery, Clarence fifteen. And because the brothers pled guilty to the robbery, they were also given an additional twenty-five years each for state time. This great injustice likewise resulted in a fatal outcome for their brother Alfred, who also participated in the bank robbery. He died in prison under suspicious circumstances in January 1964.

When you add all these elements into the equation, it is easy to see why we have been less than cooperative with the authorities over the years. And so, we have kept the secret my family has known for years, that my uncles didn't drown when they put their homemade raft into the frigid San Francisco waters on June 11, 1962, but made it to freedom. Though the exact location where they lived after the escape has been sought by the FBI, the U.S. Marshals Service, and amateur sleuths since, no one has ever found them. Nor were they aware that my uncles built lives for themselves as farmers, even getting married and having children. But as ingenious as their escape plan was and is, John, Clarence, and Frank needed help pulling it off. One man in particular, famous mob boss Mickey Cohen, proved indispensable. And it is this important relationship and his connections in the underworld that set my uncles' plan of escape in motion.

But the trail of accomplices doesn't end there. My uncles also crossed paths with other important people not lost on history, such as notorious criminal James "Whitey" Bulger, Cohen's girlfriend the exotic dancer Candy Barr, Chief Justice Earl Warren, and Robert Kennedy, along with other notable figures who impacted my uncles' lives in countless ways.

The full story of John and Clarence Anglin has waited decades to be told, and it's bigger than three inmates who broke out of a prison everyone thought escape proof. It is my hope you too will come to believe, as I do, that they did not die during their extraordinary escape from Alcatraz, but made it to freedom and started new lives. Why? Because it's all true.

Ken Widner

Disclaimer: Mike and I have spent thousands of hours over the years searching for and researching every piece of information we could find on John and Clarence Anglin and Frank Morris. Our goal from the beginning has been a depiction of the escapees that is both thorough and accurate. Unfortunately, as with all things historical, the source material will never provide a complete picture since there are always gaps. And so, in an effort to tell the whole story, there were occasions when we bridged those gaps through the use of narratives extrapolated from photographs, historical records, family history, letters, and personal recollections.

Chapter 1

June 11, 1962

THE LIGHTHOUSE BEAM SWEPT ACROSS CELLBLOCK B'S CONCRETE ROOF, briefly illuminating a ventilation shaft before moving away in a different direction.

When the roof fell dark again, the vent cover jerked up a few inches, then stopped when the beam briefly returned. After several moments, the cover slowly moved up again, until a lone arm pushed it over the side and it landed hard on the roof with a heavy thud. The noise startled several

John and Clarence Anglin
UNITED STATES PENITENTIARY, ALCATRAZ

dozen seagulls perched nearby, and they flew off, their high-pitched cries filling the air.

A small periscope appeared above the shaft's lip and scanned the area. The handmade device slipped back down when the searchlight swept across the roof a third time.

After several moments, John Anglin, aged thirty-two, pulled himself out of the shaft and crouched down next to it. Looking upward at the gulls flapping about, he watched as they disappeared into the night. The roof silent again, John peered into the opening.

"All clear," he whispered.

Dressed in the same blackened garb as his brother, Clarence, thirty-one, appeared next. He handed John two hundred-foot extension cords, a bed blanket, rubber raft, three life vests, and wood oars. Clarence lifted himself out of the vent, followed by Frank Morris, thirty-five. Brief smiles appeared on all three.

"We did it," Clarence declared. "We actually made it out."

"We're not home yet," John shot back. "Get goin' before a searchlight catches us."

The three divvied up their things and made their way to the roof's edge. A bitter wind stung their faces as John scanned the bay. His eyes lit with recognition.

"I think that's it," he said, then pointed.

"You sure?" Morris asked.

He looked in the same direction.

"Must be. A white boat. And I saw some lights flash."

Clarence stepped between the two. "Let's not stand here arguin'. We'll know soon enough when we're in the water."

Locating the metal drainpipe that went from the cellblock roof to the ground below, they lowered their things with one of the extension cords, then shinnied down the cellblock to the bottom, their actions slow and measured so as not to make any noise.

Taking a quick look around, John, Clarence, and Frank stood before a twelve-foot fence topped with barbed wire. Prepared for the setback, Clarence climbed up with the blanket and laid it over the top, then tossed their things onto the other side. John went next, then Frank. The three grabbed their gear and started for the water. When one of the search-lights briefly illuminated the area, they ducked behind the water tower until the beam passed them by.

"That was close," John said between winded breaths.

The three grabbed their gear and hurried down the steep incline straight for the water's edge, the sounds of small waves hitting the rocky shore growing louder after each step.

When they reached the seawall, Morris laid out the raft stitched together from prison-issued raincoats and attached it to a concertina he had converted into a pump. After several pushes, the raft began to fill with air.

Knowing the guards in the towers could spot them at any moment, the three wasted no time filling it to capacity.

"You sure this is gonna work?" Morris asked. "Angel Island's right there. Less risky."

"Keep your voice down," John snapped back. "The guards will pick us off for sure if they hear us. We stick with the plan."

Morris let out a hot breath but acquiesced.

Without a word, the three put on their life vests and inflated them, then threw their things into the raft as Morris pushed it away from shore.

"Man, this water's cold. You sure we can trust Cohen?"

"Quit your complainin'," Clarence groused. "He said they'll be waitin'. But that won't mean spit if we get to the dock and the boat's gone."

"They'd better be waitin'," Morris declared. "That's all I gotta say."

The three got into the raft and paddled to the south side of the island. With each push of their oars the very real fear a guard might take a good look at one of the dummy heads placed on their pillows before leaving never lingered far from their thoughts. Could they get to the transport in time if the alarm sounded?

Through the haze a faint outline appeared in the dim light: the boat pier. To the right of the dock, the guardhouse stood like a dark silhouette. Between the building and pier, a lone guard took a drag from a cigarette, the smoke from his lungs billowing into the brisk air when he exhaled. But a more immediate problem stretched upward a good fifty feet, the pier guard tower. Equipped with a searchlight and an unobstructed view of the eastern side of the island, guards had orders of shoot to kill any escapee on sight.

"Didn't expect the tower to be that close," Clarence murmured. "Do ya think we can get by it?"

"Don't know," Morris replied. "Could be tricky."

"Shut up, you two," John barked back. "You want 'em to hear us? We go for the boat."

All three sank down like Navy SEALs as they paddled their way toward the dock.

In the distance, a foghorn blared into the night, which momentarily masked the sounds of their oars in the water. They slipped past the tower unseen and slowly approached the transport. John had Clarence ready the second extension cord. But when he searched for it among their things, Clarence realized he had left it on the beach. Morris looked like he was fit to be tied, as did John. Their entire plan rested on that cord, and with it their rendezvous with Cohen's boat waiting for them in the middle of the bay.

"Maybe we can find some rope on the dock," Clarence whispered. "Must be somethin' there we can use."

John thought it over a moment, then nodded in agreement.

They positioned the raft a short distance from the dock. Clarence then rose up and scanned the wharf. Fortunately for them the guard had gone into the guardhouse, presumably to warm himself.

"Don't take too long," John admonished his brother. "The boat will be leavin' soon." Not that they didn't already know that.

Clarence climbed onto the pier and looked about. His heart was pounding in his chest, and nothing ropelike showed itself. He decided to take a chance and went toward the defensive barracks used by the guards. The light was better there, but so were his odds of getting caught. Clarence stopped when he saw something that looked like a wheelbarrow and darted over to it. In the bucket he found power tools, gloves, and most important, another hundred-foot extension cord. He grabbed the cord and hurried back to the raft.

"Look what I found," he declared in triumph.

"Perfect," John replied.

Clarence looped the extension cord around the boat's rudder and held on to both ends. They then pushed back a little and waited in the dark.

At about 11:15 p.m. a guard came out of the guardhouse. He untied the rope from the cleat holding the boat in place and jumped on board. After a quick check on deck, he went into the wheelhouse and started her up. Moments later the extension cord grew taut as the boat headed for Municipal Pier, located at San Francisco's edge. The three held on tight as the raft bounced off the wake created by the engines' propellers, the water's cold spray slapping their faces.

The transport made a sudden turn toward the right, then straightened out again when Municipal Pier came into view. At that moment the white boat sitting on the water not far away flashed its lights, then went dark again.

"That's it!" John shouted above the engines.

Clarence let go of one end of the cord, which spun around the rudder in an instant and released them from the transport. Coming to a stop in the choppy water, the raft bobbed up and down several times until the waves slowly calmed. All three collectively turned their attention toward the transport. Fearing the worst, they watched and waited, but the vessel held its course straight for the pier.

"He's not coming back," Morris finally declared.

A slow realization they had actually succeeded washed over them, but they weren't home yet. John, Clarence, and Frank put their paddles in the water and went as fast as they could toward the white boat.

Several men on deck spotted their approach and waved in reply. "Ahoy," one of them called out.

Clarence waved back, pushing even harder with his paddle.

Their hearts pumping with excitement, the three finally made it to the boat. A rope ladder dropped into the water, and they climbed on board.

"Welcome to freedom," one of the men said, patting John on the shoulder.

John looked back at Alcatraz and smiled.

A few short hours before, the lives of John Anglin, Clarence Anglin, and Frank Morris could not have been more different.

Just before lights-out at 9:30 p.m., John quietly laid on his bunk in cell B-150. In the cell next to him, Clarence had already made his way into the utility corridor between the cellblocks. For the past six months the culmination of the clandestine activities orchestrated by John and Clarence, along with their associates Frank Morris and the fourth man in their group, Allen West, had led them to this moment—escape from what everyone considered inescapable: Alcatraz Federal Penitentiary, also known as the Rock.

Everything had been prepared to the last detail. When the guards went down the cellblocks while the prisoners slept, they were ready, the tools and equipment the four had meticulously fashioned or stolen lying in wait. Included in their arsenal were the dummy heads fashioned by John and Clarence from soap, concrete dust, paint, and even hair smuggled from the barbershop where Clarence worked. Appearing lifelike to the casual eye, these were placed on their pillows, half covered with a blanket, tricking the guards into thinking the escapees were asleep.

The four had also spent the past few months acquiring raincoats given to them by their fellow inmates, more than fifty in all, which they cut and fashioned into a fourteen-foot rubber raft, along with Mae West life preservers for each man.

John met Allen West, a previous acquaintance, shortly after he arrived at Alcatraz in 1960. The two had served time together at the state penitentiary in Florida back in 1957, and John believed, despite West's unpredictable and arrogant nature, he was a man he could trust. As he had likewise attempted numerous prison escapes over the years, it's not hard to understand why John brought West into the fold. The same could be said for Morris. He and Clarence first met at Raiford Prison in Florida in the late 1940s. A convicted bank robber who successfully escaped from Louisiana State Penitentiary before being recaptured, Morris's high intelligence and resourcefulness were exactly what the group needed.

The four often met in the exercise yard, one of the few places they could talk openly about their plan of escape.

As the leader of the group, John determined the first order of business was dividing up the tasks required of them, such as making wooden paddles, fashioning dummy heads, and acquiring as many raincoats as possible for making a raft and life vests. They also required tools for their work, like spoons for digging and paint and brushes for the dummy heads and fake air vents. As for masking the noise while the others dug, Morris played his accordion in his cell.[1]

The years of cold, humidity, and salt air had taken their toll on the concrete at Alcatraz, which was opened on July 1, 1934. The elements ate away at the lime and aggregate, softening the mixture over the years. By the time John, Clarence, Morris, and West arrived, the vents in the back of their cells were ready for the diggers' tools.

On the night of June 11, 1962, everything had been set. Yet, despite months of planning, the escapees also understood the risks facing them: seven inmates shot and killed by guards during previous escape attempts, two others who drowned, shark-infested waters, and years added to their sentences if caught. But their longing for freedom outweighed the obvious dangers.

Frank Morris and Allen West
UNITED STATES PENITENTIARY, ALCATRAZ

7

By lights-out at 9:30 p.m., John, Clarence, and Morris had removed the false grilles in the backs of their cells and collected their things. As soon as the cellblock went dark, West likewise started on his, but then encountered a problem.

He had been given the job of constructing the life preservers and paddles for the raft, which he did atop the cellblock during the day while assigned the job of painting, and so never finished digging out his vent until the night of the escape.[2] Unfortunately for West, he underestimated the time it would take to widen the hole sufficiently and meet up with the others.

In the meantime, Morris went to the top of the cellblock and retrieved the dummy heads. He, John, and Clarence dressed up their beds so it appeared they were asleep.

When the three realized West was having trouble, Clarence tried kicking out the grille from his side of the utility corridor, but it didn't budge, not to mention the noise he made could give them away. Morris and the Anglins had no choice but to leave without West.[3]

The water pipes that fed into each cell aided the escapees as they made the thirty-foot climb to the cellblock roof. The raft, life preservers, paddles, and extension cords they had stashed there were ready to go.

All three squeezed through the ten-inch-wide ventilation shaft and pushed the cover onto the roof. Keeping to the shadows as much as possible, John, Clarence, and Morris scurried across the roof toward the drainpipe affixed to the side of the building. They shinnied down fifty feet to the ground below near the shower area entrance. Keeping a wary eye on the guards in the towers, the three scaled a twelve-foot-tall fence topped by barbed wire to an area on the northeast section of the island that worked as a blind spot from Gun Tower No. 1's searchlight.[4] Finding themselves on a hill that overlooked the bay, the escapees hurried down the steep rocky slope to the water's edge.

Morris then used a converted concertina and inflated the raft as fast as possible, lest they risk getting shot by one of the guards. They then inflated their homemade life preservers.

The three climbed into the raft and paddled toward the boat dock on the south side of the island. Unknown to them at the time, they had

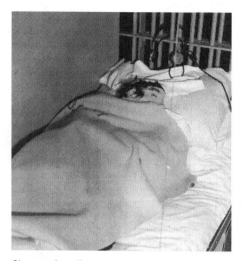

Clarence's cell
FBI

left behind the hundred-foot extension cord needed to hitch a ride on the transport boat.

In West's account of the escape, he told the FBI they planned on paddling to Angel Island, stealing a car, and heading to either Washington or Mexico. However, a recording made in 1992 by Fred Brizzi, a childhood friend of the Anglins, tells a very different story. In his account, John, Clarence, and Morris attached an extension cord to the last transport of the night and met up with a boat provided by LA crime boss Mickey Cohen, whom the brothers had known prior to their incarceration at Alcatraz.

When West had finally chipped away enough concrete from the grille opening, he slipped into the utility corridor and reached the cell-block roof around 1:45 a.m. But it was too late. The three were gone. West had no choice but to return to his cell, where nearby prisoners heard him sobbing.[5]

Most people today, including the FBI and the U.S. Marshals Service, believe the three drowned during their bid for freedom and were likely swept out into the ocean by the tide, never to be seen again. Authorities base their conclusion on certain items found in the waters around the island in the days after the escape:

> On June 14, a Coast Guard cutter picked up a paddle floating about 200 yards off the southern shore of Angel Island. . . . Workers on another boat found a wallet wrapped in plastic complete with names, addresses, letters, and photos of the Anglins' friends and relatives. . . . On June 22 a prison boat picked up a deflated life jacket made from the same material 50 yards off of Alcatraz Island. No other evidence of

the men's fate was ever found. According to the final FBI report, the escapees' raft was never recovered.[6]

Anyone else examining the same evidence would likely draw the same conclusion. For most inmates, photos of family and loved ones are some of their most prized possessions. If the escapees had gone to all the trouble of bringing those cherished items with them, they wouldn't be so careless as to let the photos fall into the water. But if the men had drowned, this would explain finding them in San Francisco Bay after the escape. This would also account for the other items found by searchers the next few days, such as the life vest and paddle. As such, the lack of any tangible evidence of their survival paints the picture that John and Clarence Anglin and Frank Morris died in the frigid San Francisco waters on June 11, 1962.

If this is indeed what happened, then the search is over, and we're left to admire the three's ingenuity executing such an escape. However, the conclusions drawn by people in general and those investigative authorities assigned to the case may be premature. A careful examination of the evidence reveals additional clues that strongly suggest the escapees in fact survived.

One, an off-duty police officer by the name of Robert Checchi, claimed to have seen a white boat with flashing lights near Alcatraz Island the night of the escape.

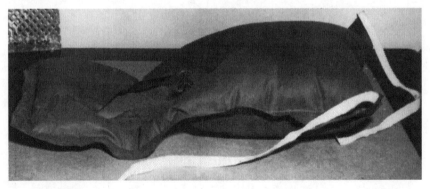

Life preserver
FBI

Two, a hundred-foot extension cord was found near where authorities believe the three slipped their raft into the water. An electrical cord of similar length was reported missing from the dock the day after the escape.[7] If John, Clarence, and Frank had drowned or planned on paddling to Angel Island, why did they replace the cord they had left behind?

Three, a dying man made a deathbed confession about the Alcatraz escape, in which he claimed he was on the boat that rescued the three and whisked them away to freedom.[8]

Four, Fred Brizzi, childhood friend of the brothers, claimed to have met them alive and well in 1975.

And lastly, Allen West asserted the four of them had planned to paddle to Angel Island and then make their way to either Washington or Mexico. The FBI sent military police to the island, who searched every inch of it. Their official report states, "No evidence was found to indicate the Escapees ever reached this island."[9] Yet if this was the case, why does a police APB dated June 12 claim the raft used by the escapees was found on Angel Island?

Both accounts cannot be correct. Either the raft was found or it wasn't. Who had more of a reason to lie?

Put all the pieces together, and this and other evidence creates a compelling case that John Anglin, Clarence Anglin, and Frank Morris did not drown in the frigid bay waters in a futile attempt to gain their freedom. Rather, their plan included the assistance of mob boss Mickey Cohen, along with other key people known by the escapees, whose connections helped these men break out of Alcatraz.

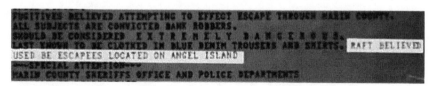

APB of raft sighting
MARIN COUNTY SHERIFF'S OFFICE

But this remarkable story goes even further. We intend to also show that John, Clarence, and Frank not only did what no one thought possible, successfully escape from The Rock, but eventually arrived in South America, where they lived for the rest of their lives.

CHAPTER 2

A Mother's Love

Mothers hold their children's hands for a short while, but their hearts forever.

—UNKNOWN

As with many stories, this one was years in the making. Some events of our lives are lived day in and day out, while others have a profound effect on us. Not surprisingly, John Anglin (b. 1930) and Clarence Anglin (b. 1931) experienced both. Years before their famous escape, they lived a quiet life in the farming community of Ruskin, Florida. And at the core of that life was their mother, Rachel. She, like so many other mothers, hoped for the best for her fourteen children, all the while knowing she could hold back only for so long the troubles and setbacks we all experience. For John, Clarence, and their older brother Alfred, this began about the time they started school. The Anglin boys were often teased because, as poor farmers, they wore hand-me-downs that had been stitched together and showed the wear of daily chores on the farm. Clarence, in particular, didn't bear the shame of being made fun of all that well. Regularly bullied, he gave back as good as they gave him. Tall and lanky, but also strong, he often found himself in the middle of a schoolyard fight.

On one occasion, fellow classmate Mark Green seemed to come out of nowhere during recess and punched Clarence in the nose. Pain shot through his eight-year-old body when he fell to the ground, blood running. Third grade was turning out to be as hard as the previous two. The Anglin family may have been poor, but the one thing they could always count on was each other, and the sound of footsteps behind Clarence meant help from his brothers.

"I told you Anglins that this side of the yard belongs to regular folks, not dirt farmers," Mark declared.

John threw a wild swing at Mark, who ducked out of the way. Time seemed to slow as Clarence moved to help, and his fist didn't miss. As Mark fell back, Clarence landed on top of him.

"Don't you ever hit me again!" screamed Clarence.

Alfred and their other brother Robert were about to join the fight when Miss Crump, one of the teachers, stepped into the fray. "You boys stop it right now!"

For the Anglin brothers, being picked on by the neighborhood kids was a regular occurrence they got used to over time, but when the same things were said by their teachers, the hurt went deep.

"Clarence Anglin, you get off of Mark, you hear!" Miss Crump faced his brothers. "You Anglins are all the same, nothing but trouble. I want all of you up against the fence right now."

Turning back to Mark, Miss Crump asked, "What happened, and I want the truth. Did these boys jump you?"

With as much of an innocent demeanor as he could muster, Mark replied, "Yes, ma'am, they did." He continued to pour it on. "I was just trying to be friends."

Furious, John yelled back, "Liar!"

Miss Crump barked at John, "You hush up. I will deal with you in a minute."

"You always take their side," Clarence snapped back.

Miss Crump had been at Ruskin Elementary School for the last ten years and was well respected by parents and fellow teachers alike. For her, having children talk back meant one thing: bad home rearing.

"That's enough from all of you." She grabbed Clarence by the arm. "I want you boys to come with me, now!"

As Miss Crump led them to the school office, she turned toward Mark. "Go on, now, while I deal with these two."

Standing on the porch with the note Miss Crump gave him for his father to sign scared Clarence spitless. He could only imagine the paddling he'd get for fighting. John told him to just go in and get it over with.

"I'm goin'. Keep your shirt on." Clarence tried to conjure up some tears as a way of softening his father's reaction. None came.

Taking in a breath for courage, he opened the door and went into the kitchen. His mother sat at the table with a bowl of string beans in her lap. The Anglin children often joked their mama was either cooking or having babies. She was good at both.

"Supper is a ways off. If you're hungry, you can get an orange off the tree out back."

She looked up and smiled at him. Rachel could tell in an instant something had happened. "Clarence, what have you done this time?"

He took out the paper from his pocket. "It wasn't my fault, Mama. That Mark started it."

She gave him a hug. "You know Daddy is going to pitch a fit." Rachel knew her husband, which proved helpful on many occasions when she shared bad news with him, especially when it helped shield her children from his anger. "Well, let me see. Can't be all that bad."

After reading the note, her hopeful demeanor faded. "Baby, you should know by now you can't give in to fightin'. It will do you no good."

Clarence hated being different from the other kids. Why couldn't their father get a job that paid better, or move to a town where the kids didn't pick on others just because they had nothing? It wasn't his fault, but they acted like it was. "But Mama, why are we so poor? I hate it when they tease us."

"Baby, I know it's not fun having other kids laughing at you. Remember, family is what will get you through tough times."

"When I get older, I'm gonna get us out of this life and make lots of money."

Rachel buried his pain in her heart. She feared Clarence was going down the wrong road, though her Christian faith also taught her a way existed for him to get on the right path again. "Baby, money isn't always the solution. God is the answer you need." For George, farming was the only life he knew. He had no time for children who misbehaved or showed any form of disrespect. When they did, that usually resulted in the only punishment for such an occurrence—the belt.

Lying in bed with John and his other brothers, Clarence expected the door to bust open any minute and see that strap they all dreaded, but his punishment never came.

"Sounds like Mama and Daddy are going to bed," John whispered.

Clarence couldn't believe it. Somehow, his mother must have smoothed things over.

Despite the family's hopes, the situation at Ruskin Elementary School didn't improve for the Anglin boys. They continued being made fun of by their classmates, and sadly, by their teachers as well at times. Outside of family, friends were hard to come by, so meeting a new kid who liked them despite their social status seldom happened. However, in the summer of 1940, things changed for John, Clarence, and Alfred. Ferdinand Brizzi and his family had returned to the Ruskin area after working at the Conchas Dam federal project in New Mexico. His eight-year-old son, Fred, took a liking to the brothers from the beginning. His experience in New Mexico hadn't been good, and so finding friends with whom he could commiserate formed the beginning of a lifelong bond. One of the things they had in common was a love of swimming.

George Anglin on the farm
WIDNER FAMILY

If it were up to John and Clarence, they'd rather jump into the Little Manatee River not far from their home the moment the sun appeared than be in school. It was only a matter of time before school officials started showing up at the house, letting the parents know that Clarence and his brothers had been skipping class. Talks and whippings from their father seemed to do little good.

Their mother hoped some divine guidance might help, so she signed the boys up for a swimming contest at their church in nearby Wimauma.

Though Lake Wimauma stretched a half mile across, the swim wasn't particularly difficult for an Anglin boy. Clarence beat out the other swimmers by a wide margin, except for John, who had been nipping at his heels the entire race. Winning that gold ribbon was one of the few highlights the boys enjoyed in their young lives, and seeing the smile on their mother's face even surpassed that achievement. Scarcely could John and Clarence have known at the time how experiences like this would prepare them for the future.

Sadly, the warm glow garnered by the brothers' performances at the race didn't last long. Continued teasing and bullying drove them back to their truant ways. After getting caught by the police multiple times, Clarence was finally arrested in earnest and appeared in juvenile court before Judge Himes.

Himes first started practicing law in 1928, after graduating from Harvard University, and became a judge in 1936. He was popular with the press and the public, and was even named Young Man of the Year by

Judge Himes
FROM "JOHN RUTLAND HIMES: THE MAN, THE JUDGE" (DIGITAL COMMONS @ USF)

the Tampa Junior Chamber of Commerce in 1939.[1] But today, he had other concerns.

"It gives me no pleasure to pull you away from family," Hime's voice resonated from the bench, "but after several warnings you leave me with no other choice." Rachel's heart sank when Judge Himes read the verdict—four weeks at reform school. If she could have peered into the future, she would've seen this was just the first of many courtroom appearances.

George, on the other hand, worked night and day on the farm and couldn't attend. Breaking the news to him wouldn't be easy. It never was.

As they took Clarence away, tears filled his mother's eyes. "Baby, you hang in there and this will pass sooner than you think. I'll come visit you this weekend, and Daddy if he can."

True to her word, Rachel showed up next Saturday at the reform school, along with John. She hated the thought of Clarence being taken from the family, even it was for only a month, but she also hoped his example might help John understand the consequences of making poor choices and turn him away from the rebellious life that seemed to be pulling on them.

"Sure do miss y'all," Clarence said.

"Looks like they feed you well in here," John commented.

Clarence smiled. "Not like Mama's biscuits and gravy."

"I don't ever want you back in a place like this," she said. "You hear?"

"Yes, Mama."

John looked around and then winked at Clarence. "So when do you think you're gettin' outta here?"

Clarence knew what he meant, part of a secret code they had created with their brother Alfred years before.

Born in Seminole County, Georgia, on February 7, 1928, Alfred was the fifth of fourteen children. Despite being in a large family, he tended to be a loner. Alfred was also considered smart, dedicated to his brothers, and like John and Clarence, often ran afoul of the law.

"Another three weeks, which should go by quick." Clarence emphasized the word "quick," which John noted.

Unknown to Rachel, Clarence had learned a lot in that place; in particular, he didn't like much there. So he and another boy planned to break out and make a run for it.

Sunday-morning breakfast always brought the family together, and Rachel never missed an opportunity to show off her cooking skills.

George, typically first at the table, often pointed that out. "Sure does look good, Mama."

Everyone had just sat down when, to their surprise, the back-door screen opened and there stood Clarence soaking wet. The look on his father's face was a cross between pulling off his belt and elation at seeing his son.

To the family's amazement, he went over and hugged him. "Mama, you better get another plate. Looks like we have one more this mornin'."

As George guided Clarence toward the table, Rachel felt happy about being reunited with her boy, but also scared. The police would certainly be looking for him and probably show up at the house sooner or later.

"I just didn't like bein' shut up like that. Me and another boy decided it was time to go, and we done just that." Clarence continued. "And I'm not going back there, no way, no how."

Despite everyone's hopes, the police came knocking the next day. As Rachel feared, the officers escorted Clarence back to the reform school. She visited him each week, encouraging him to stay put until the completion of his sentence, which he did this time.

Rachel had no way of knowing this would be the beginning of many heartbreaks she'd endure the rest of her life.

CHAPTER 3

Ruskin, Florida

You stand out too much in a small town.

—Jen DeLuca

Before anyone can really have an idea of who John and Clarence Anglin were, they must first understand the place from which they came. Like all societies around the world, the communal impact on people has a powerful effect on what a person believes and how they act. The small town of Ruskin was no different. Though the Anglin family didn't move there from Donalsonville, Georgia, until 1940, the forces that shaped the town first made their impact hundreds of years before.

Nestled on the west coast of Florida, some twenty miles south of Tampa, the Ruskin community of today, with its restaurants, parks, hotels, and water sports, stands in stark contrast to its humble beginnings. The area was once inhabited by the Uzita tribe from the Little Manatee River to the Sarasota Bay farther south, first encountered by the Pánfilo de Narváez expedition in 1528. Utilizing the local resources available to them, the Uzita constructed their houses out of wood and palm thatch. Their primary weapon of choice was the bow and arrow.

When Pedro Menendez de Aviles arrived in 1567, the Uzita had been replaced by the Tocobago people. They in turn were replaced by the Pohoy, who are last noted in historical records in 1739. By this time the indigenous peoples had been subdued by the Spanish crown, many of them abandoning their tribal beliefs and converting to Christianity.

In 1763, when the Spanish traded Florida to England, British soldiers were given land grants as a form of payment for their service in the French and Indian War (1754–1763). A large number of British colonists immigrated to Florida, hopeful for a better life in the New World. However, after suffering from privation, hurricanes, swamps, and stifling heat and humidity, most of the colonists returned to England within a few years or moved north to one of the British colonies. This allowed the recolonization of Florida by the Spanish in 1783, which they held until 1821. Americans of English, Scottish, and Irish ancestry from the neighboring colonies of Georgia and South Carolina also moved into sparsely populated Florida at this time.

Constant fighting among the different groups, which occasionally flared up into open revolt against Spain, made the territory difficult to control. The United States had an eye on Florida for years and recognized this as their opportunity for wresting prized real estate from the Spanish crown.

Andrew Jackson led an incursion against the Seminole Indians in 1817, which gave control of Pensacola to the United States in 1818. The Spanish government recognized they no longer had the will or resources to protect their territory four thousand miles away, so they ceded Florida to the United States under the terms of the Adams-Otis Treaty, signed in 1819.

With millions of square miles of unclaimed land ripe for the taking, Americans flooded into Florida with the same hopes as the British had decades before. Almost immediately, however, tensions arose between them and the Seminoles. Many of the settlers carved out plantation-style farms for themselves, effectively ignoring the natives' claims to the land. It didn't take long for resentment to flare up into local skirmishes.

The U.S. government sent James Gadsden in 1832 as an ambassador, tasked with working out an agreement with the native chiefs.

The Seminoles were called to a meeting at Payne's Landing on the Ocklawaha River. The treaty negotiated with the U.S. government called for the Seminoles to move west. A delegation of seven chiefs toured the area for several months and, on March 28, 1833, signed what they believed to be a statement that the new land was suitable for consideration.

Upon their return to Florida, however, a disagreement as to the terms of the treaty arose. Many of the chiefs stated that they had not committed to move their people to the new territory and that they had been coerced through force and misinterpretation into signing.

The refusal of most Seminoles to abandon the reservation . . . and to relocate west of the Mississippi River led to what was known as the Second Seminole War, which began with what is now known as Dade's Massacre in December 1835.[1]

The U.S. Army marched into Florida with orders to remove those who refused to leave. With many dead on both sides, the fighting lasted until 1842, when the last remaining Seminoles were forcibly taken to Creek lands west of the Mississippi River.

Florida became the twenty-seventh state in the Union on March 3, 1845. With its large sugar and cotton plantations as the state's main economic engine, half the population was composed of slaves.

Florida sided with the South when the Civil War began and ceded from the United States on January 10, 1861. The Union Army responded with a naval blockade at key ports, which greatly diminished Florida's impact for the rest of the war.

Moderate Republicans took control of the state during the Reconstruction era. But when Federal troops withdrew from the South in 1877, state and local governments in Florida set about suppressing rights given to Blacks by the Fifteenth Amendment in 1869. Vigilante groups such as the KKK used fear, violence, and intimidation to keep Blacks and poor Whites from voting, thus maintaining their political and economic power.

The Florida legislature also enacted a number of Jim Crow laws in the late 1800s that established and maintained racial segregation. Blacks soon became marginalized as second-class citizens, kept subdued through the use of poll taxes and legalized segregation in all public facilities. They could not run for office and were forced to live in the poorest parts of towns and cities.

The lost cause, worse than slavery
HARPER'S MAGAZINE 1874 (LIBRARY OF CONGRESS)

Since Florida did not suffer the devastating effects of the Civil War as did most of the South, the agricultural economy remained largely intact. This changed in the 1920s, when the great land boom occurred. Florida real estate shot up in value when vacationers and speculators gobbled up huge swaths of cheap land. New railroad lines funded by the state government created a badly needed infrastructure that moved goods and people between towns, which became the impetus for the creation of large cities for the first time in Florida's history.

The good times came to a crashing halt when the stock market collapsed in 1929, and the price of land plummeted with it. The state's economy was kept afloat by the Federal Emergency Relief Act enacted by President Roosevelt after he came to office in 1933, in which millions of dollars poured into Florida's various governmental agencies.

Though the Depression had a negative impact on the country as a whole, Floridians generally fared better than most. Even though jobs were hard to come by, people still needed to eat, which meant the agricultural industry that had sustained the state for decades remained more or less intact. Prices were cheap, but the expansion of the railroad system the decade before meant goods and produce could be shipped to buyers elsewhere in the country.

Developers lured people to Florida with the
promise of cheap land.
STATE LIBRARY AND ARCHIVES OF FLORIDA

With a constant demand for their crops, farmers enjoyed relative security in the 1930s, but life was still hard. Having large families to support, most squeaked by with just enough money to keep them on the land. This is the life the Anglins experienced when they moved to Ruskin in 1940 with the hope of a better future.

Ruskin was founded in August 1908 near the Little Manatee River, but the town's roots actually go back two years earlier. In 1906, lured by the promise of cheap land, Dr. George Miller and his wife traveled to Florida, where they hoped to build a college similar to the one they had founded in Trenton, Missouri, in 1900. Their search brought them to the north shore of the Little Manatee River near Gulf City. "Dr. Miller began trying to establish the school. When Albert Peter Dickman, Miller's brother-in-law, joined him in 1907, the two negotiated with Captain C.H. Davis for 13,000 acres stretching from the north shore of the Little Manatee River to Apollo Beach. . . . Thus the seeds were sowed for the Ruskin community."[2] As to the actual formation of Ruskin, Wikipedia states: "Addie Dickman Miller, Dr. Miller's wife, founded a post office on August 7, 1908, the day recognized as the official founding of the town."[3]

The needs of the town and college grew relatively quickly. By 1913, a general store, canning factory, telephone system, electricity, and newspaper had been established. Unfortunately for the college, most of the campus was destroyed by fire in 1918.

Ruskin College was never rebuilt, but the town Dr. Miller had planted turned out to be far more resilient. In 1926, U.S. Route 41 had been created, which stretched the length of the state. Backed by the growing farming industry in the 1920s, these and other roads were needed as a way of moving produce to local markets, cementing Ruskin's growing importance as Florida's population swelled during the land boom.

Despite the importance of Ruskin's agricultural economy, however, the population had only grown to 200 people by 1925. Though the community remained small, the town still boasted six hotels, two sawmills, a turpentine still, a public library, four grocery stores, a garage, two restaurants, and a dry goods cleaner, along with a number of farms that grew cabbage and onions.[4]

"Paul B. Dickman planted his first acre of tomatoes in 1928 following the collapse of the Florida real estate market. After making 'a fair return' on that initial crop, he doubled his tomato crop every year."[5] When other local farmers recognized how suitable the soil was for tomatoes, they soon followed. As a result, the success of their efforts meant the town needed a canning plant. The facility employed sixty-five workers in the 1930s, which was no small feat at the height of the Depression.

In the end, much of the area's post–Ruskin College success is attributed to one person, Albert Dickman. As the land boom peaked and crashed in the late 1920s, he returned to the agricultural community and would eventually place Ruskin on the map as "America's Salad Bowl."[6]

As a result of this added economic uptick, Ruskin's population grew to over seven hundred people in the 1930s. Proud of their agricultural heritage and success, the community instituted the Ruskin Tomato Festival in 1935, where farmers displayed their prized vegetables and people voted for the festival queen. The tomato festival still takes place every May.

Born on February 28, 1896, in Henry, Alabama, George Robert Anglin was just twenty-one when he married Rachel Van Dora Miller in Decatur, Georgia, in 1917 (he soon shipped out with the army and served in Europe during World War I). When he returned, George and Rachel

George Anglin and his wife, Rachel
WIDNER FAMILY

started a family while earning a meager living as farmers. Moving from Donalsonville, Georgia, to Ruskin, Florida, a decade later was no easy task with eleven children in tow.

So what brought the Anglin family to this small farming community? According to the stories I (Ken) heard at family gatherings over the years:

> They moved because of the better farming land. My Granddaddy took the money he had saved from the war and purchased the farm and built the house we came to know. It was around thirty to forty acres, and he dug a pond. The family grew all kinds of vegetables, which he sold at the local farmer's market. He also raised a few cows and pigs. Later, after he retired from farming, my Granddaddy gave a lot of his land to his kids. I remember going there and seeing it was kind of like a compound. The Anglin family house was at one end, and surrounding it were four of his children's homes and their families.

Ultimately, George and Rachel had fourteen children, which was common for farming families at that time.

And like most parents, they wanted the best for each of them, their hopes spurred by their Christian faith. As members of the Church of God in the town of Wimauma, not far from Ruskin, George and Rachel taught their children the Ten Commandments and the importance of honoring their parents, which they believed, along with a moral upbringing, provided their children with everything they needed to live honest and upright lives. But another influence just as powerful also had a profound impact on the Anglins' children—poverty.

Prejudice against different peoples and groups had left deep and painful scars within the culture, and when one learns to hate others, bitterness and anger are usually the result. As farmers who wanted nothing than a better life for themselves, the Anglin family experienced firsthand what it was like to be looked down on by their neighbors simply because they were poor.

Most of George and Rachel's children embraced their parent's example and followed the straight and narrow, but for brothers John, Clarence, and Alfred, the forces that shaped their lives pushed them in a very different direction.

Recent arrivals to Ruskin (Alfred, Clarence, and John on far right)
WIDNER FAMILY

CHAPTER 4

Fred Brizzi

There's nothing like a really loyal, dependable, good friend. Nothing.
—JENNIFER ANISTON

SEVERAL YEARS BEFORE JOHN, CLARENCE, AND ALFRED HAD EVEN MET Fred Brizzi, who would play a pivotal role in their lives, faced the very real possibility of leaving Ruskin forever.

The sun sat high in the sky as thousands of common terns cawed and screeched at the edge of the Little Manatee River. Their smaller companions, red-eyed vireos, sang incessantly in nearby trees. The red-tinted water, caused by tiny algae spores, flowed eastward some twenty-five miles through Hillsborough County, Florida, and deposited into Tampa Bay. Spanning a quarter of a mile or more in places, the river ambled along at a gentle pace under a canopy of red maples, water oak, cabbage palms, and Carolina willow trees amid tall grasses growing at the water's edge. But on this day, Fred and his older sister, Evelyn, paid the beauty before them little attention. Without exception, a swim in the cool water provided a respite from the oppressive heat the people of Ruskin endured this time of year, but his troubled thoughts prevented such indulgences.

Though Florida had escaped the full force of the depression that had impacted most of the country since the early 1930s, many local families still struggled. Evelyn, born in 1930, and Fred, born two years later, enjoyed something of a good life, but that didn't protect them from the news that shook their world, Fred's especially.

When the two reached the sandy shore near the remnants of a boat dock, Fred threw his towel down and sat in silence. Evelyn took note of the melancholy that hung over him.

"What is it, Fred?" she asked, concern tinting her tone. "You haven't said boo the whole day."

His arms clutched tight around his knees as he sat forward, Fred's gaze remained fixed on the water. "Do ya think we're really gonna go? New Mexico is awful far away."

"I don't know. You heard what Mama said. The electrician job isn't for sure. Dad might not get it."

"I hope he don't. I know he sometimes can't find work, but things will get better here. They gotta."

Evelyn's gaze settled on the river. "Aren't many jobs around. And if you're not a farmer, there's not much else."

Their father was an honest man who did what he could to provide for his family, and when a job came his way, life was good for a time. But it seldom lasted, and the Brizzis went back to struggling like before.

Evelyn got to her feet. A sinister smile formed, and she punched her brother's arm. "Can't catch me." She laughed, then ran into the water.

Little Manatee River

"Oh yeah?" Fred got up and chased after her.

The common terns hugging the shore scattered into a thousand directions as the two laughed and splashed in the water. A few weeks later, Fred, Evelyn, and the rest of the Brizzi family traveled cross-country to a place that couldn't be more different than Ruskin.

Located in San Miguel County, New Mexico, the Conchas Dam project had been approved in 1935 after "the passage of the Emergency Relief Appropriation Act, which authorized several public works projects in New Mexico to provide relief to unemployment. Initial site work began in 1935, with construction on the actual dam starting in 1936."[1]

Now with federal money earmarked for the project, plumbers, cooks, engineers, and construction workers, including those with the electrical skills Fred Brizzi offered, were needed right away. But filling the hundreds of jobs wouldn't be easy. Situated fifty miles northeast of Santa Rosa, the dam was to be built on the Canadian River, but with little in the form of roads, housing, or any other semblance of infrastructure at the remote site, the call went out across the country for workers with the skills needed for such an endeavor. For Ferdinand Brizzi, the lure of a steady paycheck was too strong to resist. He packed up the family and drove 1,600 miles to the sunbaked land of scorpions, scrub brush, and isolation.

The plan for the dam was simple. Constructed mainly out of concrete, the earthen wing dikes that stretched across the Canadian River created Conchas Lake, which would serve as a water source for farming and irrigation purposes.

But before construction could begin in earnest, workers and their families needed homes to live in, and so a makeshift town sprang up in the desert. Ultimately, eighty-nine adobe brick buildings were constructed with all the amenities, such as a movie theater, schools, clubs, hospital, church, cemetery, and post office, that made modern life in a remote location possible.

For the feeding of the workers, a mess hall had been constructed, equipped with a kitchen, dining area, and cold storage locker. On the social side, dances were held in the Service Building. The town also

Conchas Reservoir Project sign
CONCHAS DAM HISTORY FACEBOOK PAGE

boasted a rifle club, camera club, garden club, golf course, and tennis court.

Though the promise of work provided the family with a measure of financial security for the foreseeable future, the transition did not go well for Fred. Having already experienced bouts of poverty and an uncertain future in Ruskin, moving away from his friends and family only added to his feelings of anger and isolation. The only hope he had was his mother's promise they'd return home after the dam had been completed.

While there, families did their best to replicate the lives they left behind. They shopped at a local market and the children attended school, enjoyed dances, and fielded a baseball team.

For the various work crews, including the one to which Ferdinand had been assigned, safety was of paramount importance. The plant repair shop ran seven days a week, and supervisors held regular safety meetings and even sponsored slogan contests as additional ways of reducing work-related injuries. In one of the contests, electrician Floyd Mercer's entry earned him a ten-dollar prize for "Let's all be careful."[2]

The town of Conchas (ca. 1937)
CONCHAS DAM HISTORY FACEBOOK PAGE

Coming in at a cost of about $16 million, an immense sum during the Depression, the dam was completed in 1939. With the work now complete, the Brizzi family should have left with the others and headed back to Florida, but they didn't, as evidenced by the New Mexico 1940 census record.

The reason was most likely economic. The town created for the workers and their families needed to be dismantled. The adobe bricks were reused to build the U.S. Army Corps of Engineers' permanent housing and administrative building, which still exist today. With guaranteed work still to be had, Ferdinand kept his family there longer than he probably originally intended, which must have had an additional negative impact on Fred.

When the Brizzi family finally returned to Ruskin in the early 1940s, the person Fred had become was much different than the one who left, which would take him in a direction his parents could not have imagined.

Ten-year-old John Anglin sat on the sandy beach along the Little Manatee not far from the tents their father had pitched after their move from Donalsonville, Georgia. Twelve-year-old Alfred and nine-year-old Clarence sat a little farther away by the river's edge.

Conchas Dam construction
ENGINEERING OFFICE (1939)

Brizzi family census record
1940 U.S. FEDERAL CENSUS OF CONCHAS DAM, SAN MIGUEL, NEW MEXICO

As much as George enjoyed the trappings of army life during World War I, he also had a wife and large family dependent on him and needed to build a house big enough for them all, as he had promised. And if there was one thing John, Clarence, and Alfred could depend on, their father never reneged on a promise. But he also didn't have the money needed for an architect or a team of carpenters. So he enlisted his sons.

First order of business, clear the land of vegetation. The oak and hickory trees were cut down and used as lumber for the house. This part didn't thrill John, Clarence, and Alfred much. They had only moved to Ruskin a few weeks before, and the lure of swimming in the Manatee proved irresistible. Swimming was much more fun than swinging an axe or splitting logs. Their older brother Rufus, who later lost his leg while serving in the Merchant Marines during World War II, shouldered the brunt of the work, but that didn't mean Robert, John, and Clarence didn't pull their share.

Every Sunday, their father let them have the day off since it was the Lord's Day, a day of rest. But rest was the furthest thing from the boys' minds.

"What do you think?" John asked Alfred. "Is this our new spot or not?"

Alfred cleaned his glasses and looked around. "Sure. Why not?"

"I don't know," Clarence chimed in. "I like it a little ways down better, just past that old pier. Some good trees there we can tie up a rope swing and jump in the water."

John looked the spot over and considered Clarence's suggestion. "Why can't we do both? We can make this beach is our base camp, and those trees are our jumping spot."

Before either of them could answer, a gangly eight-year-old boy appeared out of nowhere. "Whatcha doin' here?" Fred Brizzi demanded. "This is my spot. Been so since I can remember."

John, Clarence, and Alfred looked at one another.

Alfred, being the oldest, spoke for his brothers. "Don't see your name anyplace." He pointed at the shore across the river. "That'll be yours. This is ours."

"I said *this* spot is mine. My sister and me been comin' here before we moved. Just got back yesterday."

John and family on the farm
WIDNER FAMILY

34

Working on the house
WIDNER FAMILY

"Where from?" Clarence asked.

"New Mexico. Hated the place."

"What did you do out there?"

"My dad's an electrician. He helped build a dam. It's finished now, so we come back."

John walked up to Fred and sized him up. "The way I see it, this might've been yours once, but you gave it up when you left. Ours now. So go on your way." He also pointed at the far side of the river.

Fred took off his shirt, gave the three a long look, then jumped into the water and started swimming. He freestyled it to the other side, then turned around and came back in short order.

Sucking in several deep breaths, Fred wiped the water from his eyes as he approached all three stunned boys.

"You got guts, kid," John said, impressed. "Clarence and me are good swimmers. Not sure we'd have made it back that fast. What's your name?"

"Fred."

"I'm John." He pointed at his brothers. "This here is Clarence, and my older brother Alfred."

"Hey," both brothers replied in unison.

"How 'bout we make you a deal? There's enough river for all of us. We share this spot with each other. What do ya say?"

"I say, the last person on the other side is a loser."

Fred again jumped into the water, followed by John, Clarence, and Alfred.

Despite the wishes of every boy, summer never lasts. With the arrival of September came school. The brothers hated going when they lived in Donalsonville. Just because they were poor didn't mean they deserved to get picked on by the other kids. Now in Ruskin, they hoped the people there would be more accepting. This was a farming community, after all, and they saw themselves as being no different than anyone else, despite wearing patched-up overalls and living in tents while building their house.

Fortunately for the brothers, their financial state meant nothing to Fred. From the day they met by the river, the four became fast friends, sharing their love of exploring and swimming until the sun set.

With only a few days left before school started, Fred was feeling itchy to do something his father didn't approve of, which he could also brag about on the playground.

"What do you think we should do?" John asked.

"That's what I'm asking you," Fred replied.

The sound of a boat's engine approaching at a high rate of speed caught their attention. The driver cut back on the throttle and let the boat drift onto the beach not far from their rope swing.

"Howdy," the driver said to them.

"Hey," the boys replied in unison.

"I'm new around here. Wondering if you could tell me if I'm headed for Tampa Bay.

"Yeah," Alfred answered. "Just keep goin' thataway and you'll make it in no time."

As the two talked, Fred glanced at the rope swing. At the foot of the tree lay twenty feet of rope they found in a garbage can behind the hardware store. He looked again at the boat, then the rope. Fred gave John a nudge. "See that rope?" he whispered. "I just got me an idea."

John smiled. "I'm game."

Crouching down low, John picked up the rope and followed Fred behind the boat. As the driver thanked Alfred for his help, Fred tied a knot around one of the handles in the rear, then slipped into the water and let the rope out.

The man, unaware what the boys had in mind, started up the engine and slowly backed up. When he had gone a safe distance from the shore, the man hit the throttle and headed west. Twenty feet behind, both boys held on for dear life, a steady spray of water hitting John and Fred square in the face.

When the driver took a hard turn at the river's bend, both boys swung sideways so hard the rope slipped out of their hands and they bounced on the water's choppy surface before coming to a stop.

As the boat disappeared behind another bend, John and Fred looked at one another and laughed.

"That was fun," John said as he bobbed in the water. "Wanna try again?"

Fred looked around. "There's another boat comin' this way. Let's try for that one."

Despite the brothers' hopes for a better life in Ruskin, the bullying and teasing started up soon after elementary school began.

Jokes about how they dressed became fodder for girls who pointed and laughed. The boys, being more aggressive, picked on the Anglins during recess or after school when the teachers weren't looking. As expected, it didn't take long before fights broke out when one of the brothers had had enough.

"I told you Anglins that this side of the yard belongs to regular folks, not dirt farmers," Mark Green declared, then gave John a shove.

Fred Brizzi, who dashed across the playground with John, stepped between the two. "Just leave him be," he said. "He ain't done nothin' to you."

Mark laughed as the kids around him watched. "Gutter trash. You're just like them."

John's anger erupted, and he threw a wild swing at Mark, who ducked out of the way. Clarence jumped into the fray, and his swing didn't miss. As Mark fell back, Clarence landed on top of him.

Miss Crump broke up the fight and hauled the brothers to the office.

His fists clenched, Fred could do nothing but watch the injustice that unfolded before him. But that didn't mean Mark Green or Miss Crump had gotten the last word.

As the children filed out of Ruskin Elementary at the end of the day, Fred waited by the playground with John and Clarence.

"What are you doin'?" John asked. "You know I gotta get the letter Miss Crump gave me signed by my daddy."

"In a minute," Fred replied.

"I don't even want to think about the whippin' we're gonna get when he finds out we got into another fight."

"Maybe this will make it a little easier. Over there."

Mark Green walked out of class and looked around. When he saw the three waiting nearby, he spat before heading for home. Fred blocked his way.

"What do you want, gutter trash?" Mark sneered.

Fred punched Mark in the nose without warning, and Mark dropped like a sack of potatoes. Fred had never done anything like that before leaving Ruskin, but he returned an angry boy, and no one again would do him or his friends an injustice.

His hand filling with blood, Mark rolled on the ground in pain as he held his nose. "What didya do that for?"

Ruskin Elementary School class photo (1945–1946). Clarence is in the top row, far left. John is in the top row, fourth from the right.
KEN WIDNER

"The next time you go after one of my friends, you mess with me." He looked at John and Clarence, who appeared both stunned and impressed. "Come on."

Standing just a little taller, the three walked together down the street.

CHAPTER 5

Boys Industrial School at Marianna

It is easier to build strong children than to repair broken men.
—FREDERICK DOUGLASS

BY 1947, RACHEL ANGLIN FELT LIKE SHE WAS IN A TUG OF WAR WITH John, Clarence, and Alfred, caught between the Christian values with which they had been raised and their desire for a better life through any means, and she was losing. Prayers, talks, whippings from their father—nothing worked. It was as though the world's temptations had their grip on them and wouldn't let go.

The boys' descent into crime started out innocently enough—skipping school at first, which soon turned into shoplifting at the local store, then breaking into neighbors' houses. By the mid-1940s, the three had been incarcerated at several local juvenile detention centers, and Judge Himes's patience was wearing thin.

Little did the brothers know their close friend, Fred, was also being pulled in the same direction. Despite Anna Brizzi's efforts, she had also been fighting a losing battle to keep her son on the straight and narrow.

The night felt warm and sticky, not uncommon for Ruskin in May. Fred hung out with his friend Ralph Wilson. As the older of the two, Ralph usually called the shots. Tonight, he told Fred he'd meet up with him on the main strip and hang out. Fred knew that was code for getting into trouble, but with little for teens to do after dark, and schoolwork the last thing on either of their minds, a little trouble sounded better than nothing.

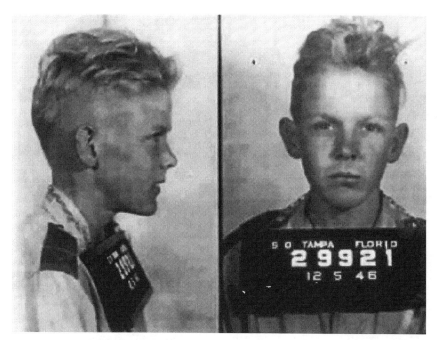

John's mug shot, sixteen years old
SHERIFF'S OFFICE, TAMPA, FLORIDA

Fred found Ralph waiting for him in front of the drugstore. At that time, the downtown area had pretty much closed up. No one around.

The two started walking down the street. Fred and Ralph hadn't gone more than a block when they came across a motorcycle parked in an alley. Fred's eyes lit up.

"She's a beaut. Let's take her for a ride."

"I got a better idea," Ralph said. "We steal the bike and sell it."

"Steal? You sure we can sell her?"

Ralph lit a cigarette. "Trust me. My friend Sam and me had no issues with one we took last week."

Ralph handed Fred a smoke.

"A bike like this will bring in fifty bucks easy, maybe more. What do ya say?"

Fred looked at the bike, then back at Ralph. "Okay. But we may as well have a little fun first."

A broad smile stretched across Ralph's face. He sat on the bike and started her up.

Fred jumped onto the back part of the seat, and Ralph tore off down the main strip. Warm air slapped their faces as he flew through a series of stop signs. At the end of the street, Ralph spun around and went back the way he came.

Out of nowhere a police car appeared from a side street, its siren blaring. The officer parked in the middle of the road, effectively blocking their path. Ralph had no choice but to slam on the brakes.

The officer jumped out and drew his weapon. "I want you off the bike. Hands in the air."

Fred and Ralph were brought before Judge Himes in juvenile court. Himes gave them three years' probation, as long as they obeyed a 10:00 p.m. curfew, didn't operate a motorcycle or automobile for ninety days, and attended a weekly court session so they'd learn the consequences of criminal behavior.

Fred and Ralph might have had every intention of staying out of trouble per Judge Himes's warning, but an empty house owned by a former Tampa attorney, Clarence "Abe" Martin, rumored to have once been the residence of famous gangster Al Capone, proved too tempting. Hoping they might recover guns and money from a long-ago bank job, the two broke into the house. When they didn't find anything, both boys had fun smashing up the place. In all, the damage was later estimated at $1,000 (about $12,000 in today's dollars).[1]

The two slipped back into the night, believing they had gotten away unnoticed. A neighbor, however, heard the sound of breaking glass and reported the vandalism to the police.

Sheriff's Deputy Viola caught Fred a short time later and also arrested Ralph riding home on a motorcycle after his high school graduation in Wimauma.

In school or out, it seemed the Anglin brothers and Fred Brizzi were destined to be together. John, Clarence, and Alfred had been caught by the police for stealing $2,200 from the Ruskin Trading Company. As the three brothers waited with their mother outside the Ruskin courthouse,

John couldn't help but react when he saw Fred head inside with his mother. With him was his accomplice, Ralph Wilson, and his mother.

"Hey Freddie," John called out.

Fred's mother slipped between her son and the Anglin boys as they passed by, preventing him from acknowledging his friends.

Judge Himes's demeanor darkened when Fred and Ralph came before his bench.

"Well, Mr. Brizzi, that sure didn't take long."

"But I didn't do nothin'."

"Are you saying it wasn't you who caused over a thousand dollars' damage to Mr. Martin's house?"

"I went to the house," Fred admitted. He glanced at Ralph. "But it wasn't me who smashed the place up."

"That's a lie!" Ralph objected.

Judge Himes banged his gavel. "You will not speak unless spoken to." He returned his attention to Fred. "I warned you the last time about disregarding the terms of your probation."

"That's not fair since I didn't do nothin'."

"I have an eyewitness that says you did."

Judge Himes shifted in his chair and faced Ralph Wilson directly. "And what is your defense?"

"No defense, Your Honor," Ralph's mother replied, jumping in, "since my son's not guilty. He was not the one driving the motorcycle when Deputy Viola arrested him."

Incredulity registered in Judge Himes's eyes. "Mrs. Wilson, you'd have this court believe your son did nothing wrong. That he was simply an innocent bystander?"

Mrs. Wilson said she had done her best to watch over her son and that she'd find a daytime job as a way of keeping a better eye on him. She went on to say, "Technically, since he was only riding a motorcycle, he has not violated his probation."

Judge Himes remained skeptical. "But in allowing him to ride a motorcycle, you essentially gave him permission to violate the spirit of his probation. Moreover, I don't understand your reasoning for doing this since he had stolen a motorcycle before. Then there's the matter of the damage done to Mr. Martin's house."

The judge paused a moment. "I don't want to be unreasonable, but I'm not going to just let him go, either. Therefore, he'll spend a week in jail without bond."

Judge Himes turned again to Fred. "Your case is different, however. Not only do you have theft of a motorcycle on your record, but you now add breaking and entering. I see no other recourse than to sentence you to the Boys Industrial School at Marianna for two years." Judge Himes added, "If you do not complete your term, I will be forced to send you to Raiford Prison for two years. Do you understand me, Mr. Brizzi?"

"Yes, sir," Fred replied.

"You are to report to the school within two weeks, and this time I pray you take my warning seriously." Judge Himes banged his gavel.[2]

After Fred and his mother left the courtroom, Rachel and her three sons entered, along with Luther Miller, who had also participated in the Ruskin Trading Company robbery.

Judge Himes looked them over before speaking. "You're the second group of boys I've had to deal with today who have a hard time following this court's admonitions."

Looking at all four defendants, Judge Himes continued, "Do you have anything to say before I pronounce sentence?"

None of the brothers uttered a word as they stood before the judge, their eyes cast downward.

After a few seconds, Rachel spoke up for them. "Your Honor, I know my boys have done wrong and they deserve to be punished, but please don't send them far off." She choked back tears. "Our family is very poor, and if they're sent far off I'm afraid I won't ever see them again."

"Mrs. Anglin, I am not an unfair person. I do my best to give young men second chances in the hope they will turn their lives around. But I also believe this court has been more than lenient with your sons, and I'm afraid a harsher punishment is required this time."

Judge Himes sentenced Clarence to two years at Marianna. John and Luther each received one-year sentences. Since Alfred was eighteen and a legal adult, Judge Himes gave him a five-year term at Raiford Prison.

The Florida School for Boys (also known as the Florida Industrial School for Boys and the Arthur G. Dozier School for Boys) was a reform school located in the panhandle town of Marianna. The school operated from 1900 until state authorities closed it in 2011.

For more than a century, thousands of boys and teens sent to Marianna suffered indescribable abuse there, such as rape, torture, and murder at the hands of guards and staff. The school was eventually closed after years of mounting allegations that could no longer be ignored, and in time the state pursued criminal charges against the perpetrators.

In recent years, searches using ground-penetrating radar have discovered dozens of unmarked graves on school property. By late 2014, researchers had recovered the remains of fifty-five African American boys. For decades the school remained segregated; Blacks were not buried with Whites. Thirty-one other boys are buried in a small cemetery, the only marked graves on the property. Most suspect many more graves are waiting to be found on the campus.

Getting settled in for John and Clarence wasn't as bad as they had feared since most of the boys there had been sent for similar offenses. The brothers had been assigned jobs cleaning the bathrooms, maintaining the grounds, and sweeping the halls.

When Fred Brizzi walked into the dorm area a week later, John's and Clarence's faces lit up.

"Hey Fred!" shouted John. "Whatcha doin' here?"

Fred was glad to see familiar faces. In a place like this, friends meant protection.

"We weren't sure you were gonna get sent to Marianna with us after seein' you in front of Himes," Clarence laughed, "but there's an open cot for you just the same." He pointed at it.

"You sure that one's empty? Don't want to start a fight with someone over a bed."

"There was a guy in it last week," John said, "but I guess he got out, because we haven't seen hide nor hair of him since."

What the three didn't realize at the time was that those who "left without warning" tended to be orphans and loners, boys no one would miss.

45

Boys at the school
STATE LIBRARY AND ARCHIVES OF FLORIDA

African American boy's funeral at Marianna
STATE LIBRARY AND ARCHIVES OF FLORIDA

Days turned into weeks, and weeks turned into months. The boys passed the time taking classes, such as machine shop, carpentry, and skill testing. Another class the three took involved unlocking combination locks, as strange as that sounds. The school believed that teaching complex motor skills like unlocking a lock was a good way of redirecting the mind from criminal activities. In the case of John, Clarence, and Fred, this had the opposite effect.

Stories also floated around Marianna about staff abusing some of the boys, which didn't sit well with the three. They feared it might happen to them sooner or later, and so they were eager to get out of there. The three also had another problem. One of the boys had struggled opening different types of locks. When Clarence refused to help him, he became angry, and before Fred could stop the two, a fight broke out.

The school had a unique way of settling arguments between boys: a boxing match set up by the staff. Having been in a number of school fights in his younger years gave Clarence an advantage, and he finished off his opponent not long after the match started.

Though Clarence won the fight, this created an additional reason for breaking out of Mariana as soon as possible. Once a boy was tagged as a troublemaker, the situation quickly deteriorated for him, or worse yet, he disappeared one day.

As the three worked on their plan of escape, they masked their clandestine activities by following the rules and staying out of trouble, the reward of which meant periodic visits from family. Despite the troubles Fred had had with his parents over the years, the one thing he counted on was them coming every chance they could. Wasn't so for the Anglin brothers. Their parents had little money, so no one usually showed up on visitation day.

However, to John's and Clarence's utter shock, their mother and older brother Robert, or as they liked to call him "Man," showed up at the visitors' center with the other families not long after the fight with the boy.

"I can't believe you came all this way," John declared. He was so happy to see them that he almost cried.

Man and his mother, along with John and Clarence, all sat down at the picnic table. They talked about how they were getting along okay at the school, though John and Clarence left out the part about the boxing match. Their mother promised she'd make them biscuits and gravy when they got out. She also reminded them about the importance of family

Boys in a boxing match at Marianna
STATE LIBRARY AND ARCHIVES OF FLORIDA

and sticking together no matter what, which would play a big part of the brothers' lives years later.

After being there for four months, the visit was just what the boys needed. But with the holidays coming up, it made saying goodbye that much harder.

Man asked his brothers if he could do anything for them before they left.

"Take us with you," John joked.

For her part, Rachel didn't make a fuss. Wouldn't do her sons any good if she had. But inside, as she walked away, her heart broke just a little more.

When Man and their mother reached the visitor exit, he turned back and nodded. Both boys knew in an instant what he meant.

Later, when they were alone, the three discussed their escape plan.

"You sure he'll help us get out?" Fred asked. "He could've been just sayin' goodbye."

"I know my brother, and he'll do whatever we need," John replied. "The only question is, when do we go?"

Having been assigned maintenance jobs around the grounds, Clarence knew the lay of the land surrounding the campus. What they needed was a way out of there. Like a car.

Fred suggested Clarence and John write their brother and double-check with him about his intentions. He had seen escape plans fail before, and the price paid by those who were caught.

"Leave that to me," Clarence declared. "We have a way of talking without sayin' anything."

Over the years, the brothers had developed codes only they understood. A particular line written on a note meant one thing, while a way of looking at someone meant something else.

The only thing remaining was deciding the day. All three agreed they wanted to be home by Christmas.

As promised, Clarence mailed a letter to Man about the escape and heard back from him a couple of weeks later. Robert said he'd wait outside the compound with a car. Another boy in the facility, Leroy Smith, had information about the room supervisor who had been assigned the night shift, and so Fred brought him into the group.

John felt a bit leery at first about adding an outsider, but he also knew this particular information might prove helpful. He also trusted Fred's judgment.

The three met with Leroy in the dorm room when no one else was around. As a way of earning extra privileges or getting in good with the staff, boys were encouraged to snitch on one another.

"Okay, what do you have?" John asked.

"I've watched the guard come into the room three times now around 1:00 a.m.," Leroy recalled, "and get this kid up a few beds down from me. They're gone for a half hour before comin' back. If we're goin', then that's our best time."

"What we really need is Audrey's dummy heads," John declared.

"Audrey?" Fred asked. "Dummy heads? What are you talkin' about?"

"You know, the kind they have at department stores in the ladies section. Clarence and me took them from our sister whenever we snuck out of the house. She put her wigs on those heads at night before she went to bed. After she was asleep, one of us would sneak in and take 'em, then put the head and wig on our pillows. Fooled Mama and Daddy every time."

"That's a stupid idea," Leroy chided John. "Whoever heard of someone being fooled by a dummy head?"

"Since we don't got any, it don't matter none anyway. We go with the plan and break out tomorrow night."

The four agreed and left the dorm.

Like clockwork, the staff member came for the boy that night. Leroy got up and went to the dorm where John, Clarence, and Fred had been assigned and signaled them it was time to go. They got their things and left without waking the others.

Once outside, it didn't take them long to reach the road in front of the school property. A little farther down near the bend, Robert waited for them. They jumped into the car and took off as quick as lightning.

Word of John's, Clarence's, and Fred's sudden reappearance in Ruskin spread around town, which alerted the authorities. They were apprehended not long after. Since the three were still juveniles, they should have been sent back to Marianna, but both mothers' pleas made an impact on the judge, who sent them elsewhere instead.

CHAPTER 6

In and Out

DRESSED IN HIS PATCHED OVERALLS, CLARENCE WALKED THROUGH THE front door of their house with John and Alfred. Though the modest four-room home for a family of fourteen was only a couple of years old, the furniture that filled it had seen better days.

Raiford prison inmates
STATE LIBRARY AND ARCHIVES OF FLORIDA

George sat in the living room with his pipe, his world-weary face looking out the window.

The three entered, though none of them spoke.

"Somethin' I can do for you boys?" George asked.

"You all right, Daddy?" Clarence asked.

The smell of pipe tobacco filled the room. "I was just sittin' here thinkin'." He took another puff. "So, what have y'all been up to?"

Clarence glanced at his brothers, who looked back at him. In Clarence's hand, another note from Miss Crump for fighting in school. "Nothin' much."

They stood there staring at their father as he puffed again on his pipe.

He finally said, "You boys should know by now that you can't let others get to you about bein' farmers. It's not an easy life but we manage."

Clarence slipped his hands into his pocket. "You know what happened?" On the wall by the kitchen hung the belt.

George looked all three boys in the eyes. "You know that Mama has never kept anythin' from me. The only thing we have in the world is our name, and I don't like us bein' talked about."

"Yes, sir," Clarence replied.

"So, yes, Mama told me what happened. I'll let you know later what I plan on doin' about it."

"That John Talbert had it comin'," John blurted out. "He won't be lookin' down on us no more jus' because we're poor. I can promise ya that."

"John! The three of you gettin' sent to reform school last year hurt your mother deeper than you'll ever know. We're Anglins. Never forget that."

John's bravado melted away. "Yes, sir."

George picked up his Bible from the table beside him and stared at it. "Have you given any thought to the pastor's invitation about bein' saved? Your mama and me believe you all gettin' baptized will do you a world of good. Set you on the right road."

The three looked at one another.

"We've talked about it," Clarence finally said.

"And . . . ?"

Clarence took the note from his pocket. "If you think it's the right thing to do, then we'll do it." He handed the folded paper to his father.

"As long as you know what you done was wrong, even if it was for the right reason." George paused a moment. "The note will be on the kitchen table in the mornin', and it better be the last."

But the bullying at school continued. Rather than get into trouble again for fighting, John, Clarence, and Alfred started skipping school. Like moths to a flame, they spent their days swimming at the train trestle on the Manatee. Many of those times, Fred Brizzi joined them.

But the Anglin Brothers traded one form of trouble for another. In 1940, nine-year-old Clarence was the first to get caught for being a truant and sent to a reform school for thirty days. For the next several years, John and Alfred often faced the same fate as Clarence. Their parents took them and their brothers and sisters to church every Sunday, hoping the pastor's teachings about honoring God and shunning the world's temptations would put them on the right path, but rather than help, the brothers' behavior steadily worsened.

As teens, the boys worked in canning plants around Tampa, but they grew tired of the hard work and low wages. John and Clarence wanted money for the things they didn't have, and so the two started by stealing car batteries and selling them to unsuspecting buyers.

Their illegal activities generally ended at the beginning of summer when the family headed north to Michigan and picked cherries for extra money. When the season ended, they'd return to Ruskin, where John, Clarence, and Alfred soon took up their stealing ways again.

In 1945, Clarence was caught breaking and entering and sent to Florida Industrial School for Boys,

Clarence, age thirteen
WIDNER FAMILY

mixing for the first time with street kids tougher than himself. Fights and abuse from guards soon followed.

Not long after his release, trouble found Clarence again. But this time he had been falsely accused. According to family history:

> After being released from Marianna, Clarence was falsely accused by a neighbor for breaking into their home. His father, George, didn't even check it out as to being true and whipped Clarence for doing it. After the whipping, Clarence looked his father in the face and said, "You whipped me for something I didn't do. Now I'm going to go do it!" The brothers would help Clarence get even with the neighbor by actually breaking in. Clarence was caught and sent again to the boys' school for a year. For their part in the crime, Alfred and John spent time in a local boy's school for thirty days.

Over the next five years, the brothers grew more emboldened in their illicit activities. Graduating from petty thefts, they started breaking into cars, houses, and businesses as a way of making quick money. But they paid a price as well, having been caught six times, but the brothers only received minor jail sentences because they were minors. Their mother

John and Alfred working on the family farm
WIDNER FAMILY

pleaded with them each time they came home about turning their life around, but the promises made never lasted. She even saved some money and bought Clarence a guitar, hoping music would fill his free time with a more positive outlet. It didn't. The three had dropped out of school at this point. When they were asked why, they said, "We don't see the need for school anymore." And with time on their hands, trouble soon followed.

Fred Brizzi, who had also dropped out of school, traveled through Florida and Georgia but still kept in touch with his friends.

In between those times when John was incarcerated, he helped harvest the latest crop with his father and brothers and also worked as a handyman. As the family remembers, his ability to fix broken machinery and cars impressed most people who knew him.

John also made toys for his younger brothers and sisters to play with, along with keeping an eye on them. He even did a little painting, including a rendition of the family house.

Anglin home painted by John
WIDNER FAMILY

Despite his and Clarence's best intentions, the brothers didn't stay out of trouble long, as their arrest records attest:[1]

RE: John William Anglin

Contributor of Fingerprints	Name and Number	Arrested or Received	Charge	Disposition
SO, Tampa, Fla.	J.W. Anglin #29921	12/4/46	Breaking & entering, grand larceny	12/24/46, released to juvenile authorities
PD, Tampa, Florida	J.W. Anglin #35794	12/25/46	Investigation B & E	Released 12/26/46
SO, Tampa, Florida	J.W. Anglin #29921	11/16/48	Petty larceny	11/23/48 discharged
State Prison, Raiford, Fla.	J.W. Anglin #49025	12/11/51	Vagrancy investigation	12/11/51, 2 yrs state prison

RE: Clarence Anglin

Contributor of Fingerprints	Name and Number	Arrested or Received	Charge	Disposition
Fla. Industrial School for Boys, Marianna, Fla.	Clarence Anglin #2002	7/6/45	Incorrigible breaking & entering, grand larceny	Until legally discharged 8/26/46 to Mother
SO, Tampa, Fla.	Clarence Anglin #29919	12/4/46	Investigation breaking & entering, grand larceny two counts	12/24/46 to Juvenile Court
SO, Tampa, Fla.	Clarence Anglin #29919	11/16/48	Petty larceny	11/23/48 released at court (discharged)
State Board of Corrections, Atlanta, Ga.	Clarence Anglin County P.W.C.	3/14/50	Burglary	1 to 2 years

State Prison Raiford, Fla.	Clarence Anglin #48454	6/22/51	Breaking & entering with intent to commit felony grand larceny	5 years
SO, Bartow, Fla.	Clarence Anglin #P-8240	1/9/52	Escaped from State Road Camp #36	Released to Taylor County SO, Perry, Fla., 1/10/52
State Prison Raiford, Fla.	Clarence Anglin #49911	6/13/52	Breaking & entering	4 years consecutively with #48454

The FBI did not document Alfred's prison record since he hadn't been a part of the Alcatraz escape, but according to family history, he frequented jails and prisons as much as his brothers. And with his numerous incarcerations came the inevitable breakouts.

One example took place in 1947, when John, Clarence and Alfred stole $2,200 from the Ruskin Trading Company (about $26,000 in today's dollars). They were caught not long after and brought once again before Judge Himes. He sentenced John and Clarence to a year at Marianna Boys' School, but because Alfred was eighteen, he was given five years at Raiford Prison.

Raiford Prison
STATE LIBRARY AND ARCHIVES OF FLORIDA

Raiford Prison, also known as Florida State Prison, is Florida's largest and oldest correctional institution. Established in 1913 to house male and female inmates, the prison routinely assigned inmates the job of farming the 18,000-acre property.

"Living conditions in the prison were very poor. The women especially lived in horrid conditions, housed separately from the men in overcrowded, wooden dormitories. Segregation existed in all aspects of prison life, from working areas to hospitals to bathrooms."[2] Over the years,

the prison farm continued to expand. The number of salaried farm employees, agricultural specialists, and factory managers increased. In 1925 a horticulturalist was hired to grow palms, ferns, and shrubs which were sold on the open market. . . . Inmates processed and packaged cigarettes and chewing tobacco to be supplied free of charge to the prison population. By the 1940s, the farm continued to be self-sustaining with an abundance of chickens, pigs and cows.[3]

Inmates working in the fields
STATE LIBRARY AND ARCHIVES OF FLORIDA

Brutality and murder also existed at Raiford. Chain gangs were introduced in 1919, partly because a cheap workforce was needed to build roads for the growing population and tourists flocking into Florida during the 1920s land boom. If an inmate committed an infraction, he'd be whipped and put into a sweatbox (solitary confinement quarters in the broiling Florida heat).

Beatings by the guards were regular occurrences at the prison, along with other forms of brutality they inflicted on the inmates. And this was the world Alfred entered in 1947. After a year, it's little wonder he asked his brothers to help him escape. Alfred often wrote home and let the family know how he was doing. Not wanting to worry his mother, he always said he got along okay. One letter, however, stood out from the others. In particular, two lines at the bottom that were code John and Clarence recognized. He was planning on breaking out soon and wanted them to pick him up.

On the prearranged day, John pulled the car he drove off the country road when he caught sight of Raiford Prison several hundred yards away. With him were Clarence and Fred. Since they didn't know exactly when he'd make a break for it, they had no choice but to wait.

A rooster's crow woke the three up at first light. The cool morning air had fogged up the windows, so John rolled his down so he could see the prison better. Perched fifty feet in the air stood the guard tower. Farther off in the distance, a thick barrier of trees encircled the entire facility like a wall.

Fred rubbed his sleepy eyes. "Wha . . . what time is it?"

Clarence let out a yawn, then looked at his watch. "Almost seven thirty."

"You sure you're right about that message?" Fred asked, disbelief tinting his tone.

"Maybe somethin' happened," John suggested.

Without any warning, the prison siren blared. Moments later, rustling sounds from the nearby woods stopped the three cold. The plaintive wails of hound dogs came up on them fast.

"Start the car," Clarence ordered.

John turned the key, and the engine sputtered to life.

A skinny youth with wavy black hair dressed in prison clothes came running out of the woods. Breathing heavy, Alfred stopped at the tree line and looked around. When he spotted the car, Alfred sprinted for it and jumped into the back seat.

Fred slammed the door shut. "Go!"

Before John could put the car into gear, two hound dogs darted out of the woods hot on Alfred's trail, yelping and barking as they approached.

John hit the gas and sped off as a guard with a shotgun followed after the dogs.

"Get down!" John ordered.

A shot filled the air but too late. Already a quarter mile down the road, the car disappeared behind a cloud of dust and into freedom.

Alfred managed to stay out of trouble for a while, but John and Clarence went right back to their old ways. A few months after Alfred's escape from Raiford, they were arrested for petty larceny but were only jailed for a week and then released.

A year and a half later, Alfred's luck finally ran out. He and Clarence were caught breaking into and entering a home on March 3, 1950, in Seminole County, Georgia, and sent to the Atlanta state penitentiary on a charge of burglary. Both were released on January 31, 1951.

In May 1951, Clarence was caught breaking and entering once again, with intent to commit felony grand larceny, in Bradenton, Florida. The judge gave him a five-year sentence at Raiford.

A year later he and five other inmates escaped from a road camp in Perry, Florida. The *Tallahassee Democrat* wrote the following about their recapture: "Two more of the six fugitives who fled from the State Road Camp at Perry on April 30 were captured in Brooksville in a stolen car,

	NAME	FILE NUMBER	CRIME	COUNTY WHERE CONVICTED	SENTENCE		DATE RECEIVED IN PENITENTIARY		
					MIN.	MAX.	MO.	DAY	YEAR
1	Anglin, Clarence	24506	Burglary	Seminole	1	2	3	14	50
2	Anglin, Alfred	24507	Burglary	Seminole	1	2	3	14	50

Felony Conduct Record from the State Department of Corrections in Atlanta, Georgia

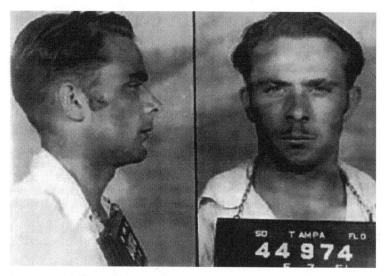

Nineteen-year-old Clarence's mug shot
SHERIFF'S OFFICE, TAMPA, FLORIDA

the Florida Highway Patrol reported last night. . . . The two listed as captured were Clarence Anglin and Robert Hayes. . . . Anglin and Hayes are being held in the Brooksville jail for state prison authorities."[4]

While Clarence and Robert Hayes were on the run, Clarence's thoughts turned toward his mother, so he wrote her a letter. Despite the letter's brevity, you get the sense of what prison life was like for Clarence at Raiford, and why he broke out with the others.

May 5, 1952

Dear Mom,

Just a few lines to say hello. And to let you all know how I am. I am getting along pretty good and I hope this will find you all the same. I guess you all feel pretty bad about me leaving don't you. Well I took all I could hoping you all would get me away from this place before I had to myself. You all should have known that they would try to do all they could to me because the only thing I could do was to leave. They wouldn't even let me have no mail. The only letter I got was one from you and from Verna the whole time back about three weeks. Mama I am going to try and make it. I am with a boy that left with me up here in Mich. I am staying with him right now Mama. I don't want you all to write me, but I am going to write you all every time I can. I am sending some after running from that same camp and going right back there. They put me in the sweat box and shot tear gas on me after they got me back and put chains on me. Trying to make me say I killed a dog, but they never found out. I tried to write you all to go to Tallahassee but they put me in the sweat box every time I wrote. So if you all blame me for leaving, well I can't help it. It was to either to leave or get smoked.

Clarence and Robert were caught five days later by patrolmen W. D. Floyd and T. W. Greene while traveling on U.S. 41. The two surrendered without a fight despite having a pistol, rifles, and ammunition in their possession. As expected, Clarence was sent back to Raiford, but with four years added to his sentence.

The *Tallahassee Democrat* filed this story on June 10 in regard to another crime committed by Clarence and Alfred:

Raiford sweatbox

Two young convicts from the state prison at Raiford, Clarence and Alfred Anglin, were each given a four-year prison term to add to the terms they are already serving. Released from the state prison temporarily to go on trial in circuit court for burglarizing the Majorette Drive-In, they were found guilty of breaking and entering by a jury this morning. Judge W. May Walker sentenced them after State Atty. W. D. Hopkins disclosed that they were already serving nine years for burglary and breaking and entering. He also reported to the court that Clarence had made two attempts to escape from the prison, and had been involved in a prison strike; while Alfred's record showed one escape attempt.[5]

The article does not explain why Alfred had been sent to Raiford, but based on the newspaper account he was also given an additional four years to his sentence after being convicted of burglarizing the Majorette Drive-In in Miami, which most likely took place in May 1951. Alfred then had a decision to make. Do his nine-year stint while enduring mistreatment by the guards and fellow prisoners, or take matters into his own hands.

The area surrounding his home in Ruskin is made up largely of limestone. Composed of calcium carbonate, limestone is utilized commercially in many ways: as a building material, as an essential component of concrete, as aggregate for roads, as a chemical feedstock for the production of lime, and as a soil conditioner.[6]

With the discovery of limestone around Ruskin by the Spanish in 1672, mining soon followed. As the centuries passed, large pits dotting the area soon formed. With an average rainfall of fifty-four inches a year, the pits filled with water. The locals stocked them with fish, and soon a local pastime had been created.

Alfred knew this while doing his time at Raiford. But the days came slow, and so he formed a plan of escape in December 1953, which he executed on the seventh, this time without his brothers' help. Clarence made it a practice of going straight home whenever he broke out of prison, which always led to his rearrest. His brother Robert recounted one example with a reporter in 2007:

Clarence was working a road gang somewhere around Ft. Meyers. Turns out Clarence's mother Rachel and another of her sons went to visit Clarence in the jail. Clarence told them not to come next week, that he would be visiting them at home. The mother and brother shrugged it off to Clarence's usual banter. The following week, Clarence, true to his word, escaped the road gang with two other prisoners. Clarence was barefoot and made his way up the Gulf Coast, wading and swimming for more than sixty miles.[7]

Upon his return home, Clarence was promptly arrested.

Not wanting to make the same mistake, Alfred knew he'd have a better chance of evading the police if he hid at the Pits until the heat died down.

While working outside Raiford prison as part of a road gang on December 7, Alfred took off running. Just like Clarence had done the year before, he went by way of rivers, dirt roads, and swamps. Several days later, Alfred finally arrived at Ruskin. Rather than go home, he hid out at the Fellowship Primitive Baptist Cemetery (founded in 1903) at the edge of town. He knew not many people frequented the area, and the large groves of trees easily covered his movements.

Alfred also knew he could sustain himself indefinitely by fishing at the nearby Pits.

Considered the smartest of the three, Alfred finally went to his house after first making sure the authorities weren't around. Though his parents weren't happy about the escape, they agreed to provide him with a tent and basic cooking and fishing equipment so he could live somewhat comfortably in the wilderness. His brothers and sisters visited him on occasion, though they referred to Alfred as "Uncle Charley" so as to keep his true identity a secret.

Neither Alfred nor the family knew at the time that this would be his home for the next five years, which the FBI later corroborated when they interviewed one of his former cellmates.[8]

He also commented that when ALFRED ANGLIN last escaped from State custody, and was out for five years, he hid out in Haynes, Florida.

CHAPTER 7

Winds of Change

When you can't change the direction of the wind, adjust your sails.
—H. JACKSON BROWN

NOT QUITE TWENTY-FOUR IN EARLY 1956, FRED BRIZZI HAD ALMOST finished his private pilot's training, which he had been talked into by his father. Turned out that Fred liked flying. His father certainly approved of him pursuing a positive outlet in his life for a change.

A letter arrived in the mail for Fred at that time from Sam Hunt, one of the friends he had made when his family lived in Conchas, New Mexico. If it weren't for him, Fred might have run away back to Ruskin.

Though they hadn't seen each other since, Sam had heard about Fred getting sent to Marianna and thought a trip out to New Mexico might do him some good. He also wanted to talk with him about something but didn't say what in the letter.

Both parents had no objections about him visiting Sam, though they also worried about him driving out there alone. His father even offered to come if Fred didn't feel comfortable going that far by himself.

Fred appreciated his concern. Despite being angry with his dad for a long time after they returned from New Mexico, Fred knew his father had done his best to spend as much time with him as possible, and their relationship did improve. But Fred wasn't a boy anymore. He had been itching to make a life for himself and thought a little time away just might be the first steps toward making that happen.

The next day Fred headed west to New Mexico. All told, the 1,576 miles from Tampa to Tucumcari took about thirty hours on the road. He traversed some of the newly constructed Interstate 75 in Florida and parts of I-10 that stretched across the country to California, though many sections of the interstate were still under construction, so he took whatever roads he could along the way, dirt or otherwise.

After three long days of driving, Fred finally entered Tucumcari, forty miles southeast of Conchas Dam, where Sam and his family had moved after the completion of the construction project. When he pulled into the driveway of Sam's modest-looking house, a brand-new convertible Cadillac El Dorado was parked out front. In a dusty blue-collar town like Tucumcari, the mint green, two-door sedan stood out from the more commonplace Fords and Chevrolets.

The Hunts greeted Fred like a long-lost son. The warmth and friendship created all those years ago hadn't diminished, and he truly felt welcomed. They had set up a room for Fred, which he appreciated.

The next morning, Fred and Sam got up early and headed into town, stopping at a local diner for breakfast.

"The place hasn't changed much since I was here last," Fred said as he looked out the window. "Never understood why you stayed."

As the two ate their bacon and eggs Sam cleared his throat then looked Fred straight in the eye. "Tell me, Fred, you like the car I'm driving?"

Fred glanced as the Cadillac parked out front. "Of course. I was gonna ask you how you managed to talk the old man into buying you somethin' like that."

"Didn't have to. Bought the car myself."

"How the heck did you get that kind of money?" Fred asked, clearly impressed. "You rob a bank or somethin'?"

Sam smiled. "Nope. Tell you what, I've got something I need to drop off tonight. I hoped you might wanna come along."

Fred thought it over a moment. "Sure, why not."

That night the two of them traveled thirty miles south of town. Sam pulled into the driveway of a house that looked abandoned. A pair of headlights appeared down the road not long after. Moments later, a car with its license plate covered pulled up behind them.

"Stay here."

Sam stepped out and opened the trunk. He retrieved four brown bags, which he carried over to the waiting car. In turn, Sam received an envelope from the driver, but not before he pointed at Fred, and the two talked for several moments. Whatever Sam said, the unknown person seemed to accept. Their transaction completed, the driver turned the car around and disappeared in a cloud of dust.

Sam stepped back into his car and set the envelope on the seat.

Fred looked at the envelope, then at Sam. "You doin' drugs or somethin'?"

"Not doin'. Transporting. I pick up marijuana from a supplier and drop it off at different locations. In that envelope is my payment."

Fred picked up the envelope and pulled out a wad of twenties. "So, you play delivery boy, but don't worry about growing or getting caught. Sounds like some easy money."

"More than you know."

The next couple of days Sam told Fred more about the operation and how he got connected with it. Sam had taken a trip to Los Angeles with some friends a couple of years back and had been introduced to a mobster who sometimes did business out of strip joint called the Largo Club. He hired them as couriers to move the marijuana between different distributers.

Drawn by the idea of making some real money for the first time in his life, Fred found himself interested. Turned out this was the reason Sam asked him to come in the first place. He had heard from Fred's sister, Doris, who wrote a couple of months before, mentioning Fred taking flying lessons, and this unnamed mobster was looking for ways to expand his operation. "Like you said, Fred, it's easy money, and with you getting your pilot's license, think of the possibilities."

Fred thought about it, a lot. Truth be told, he didn't see much of a future for himself in Ruskin, and the last thing he wanted was to live life begging for jobs like his father.

He packed up and was ready to go the next morning. When Fred slipped into the front seat of his car, Sam took out a magazine ad from his pocket and handed it to him.

"I called my boss, Mickey Cohen, and told him you were comin'." Sam also gave him several twenty-dollar bills. "And this is for expenses."

"Wow. That's a lot of money."

"All you have to do is show up at the Largo Club two nights from now. If he likes you, you're in. The money will start flowin' your way not long after. You can trust me on that."

Fred pulled up two days later in front of the club, located on Sunset Boulevard in the heart of West Hollywood. When he walked inside, he stopped and gave the place a long look.

An unseen voice startled him. "You looking for someone pal or come for the show?"

Fred turned and stood face-to-face with the club's owner, Chuck Landis.

Key magazine ad

Landis moved to Los Angeles in 1945 from Minneapolis and opened the Morocco, hoping to capitalize on post–World War II prosperity. The nightclub soon became a success, and over the decade he opened several others in West Hollywood. In the 1950s he converted an old market on Sunset Strip into the Largo, which he billed as the nation's "class" burlesque house.[1]

Landis stood a little taller than Fred, but much heavier. Thick brown hair and bushy sideburns complemented the man's burly persona.

"Not sure. I was told I'd be meetin' someone here and ask for table number five."

Landis's eyebrows furrowed together. "You Brizzi?"

"I am, and you are . . . ?"

"The name's Landis. This way."

Chuck brought Fred to a small table with a pair of chairs in the middle of the establishment. A stage a few feet away graced the front. Shimmering curtains hung from the ceiling, and floor light faced upward.

Chuck snapped his finger and a pretty waitress walked over to them. "Give my friend here whatever he wants. On the house."

"Yes, Mr. Landis," she replied with a smile, then turned and went toward the bar.

He patted Fred on the shoulder and told him to enjoy the show. An hour later Fred had watched two strippers do their act while waiting for Cohen, when a minor commotion on his right caught his attention—a short balding man in his forties dressed in a business suit and tie approached, Landis at his side.

"Here's your favorite seat, Mr. Cohen. Enjoy the show."

The man in the suit smiled in reply. "Chuck, anything my Candy does is always the best."

As the man took his seat, Fred noticed someone who looked like a bodyguard standing behind him, along with another at the door. Cohen looked over at Fred and extended his hand. "Name's Mickey Cohen, and you must be Fred."

Meyer Cohen was born on September 4, 1913, into an Orthodox Jewish family. He started working at age six selling newspapers. In 1922 a petty crime landed him in reform school. Cohen took up

Mickey Cohen
KTTV-FOX 11 NEWS

boxing and turned professional at the age of fifteen. In 1931 Cohen fought against future world featherweight champion Tommy Paul. He was knocked out in the first round but fought well enough to earn the name "Gangster Mickey Cohen." When his boxing career ended in 1933, Cohen found himself drawn into the world of organized crime. He moved back to New York and became involved with racketeering. Later he went to Chicago and helped run Al Capone's gambling operation. Then Cohen moved to Los Angeles and met up with Bugsy Siegel. In 1947 Cohen helped set up the Flamingo Hotel in Las Vegas, where he ran a sports booking operation. From the 1950s onward he also trafficked in marijuana and heroin from Mexico. Mickey's life as a gangster also brought him some celebrity, but not without paying a price: wars with other gangsters, numerous attempts on his life, and eventual imprisonment.[2]

"I am. Nice to meet you, Mr. Cohen."

"Please, call me Mickey."

The stage lights came on and Landis walked onto the stage.

"Tell me, Fred, have you ever had a chance to see the lovely Miss Barr before?"

"No, sir, I haven't."

Mickey leaned close. "I promise you this, you'll never see anyone more beautiful."

Candy Barr was born Juanita Dale Slusher on July 6, 1935, in Edna, Texas. She was nine years old when her mother died after falling out of a moving car. Her father then married Etta Holden. Juanita's early years were reportedly scarred by the trauma of sexual abuse by a neighbor. At thirteen she ran away from home and went to Dallas and began working as a prostitute. At the age of fourteen she reportedly married her first husband, Billy Joe Debbs, an alleged safecracker, but the marriage ended after he was sent to prison. She also worked as a cocktail waitress and cigarette girl before eventually becoming an exotic dancer.[3]

The lights dropped, the curtain opened, and Miss Barr stepped out wearing her trademark cowboy hat, pearl-handled six-shooters, cowboy boots, and not much else.

Mickey leaned over a second time. "We'll talk more after the show. Enjoy."

Fred turned forward and watched Candy's act. He wondered how he could take pleasure seeing a woman take off her clothes when the man who loved her sat beside him. Strange indeed.

When her fame grew as an exotic dancer, she and Cohen started dating, and he fell passionately in love with Candy and wanted to marry her. In 1957 she was arrested for a marijuana charge and sentenced to fifteen years in prison. During her appeal, Mickey hid Candy at his farm in Mexico. Cohen sent her money for expenses, until she returned to the United States against his wishes. The authorities arrested her and she served three years at the Goree State Farm for Women in Huntsville, Texas. While there, she testified against Cohen during his tax evasion trial in 1961.[4]

Candy Barr in her cowboy outfit
MIKE LYNCH

When the lights came back on, Miss Barr stepped off stage accompanied by whistles and clapping. Cohen was right. Fred found himself mesmerized by her performance.

Mickey scooted this chair toward Fred's. "Didn't I tell you she was good?"

"You did. I've never seen anything quite like it before."

Cohen's demeanor shifted. "Enough of the pleasantries. We both know why we're here, so let's get down to brass tacks. I understand you're interested in being a part of my operation."

"If you're talkin' about the drugs Sam moves, then yes, I'm interested."

Cohen put his hand on Fred's shoulder. "Let's get one thing straight. We don't refer to the things I transport as drugs. We refer to it as merchandise. You got that?"

Fred replied with a hesitant nod.

A soft smile pushed on the corner of Cohen's mouth. "Don't worry about it, kid. An associate of mine will contact you in the next couple of days and instruct you about the operation. Later, when you get your pilot's license, we'll discuss how we do pickups and drop-offs. I have some thoughts about expanding, and you just might fit in well with that."

An idea popped into Fred's head, one that could benefit both his new benefactor and his friends: the Anglin brothers. "Mr. Cohen, I just had a thought, something that may interest you."

"Of course. Always interested in someone's ideas."

"I have some friends back home who can grow just about anything. You should see some of the tomatoes their family produces every year. They'd be a great addition to your operation. Trust me, they'd produce some quality merchandise for you."

Cohen sat back in his chair and studied Fred. After a moment, a muted smirk softened his features. "I don't normally trust someone without seeing what they can do first, but I have a feeling about you. I'll give your boys a shot on a limited scale. If they do well, we increase their output. You think they might have something for me by end of summer?"

"I'm sure of it. When I get back I'll talk with them and get everything set up."

Cohen looked back at a man with Hollywood good looks and confident swagger standing in the rear of the club. Cohen motioned for him to come over. "This here is Johnny Stompanato, and he handles a number of my business dealings."

The man offered Fred a restrained nod.

"Brizzi here will need a little seed money." He laughed at his own joke. "I think a thousand dollars should be sufficient."

Fred looked with amazement as Stompanato counted out ten one-hundred-dollar bills and laid them on the table. He had never seen that much money in his life.

Cohen rose up from his chair and started for the front entrance when he suddenly turned back. "Summertime, Mr. Brizzi. Don't disappoint me."

Candy met him at the door, now dressed in more modest clothes. She kissed him, and the two left. For Fred, he somehow knew his life would never be the same.

After a long drive home, Fred looked for the Anglins at his first opportunity. He finally found them parked near the Little Manatee River. Alfred and John sat on the hood of their car, smoking cigarettes. Clarence was just coming out of the water.

Mickey and Candy Barr
KTTV-FOX 11 NEWS

"Fred, you old dog," John said with a smile. "Where the heck you been? We've all been wonderin' if you got caught or something."

"Naw, nothing like that. Been out of town visitin' an old friend in New Mexico."

"Sounds like fun," Clarence commented. "Maybe we should plan a trip out there one day."

"That's kinda the reason I came by lookin' for y'all."

Fred cleared his throat and was about to tell them about Sam and Mickey when a car pulling a boat crept into the parking lot. The mother and father sat in the front seat, a girl in her teens sat in the back.

Alfred gave John a playful hit on the back. "Hey John, isn't that Helen in the car? Looks like the family's goin' for a boat ride. Here's your chance with her, little brother."

"I just may talk with her."

Fred pulled out his wad of cash, which got the brothers' attention.

"Where'd you get that?" Clarence asked, his eyes wide. "You rob a bank or somethin'?"

"You guys interested in makin' some money? Not the usual nickel and dime stuff you pull around here. I'm talkin' real money, like this."

"Hell yeah," Clarence replied without hesitation. "What you got in mind?"

"I'm in, whatever it is," Alfred added. Hiding out at the Pits the last few years had lost its luster a long time back, and he was ready for anything different.

"You Anglins are some of the best farmers around these parts. Hell, I bet you can grow just about anything you put your minds to."

"Guess you could say it's in our blood," Alfred declared. "What did ya have in mind?"

"I met someone in California. He's willing to buy all the marijuana you can grow, as long as it's good stuff."

"Marijuana?" Alfred considered Fred's proposition. "Never thought about doin' that before, but if he pays top dollar . . . We've been talkin' about buyin' our own farm for years. Maybe this is our chance."

"Hang on, Al," John objected. "Where are we supposed to grow a crop like that?"

"How 'bout the farm? There's that patch in the back Daddy ain't usin'. The trees should cover that area real good."

"You know what will happen if we get caught," Clarence said with foreboding. "Daddy would thrash us good if he ever found out."

"Then we do it careful."

"Well?" Fred asked. "You in or not?"

"All right," Clarence replied. "If we can keep it hidden, I'm in."

"Fine." John shifted his attention toward Helen as her father slipped his boat into the water.

"Slow down, lover boy," Alfred chided him. "Not sure a rich girl like her would give someone like you the time of day."

"Oh yeah," John declared. "Watch me."

He marched over to Helen and started up a conversation. A moment later she laughed at something he said. John turned back and nodded at his brothers.

For the sake of appearances, John, Clarence, and Alfred tended the farm as they always had, but when their work brought them in the vicinity of the fields where the tree line made for good cover, they cleared out an area and planted their first crop of marijuana.

The brothers working on the farm
WIDNER FAMILY

With rains and sunshine plentiful, Ruskin was also blessed with the type of soil that could grow most vegetables, which also happened to be the perfect ecosystem for marijuana. The brothers discovered they were good at growing that too.

CHAPTER 8

Romeo and Juliet

These violent delights have violent ends.
—*ROMEO AND JULIET*, ACT 2, SCENE 6

THE LOVE STORY BETWEEN JOHN ANGLIN AND HELEN TAYLOR STARTED out just like Romeo and Juliet. John first met Helen in elementary school at Ruskin, and like many kids at that age, a crush soon followed. As has been previously discussed, the Anglin boys experienced bullying by the other children, and their teachers often singled them out for things they did and didn't do. One of the playground teachers even informed Fern Taylor, Helen's father, he might want to speak with his daughter about her choice of friends, as he probably didn't consider the Anglin boys the suitable kind of people for an upstanding girl like her.

Despite their obvious differences, what John loved about Helen was how she never made fun of the way he dressed, and usually played with him at recess, that is, until her father got involved. John had grown used to the mistreatment from others, but he took it hard the day Helen told him she couldn't play with him anymore. What John didn't know at the time was how Helen tried to change her father's mind about him. But he would have none of it, and so she had no choice but to play with other kids. True love, however, cannot be squelched so easily, and John and Helen found other ways of seeing each other beyond their teachers' prying eyes.

Running a farm and raising a family of fourteen was a constant chore, and George Anglin needed all the help he could get, which is why his sons were often pulled out of school and asked to do their share of the work. George and Rachel hated doing this, but hard times required sacrifice.

John didn't miss the fights at school, but he sure missed seeing Helen there. But that didn't keep him from visiting with her in town. More than once Helen's father saw John hanging around and kept warning his daughter about him, but as she grew older those warnings didn't carry the weight they once did. Helen was interested in John, and her father knew it. Fern had hoped John dropping out of school would keep the two apart, but the growing love between them had a way of pulling them back together.

Most families in Ruskin didn't give their teenage children expensive gifts, but the Taylors weren't just any family. Helen's father had money, and he used it as a way of displaying his status in the community. An example of this is when he bought Helen a car on her sixteenth birthday. The following Sunday, she drove to the church John and his family attended. From the parking lot, Helen caught his attention through the window with a couple of quick waves.

John looked at the far end of the pew. His parents' attention fixed on the preacher behind the pulpit, he recognized his opportunity and slunk down low and started for the exit. But Clarence grabbed his arm.

"You crazy? You better sit back down before Daddy catches you."

Sitting down was the furthest thing from John's mind. "Cover for me." And off he went.

Despite her father's objections, John and Helen tried to see each other whenever possible, until Fern finally had enough. He figured sending her off to family in Ohio was the only way of breaking them up for good. At first, they kept in touch with each other through her sister, Ruth, but the miles and time apart proved difficult for the pair. Though they missed each other terribly, as with many teenagers, the two started seeing other people. Even when Helen finally returned to Ruskin just before her high school graduation, their interests lay elsewhere.

Helen's father could not have been happier when she agreed to marry Jim McIntosh, a local boy who had been interested in her for a while. Even though John dated other girls, he didn't take the news well, especially when he found out through Ruth the couple had moved away. A few years would pass before Helen talked Jim into returning to Tampa, but with their marriage already having issues because of their age and lack of compatibility, she secretly hoped John still had feelings for her.

Helen Taylor
WIDNER FAMILY

When John found out Helen had returned and her marriage was on the rocks, he stopped seeing the girl he had been dating and focused his attentions on winning Helen back, marriage or no marriage.

Situated along the shores of the Little Manatee River, Bahia Beach served as a resort community for locals and visitors alike, including marinas designated for boating and other types of water activities. John knew that Helen often spent time there with her family, and he made himself available.

Before heading to the resort on a warm Saturday morning, John promised his younger sister Marie he'd take her daughter Sue to the beach. He knew how much Helen loved children, so having his niece with him would be an easy way of starting up a conversation.

Pulling into the parking lot with Sue, John spotted Helen's car and went about searching for her. It didn't take long before he found Helen with her husband and Ruth.

"Hey Helen," John called out. "What a surprise."

Bahia Beach postcard, near Ruskin (four miles from the Anglin home)

Engaged in a conversation with her sister, Helen turned around and smiled at John, then glanced at her husband. Her demeanor stiffened. "John, what are you doing here?"

He put his hands on Sue's shoulders. "Oh, just takin' my niece out for some fun in the sun." He caught himself. "Where are my manners? This is Sue, my sister's kid."

When Sue smiled in reply, Helen just fell in love with her. "Sue. That's a pretty name. Do you wanna come join us?"

John agreed for her, and the two sat beside Helen.

"John, you remember Ruth, and my husband."

John tried to be polite, though he really wanted Jim gone. John shifted his attention toward Ruth, specifically mentioning that Clarence asked him to say hello, which she appreciated.

With the distraction of the waves hitting the beach, the conversation soon faded into silence. John sat as far away from Jim as possible but felt his glare on him the second he sat down. Rather than let him hold the dominant position, John decided he'd take Jim down a peg. "So, I hear you two might be ending things soon."

The temperature dropped in an instant as Jim locked eyes with John. "Well, it might work out if we could get some alone time."

"Jim and I were just talkin', and we both agree some time apart might be good. We'll see what happens after that."

What Jim didn't know was that she had already made up her mind about leaving him, and no amount of talking would change things. And since there wasn't much point in dwelling on the subject, she shifted her attention to John, which Jim grew tired of in short order.

"I think I'll get going. Got some things I need to do." As Jim stood, he couldn't help but throw in one more condescending remark at John's expense. "Tell me, what kind of work are you into these days? Still farming dirt?"

His insult felt like school all over again, and in front of Helen no less. John's hands balled into fists and he considered punching Jim in the face, but he also knew Helen wouldn't like it, so he pulled out the one trump card he knew her husband couldn't top. "Actually, my brothers and me are workin' with someone in Los Angeles on a special job that's been very profitable."

"Oh really," Jim chided him. "What kind of business needs a dirt farmer? Pig slop comes to mind."

John jumped to his feet. "Believe me, I'll have enough money soon enough where I can treat Helen right. Better than you, anyways."

Jim laughed. "Yeah, sure." He got into his car and sped off.

"Good riddance," John said under his breath. He shifted his attention toward Helen and helped her up. "How about we take a walk on the beach? Sue, you mind playing on the beach by yourself for a while? We won't be gone too long."

"I guess so."

John and Helen started down the beach. "I tell you, Helen, I never knew what you ever saw in him. He just ain't right for you."

She gave John a long look. "Oh, and you are, Mr. Anglin?"

"You bet I am. I'll shower you with all the love in my heart, sure enough, and do just about anything for you." He grabbed her hand. "You know I've had feelings for you all the way back when I first saw you on the playground in school. I never thought our lives would turn out this way, but here we are."

"Yes, here we are." Helen stopped and looked deeply into John's eyes. The two drifted toward each other and kissed.

As they walked along the water's edge John suggested they go on a double date with Clarence and Ruth the next day. Helen accepted, certain she could get her sister on board.

The double-date turned into an all-day event driving around Tampa: out to Ybor City for lunch, over to St. Petersburg, across the Skyway Bridge, and back to Ruskin. Other dates followed, which deeply troubled John's parents. Helen was still married, though John tried to assure them she planned on divorcing Jim. Divorce or not, the fact that they were together didn't sit well with his mother. She had definite feelings about what the Bible said regarding being involved with a married woman.

Days turned into weeks, and before long John and Helen spent most days together. Their feelings for each other grew more serious, and John knew he wanted to be with her the rest of his life. But he also feared telling her about the marijuana he and his brothers grew for Cohen.

John and Helen, the happy couple
WIDNER FAMILY

How might she react when she found out? But if they did have a future together, he should be honest with her.

John decided to take Helen to the park, where they could talk in private.

He hemmed and hawed as they sat on the grass. Two days before he had received a letter from Cohen. He wanted the brothers to drive out to California and discuss an important business matter with them, something he said would make the three a lot of money. Every time the words formed on his lips, they seemed to get stuck there.

"My, my, you're as nervous as a piglet at a hog roast," she joked.

John knew it was now or never. "Helen, I need to talk to you about somethin'. Somethin' important."

She let out a nervous laugh. "You're not going to break up with me, are you? If it's about Jim—"

"No, no," he interrupted. "This has nothing to do with him."

"Good. I was afraid . . ." She caught herself. "You know you can tell me anything."

"Okay. Here goes. I'm leaving with my brothers so we can travel out west. We're planning on meeting with our business associate, the one I told you about."

Helen's gaze drifted downward. "How long you think you'll be gone?"

John saw the worry in her eyes. "A couple of weeks, and I promise I won't stay one minute longer than I have to."

She hugged John tight. "That's a long time, and I'll miss you terrible."

John's heart melted, and he gave her a kiss. "If this works out as good as I hope, you won't want for anything ever again."

"I guess I can wait until you get back."

They hugged again.

John would miss her as well, though he still couldn't bring himself to tell her who he was meeting with and why. Maybe when they returned he'd have the courage then.

CHAPTER 9

The Trip West

ON FEBRUARY 26, 1957, THE MCCLELLAN COMMITTEE SENATE HEAR-
ings commenced with its investigation of corruption, criminal infiltra-
tion, and illegal activities in the nation's labor unions.

Chaired by Democrat John McClellan, the committee included John
F. Kennedy and Barry Goldwater, along with Robert Kennedy as chief
counsel. The committee's investigation focused on the International
Brotherhood of Teamsters, teamster president Dave Beck, and Beck's
successor, Jimmy Hoffa. In televised hearings watched in over 1 million
American households, the committee detailed the Teamsters' misuse of
union funds and ties to labor racketeers and organized crime.[1]

Alfred, Clarence, and John
KEN WIDNER

In all, the committee conducted 253 investigations, served 8,000 subpoenas for witnesses and documents, and took testimony from 1,526 witnesses.

With the heat ratcheted up against organized crime, and the national recognition gained by the Kennedy brothers as a result of those hearings, they soon turned their attention toward prosecuting other reputed mobsters, one of them being Mickey Cohen. Unfortunately for the Anglin brothers, their trip west could not have come at a worse time.

Dressed in a pair of work jeans and T-shirt, Clarence grabbed his suitcase and put it in the trunk of his brother's car, while John, tanned and lean and sporting no shirt, was eager to get going. Helen stood nearby and wiped away a tear.

"Promise me you'll call," she said. "Let me know you're okay."

John promised he would, and maybe send a postcard or two.

Alfred held hands with Jeanette Anderson, his girlfriend of a few months. Though the thirteen-year age gap between them raised eyebrows, both paid the talk around town little attention. They were in love and didn't care who knew.

"Mama said I should forget about you, bein' an Anglin and all, but my heart just can't let me," Jeanette declared. "Makes no never-mind what folks say. You're a good person, Alfred Anglin, and I'll be waitin' for you." She threw her arms around his neck and hugged him tight.

The brothers packing for the trip
WIDNER FAMILY

From the porch their parents and siblings watched in silence. They had said their goodbyes before the girls showed up, and to do so again would only drum up emotions already expressed. They waved, then went into the house.

John kissed Helen, then got into the car with his brothers. Alfred started up the engine and headed toward downtown Ruskin and onto US 41, which eventually connected with I-75, then west on I-10, and if they didn't have any major problems along the way, they'd arrive in Los Angeles a week later and finally meet their benefactor, Mickey Cohen. The three assumed Fred would meet them in LA as well, as no one had heard from him in weeks.

The miles passed by one blurry hour after another. With the journey over 2,500 miles long, the brothers took turns behind the wheel. Every few hours they'd pull over and get something to eat or gas up the car. During those stops, the brothers sometimes took pictures of themselves. Since the family had never seen this part of the country before, they figured everyone would enjoy looking at photos of the places they visited.

The trip, for the most part, fell into a routine not long after they left. The brothers switched drivers when one of them got tired. They listened to music on the radio from a nearby station or watched the vistas drift by. When they stopped for a meal, John and Alfred sometimes made calls to Helen and Jeanette, just as they had promised. The girls were always glad to hear from them and bombarded the brothers with a thousand questions. But the two kept the calls short and got back on the road at their earliest opportunity.

Every so often, the conversation invariably gravitated toward what they thought might be waiting for them in California, what Mickey Cohen was like, and their thoughts about what kind of deal he had for them. They figured it must be something big, or he wouldn't have asked them drive out all that way. And by big, that meant the money that went with it, and perhaps make enough to buy a farm for themselves, which the brothers had wanted for years.

When the three came upon something interesting, they'd stop and take in the scenery.

Posing by the car
WIDNER FAMILY

Perhaps the most eventful part of their trip was a daring stunt they pulled off during a gas stop. According to family history, somewhere out west they stopped for gas and drove off without paying. Later they were pulled over by a highway patrolman and talked the cop into letting them help him find the guys who did it. The brothers told him they saw a car back a few miles turn off the road onto another one, and the cop believed them. Even though the three had gotten away with the theft of gas, the brothers decided they shouldn't take a risk like that again. The police officer could have just as easily arrested them on the spot and thrown them in jail, and where'd they be then? The biggest opportunity of their lives squandered because of a stupid stunt. From this point on, the only thing that mattered was getting to California without incident.

When John, Clarence, and Alfred finally crossed the state line near the town of Blythe on I-10, they found the landscape nothing more than desert and scrub brush. All their lives the brothers had heard about the wonders of California, such as palm trees, sandy beaches, large cities, and Hollywood. But a desert, no one ever talked about that.

Visiting nature's wonders
WIDNER FAMILY

After checking at a gas station in Los Angeles, the brothers found Mickey Cohen's house in an upscale neighborhood called Brentwood. For being a crime boss running a West Coast syndicate, they were a little surprised when they saw his home for the first time.

The brothers expected something big and splashy, akin to a Hollywood mansion in Beverly Hills. On the other hand, they also understood the value of hiding in plain sight. An obvious display of wealth drew unwanted attention, something not easily explained as the owner of small businesses in the Los Angeles area, such as the About Towne clothing store located on Sunset Strip.

As the three brothers walked up the driveway, John took note of the manicured lawns and hedges. Same for the houses packed close together on the sun-drenched street. Back in Ruskin, acres of land separated people's homes, most without fences. And with fields of crops between farms, few bothered manicuring anything.

Alfred reached the door first and knocked. Someone stirred inside, and several moments later the most beautiful woman they had ever seen before answered—Candy Barr.

"Hello."

The three brothers stood slack-jawed as they took in the shapely beauty dressed in a bikini covered by a kimono robe.

"Something I can do for you?" she asked with a warm smile.

"I, uh . . ." Alfred stammered. "Does Mickey Cohen live here?"

Cohen's home in Brentwood
KTTV-FOX 11 NEWS

She looked back over her shoulder. "Hey Mick, three, uh . . . gentle-men are here to see you."

The way she said "gentlemen" hinted at a mild slight, but the brothers didn't care. They just stood there enjoying the view.

"What do they want?" a man replied from another room.

Candy turned back and faced them. "Is this personal or business?"

"I'm Alfred Anglin, and these here are my brothers, John and Clar-ence. We drove out from Florida to meet with Mr. Cohen. We received a letter from him."

A short chubby man with thinning hair turned off a television set showing the McClellan hearings and walked toward the door. Though they had never met before, something about him commanded attention. "Are you the Anglins?"

The three nodded in unison.

"Well, about time you got here. I told Candy this morning I was wonderin' when you'd show up, didn't I, Candy?"

"Yeah, sure, Mick."

A broad smile stretched across his face. "Come in. Come in. Don't just stand there."

Candy opened the door a little wider.

"Well, here they are, my three green thumbs. I must say, Fred didn't lie when he bragged about your farming skills. What you produce is some of the best stuff I've ever seen."

"Thank you, Mr. Cohen," Alfred said. "We didn't want to disap-point you."

"Please, call me Mickey." Cohen caught himself. "Where are my manners?" He tipped his head toward Candy. "This is Candy Barr, my girlfriend."

"Hello, again."

"Hello," Clarence replied with a smirk, followed by Alfred and John. "Candy Barr. That's an interesting name."

"Her professional one," Cohen stated matter-of-factly. "She's a dancer. The best in town."

She gave them a quick dance, then laughed.

"Very nice, Baby, but me and the boys have some things we need to discuss."

"I know, I know," she said playfully. "Make myself scarce." She blew a kiss at Cohen and disappeared in the kitchen.

"Why don't we go out back and talk there."

Cohen led the three into a yard similarly manicured as the front. He guided them toward a patio table and chairs.

"Anything I can get you fellas?" Cohen asked. "Candy mixes a mean cocktail."

The brothers settled on beer, which she brought on a tray.

"You have a fine place here, Mr. Cohen," John complemented. "Much better than what we have in Ruskin."

Cohen looked around, clearly proud of his home. "This can be within your reach as well, which is why I had you come out. Nothin' tells the truth more than results."

"We talked about the same thing on our way here," Clarence stated, speaking for the first time. "The money you paid us for the . . ." He looked into the house.

"Marijuana," Cohen finished for him. "It's okay. Candy knows all about what I do."

"Well, it's nice to finally get some real spendin' money."

"There's more of that for you three. A lot more. I have something in mind I'd like to show you. I think you'll agree it will be a better setup than your little dirt patch in Florida."

Mickey drove Candy and the brothers to Van Nuys Airport about a half hour away. There a twin-prop Cessna had already been fueled up. The cabin was a tight fit for the five, plus the pilot, John Kelly, but they managed.

Kelly radioed the tower and received permission to taxi to the runway. The plane rolled out onto the tarmac and positioned itself at the far end.

"Hold on," Cohen said from the copilot's chair. "This is where it gets fun."

A firm grin formed on Cohen's face when Kelly pushed forward on the throttle controls and both engines revved up in an instant. All three brothers clutched their armrests tight as the plane shot forward in a burst of acceleration.

Candy threw her arms around Cohen's neck and held him tight, both eyes shut. "I hate this part."

Kelly pulled back on the controls and the Cessna lurched into the air. All three brothers felt their stomachs practically drop out of their bodies.

Only when Kelly leveled out at about 12,000 feet did the brothers finally relax.

"How long before we reach where we're goin'?"

"Not long," Cohen replied. "We'll be at the place before you know it. Though it's a shame Brizzi won't be there to meet you."

The brothers looked at one another, uncertain what he meant.

"I assumed you knew. Arrested in Utah. He and a couple of his friends tried robbing a telephone company. Police caught them in the act. Should get out in a year."

"I guess that explains why we haven't heard from him in a while."

A half hour later Kelly banked hard and pushed the control forward. When he did, the plane's nose dipped and the ground slowly rose toward them. A dirt runway appeared near a cluster of small houses.

Candy buried her face into Cohen's neck like before. "I changed my mind. I hate landings more than takeoffs."

Kelly lined up the plane with the runway and hit the ground hard. The Cessna bounced a couple of times before finally coming to a stop. Kelly then taxied toward several houses made out of mud brick with red tiled roofs. A group of children watched from one of the porches, pointing and laughing.

"Thank you for flying Cohen Air," Kelly joked. "Please put your trays in an upright position and prepare to disembark."

The brothers jumped off the plane after Cohen and Kelly and took in their surroundings.

"This will be the hub of my West Coast operation," Cohen declared. "Before Fred was arrested in Utah, he flew drugs for me into the U.S. from Mexico City, but I can no longer keep up with demand so I'm expanding out west." He turned and faced them directly. "What do ya think, boys? Can you make somethin' out of this place?"

The brothers looked at the sunbaked land filled with scrub brush.

John crouched down and picked up a handful of dirt. "This is bone dry."

Alfred's gaze drifted upward, the sun's rays pounding down on him. "There's certainly plenty of sun around here, but what we need most is water." He kicked at the ground.

"Don't you worry about that," Cohen assured him. "I had a well dug over by those houses. Tapped into an aquifer that should be more than enough for your needs. What you see is five acres, which translates into approximately twenty thousand plants. At today's prices, we're talking a million dollars at harvesttime. If you farm the land right, we can have yields all year round. Best part, you get a cut of everything you grow."

"How much?" Clarence asked.

"For now, one percent of the profits, then I'll see how you boys do after. You keep me happy and I'll increase your cut. It's as simple as that. What do you say?"

Alfred looked at John, who looked at Clarence.

"Can you give us a minute?"

Cohen nodded. "Of course."

The brothers walked about the property, discussed the offer, then returned to Cohen.

"Well?"

"Okay, we're in."

A broad smile parted Cohen's lips. "I was hoping you'd say that. And just so you know, I'm a man of my word." He pulled out an envelope from his coat pocket and handed it to Alfred. "This here is three thousand dollars. Call it an advance on your first crop."

"I don't know what to say, 'cept thank you, Mr. Cohen, I mean, Mickey."

"Yes, thank you," John and Clarence added in unison.

"Say, I have an idea. Why don't you take a little trip into Tijuana? Celebrate the partnership. I'm sure you'll find the right kind of entertainment that suits your tastes."

Downtown Tijuana hummed with people, and music they had never heard before, called mariachi, poured out of bars. When the brothers came upon a street vendor selling various leather crafts, Alfred looked at what the man had on display. One with a horse caught his attention. After a brief negotiation, he purchased the item.

A little farther up the street, John bought a souvenir license plate placard that spelled out MEXICO in big, bold letters.

With a blare of the horn and a cloud of dust behind, the brothers returned to the farm in the car Cohen had loaned them.

He appeared in the doorway, Candy behind him. "Hope you boys had a good time."

Leather horse purchased by Alfred
KEN WIDNER

"Not too bad. Had a few beers. Walked about town. Alfred got himself a nice leather piece."

"Good, though I'm afraid I have a bit of bad news," Cohen announced. "I just got a call from one of my associates back east." His affable demeanor darkened.

"Nothing about the farm, is it?" Clarence asked.

"In a way. Those damn Kennedys are trying to make names for themselves, so they're going after Jimmy Hoffa and the Teamsters, along with some people I'm associated with in my East Coast operation. I need to get back to LA and assess the damage. You understand."

"Of course."

The six flew back to Van Nuys Airport and drove straight to Cohen's house. Upon his return, he made a couple of calls. It didn't long for him to realize the heat the Kennedys had put on his associates was worse than he feared. They were doing real damage to his business interests, which meant he might have to shut things down for a while, including the farm in Tijuana.

Rather than return the way they came, Cohen suggested the three head north to San Francisco. They had come all this way, why not go somewhere nice before heading home? He promised them the trip up Highway 101 as it hugged the Pacific Ocean was one of the most scenic routes in the world. Then they'd be rewarded with the most picturesque city on the West Coast.

Cohen also offered them his 1956 Pontiac Star Chief as a way of making up for cutting the trip short. They refused at first, too generous, but he insisted.

Clarence held up the keys and grinned. "I got first leg."

They reached San Francisco by early evening. Before finding a hotel, the brothers drove to Fort Point at the water's edge so they'd have a perfect view of an engineering marvel the three had heard about for years, the Golden Gate Bridge. They weren't disappointed.

In an unforeseen twist of fate, a small island in the middle of the bay caught John's attention. A powerful searchlight spun around at regular intervals, both as a warning for planes taking off and landing from San Francisco Airport, and for the ships navigating the port of Oakland across the bay.

"That must be Alcatraz," he declared. "Never want to find myself there."

"Yeah, right," Clarence chided him. "Alcatraz."

The three arrived home a week later. Flush with cash, the brothers purchased new clothes for themselves that impressed family and friends

Alcatraz
CASEY HORNER (UNSPLASH.COM)

alike. But John didn't let the public display of their newfound fortune stop there. He checked several car dealerships looking for something that told the world he was now a person of means.

Everyone remarked on the brothers' transformation, and for the first time in their lives people in Ruskin treated them with respect.

John's 1951 Ford Custom black convertible
WIDNER FAMILY

Clarence looking sharp
WIDNER FAMILY

John with a new car (note Mexico license plate)
WIDNER FAMILY

Columbia Bank Robbery

Bank robbing is more of a sure thing than farming.
—ALLAN DARE PEARCE

AFTER HIS RETURN FROM TIJUANA, COHEN DID LITTLE ELSE BUT watch the hearings on TV, his anger simmering just below the surface. The Kennedys had declared war against him and the other crime bosses, which hurt their collective business interests more than Cohen expected. Something had to be done about them.

A knock on the front door ripped his attention from the television.

Cohen turned down the volume. Two Los Angeles police officers stood on the porch.

He jerked the door open. "I don't believe it. This is bordering on harassment."

"The chief wants to talk with you."

"I haven't done anything, just like when you pulled me over for no reason last week, or when you arrested me in Beverly Hills for not registering as an ex-con. Why don't you go after some real criminals?"

"The chief said something about bookmaking. Wants to have a little chat."

"Fine, but I have half a mind to file a civil lawsuit against the police department."

The officers held their spot.

Cohen grabbed his hat and brushed past the officers. "Damn Kennedys."

Alfred, John, and Clarence waited at their sister Verna's house. Of all the children in the Anglin clan, she was the only one with a telephone. The telegram they received from Mickey two days before only said they needed to call him on an important matter, which included a phone number and time for the call. Normally, Verna would be home with her husband and children, but Alfred gave her some money so they could eat out.

At the appointed time, Alfred dialed the number. A woman answered, then transferred the call to Cohen.

"This is Cohen."

"Hello Mickey. It's Alfred Anglin. Can you hear me okay?"

"I appreciate a man who's prompt."

"We're all here, just like you wanted. Your telegram said it was important."

A short pause followed. "I'm afraid I have some news for you boys. I know you planned on coming back and getting the farm up and running, but the heat from the hearings is getting worse, and the cops have been all over me. I think it's best if we laid low for a while."

"Are you sure, Mickey?" Alfred asked. "We can get there real quiet like. If no one's found out about the crop here, we can do the same in Mexico."

"I wish that were true, but I've got the Kennedys breathing down my neck. I can't order Chinese without the Feds hearing about it."

"I see."

"I know you're disappointed, but this will blow over in time. When things calm down we'll get the farm going then." Another pause followed. "Look, I gotta go. I have an appointment with my lawyer, and he charges me fifty bucks an hour whether I show up or not. I'll talk to you later." The phone clicked.

Alfred put down the receiver and looked both brothers in the eyes.

"Well, are we goin' or not?"

"Yes," Alfred replied. "But not now. The heat's on him pretty bad, and he thinks we'll get caught if we start up the pot farm in Tijuana."

Clarence punched the couch with his fist. "Fred gets busted in Utah, and now this. What are we supposed to do with all that marijuana? We're growers, not dealers."

"We can't just wait for Cohen before he says it's safe. Could take months. Maybe never."

Alfred went to the window and stared outside. "Maybe there's another way." He turned back. "Even with Cohen, we would've been in Tijuana for a couple of years easy before we had enough money for a farm. What if we got it all at once?"

"That's a great idea," Clarence said in a sarcastic tone. "Just how do we do that?"

"You remember the town of Columbia when we were kids?"

"Sure. We stayed there a few summers with our cousins. Not much around, exceptin' crickets and june bugs."

"And the bank."

Clarence's head snapped in Alfred's direction. "Wait. Are you suggestin' what I think you're suggestin'?"

"You can't be serious." John balked. "Rob a bank."

The brothers talked for a long time before Clarence finally agreed to go along with Alfred's idea. John, however, needed more convincing. He finally said yes, but on one condition. They wouldn't use a real gun, only a toy one. He didn't want to take a chance of shooting someone by mistake. Though Alfred and Clarence had their reservations, they accepted John's terms. They also decided Clarence should check out the bank first before finalizing their plan.

When he visited Columbia not long after, Clarence noted how few townspeople frequented the downtown area, just as the brothers had hoped. A single road cut Columbia in half, small shops and stores pressed together on either side. The bank was just as unassuming. Only three people worked there: the president (Walter Oakley), his wife (Florie Oakley) who was the secretary, and the teller (C. L. Williams). Even more important, no security guard.

Based on the report Clarence gave when he returned, they figured the job could be done without much trouble. They also chose a Friday as the best day for knocking off the bank since the vault would have extra cash on hand needed by the townspeople for weekend shopping. Just one question remained: when they'd do the job. After further discussion, the three decided on January 17, 1958, scarcely aware at the time how that fateful decision would change the three's lives forever.

In the meantime, John and Helen continued seeing each other. For the sake of secrecy, the brothers decided not to tell anyone about their plans, including their girlfriends.

Alfred had also been spending more and more time with Jeanette. The more their lives intertwined, the deeper his love for her grew. Even though she was only sixteen and Alfred twenty-nine, they had discussed marriage a few times, but with Christmas just around the corner and the prospect of leaving Ruskin for good after the bank job, having her as his wife could no longer wait.

Alfred went to her house after they finalized their plans. He drew in a deep breath and knocked on the front door; her father had made his feelings known about spending time with his teenage daughter.

John and Helen dressed for a date
WIDNER FAMILY

Dressed like an angel, Jeanette opened the door and a broad smile parted her lips. "Alfred. I wasn't expectin' you."

He gave her a kiss and then proposed on the spot. "Jeanette, I know we haven't been datin' for very long, but that don't matter to me. I think about you all the time, and I can't stand bein' apart from you." He produced a gold band he recently purchased. "Marry me."

She took the ring from his hand and looked at it with tears in her eyes. "Yes," she replied without hesitation, and he helped her slip it on.

Rather than wait, they went to Georgia and were married by a justice of the peace on December 16, 1957, most likely because the state did not require witnesses.

Though Alfred wished he could have told his new wife about their plans, he had promised his brothers he wouldn't. One little slip, and they'd spend the rest of their lives in prison.

On January 17, John parked in front of the bank just before 10:00 a.m. in a 1952 Chevrolet they had stolen a few miles away. All three looked

The newlyweds
WIDNER FAMILY

through the front windows. To their relief, they saw no customers inside. And even better, no security guard.

"Okay," Alfred stated in a stern tone, "in and out in five minutes."

Clarence took out the toy gun John gave him back in Ruskin.

The brothers looked at one another, nodded, then stepped out of the car. Clarence reached the front door first, jerked it open, and burst into the Bank of Columbia.

"Don't anybody move!" he shouted. "This is a robbery." He produced the gun and pointed it at the teller.

Williams immediately went white and put his hands up.

Alfred and John went behind the counter, where Walter Oakley, the stunned president, sat at his desk.

"Come on," Alfred barked. "Get up. Over here."

He led Walter into the middle of the bank.

John turned toward Florie Oakley at her desk. She likewise had her hands up, terrified.

"You too. Out front."

After Alfred herded them together, he had all three lie on the floor.

"Anyone try anythin'," Clarence stated matter-of-factly, "and they'll be sorry." He stood over them with the gun prominently displayed to show he was serious.

John went straight for the vault but found the steel door locked. He looked over his shoulder. "You," he said, pointing at Williams. "How do you open this?"

Williams looked up but didn't move; a light sheen of sweat covered his face.

"It's okay, you can get up." Clarence took a step back and motioned for him to do as he was told.

The scared teller slowly got to his feet and approached John with his hands in the air.

"Quick," John ordered him, "get this door open."

Williams took a key out of his pocket, slipped it into the lock, and opened the vault. Inside, bags of cash sat on shelves. John kept Williams in view as he grabbed the money, then forced him to go to the teller's window and stuffed the bills from the drawer into one of the bags.

When they both came around the front, Clarence noticed that Florie had started hyperventilating. Clarence's demeanor softened and he knelt down next to her. "Are you okay?"

"I—I can't breathe."

He looked around. Behind the president's desk he noticed a water cooler with paper cups on top. He hurried over to it and poured her some water.

"Come on," Alfred scolded him. "We don't have time for this."

Clarence ignored his brother and helped her sit up. "Here."

After Florie took several sips, her breathing eased.

Certain she was okay, he spun around. "Okay, let's go."

The three bolted for the door. A teenage boy happened to be walking toward the bank from across the street. When he saw John, Clarence, and Alfred, he opened the door as an act of courtesy and held it for them. The brothers jumped into the stolen car and sped away.

Not long after, the townspeople realized something extraordinary had occurred.

Dr. Adair Gilbert, a young girl at the time, later recalled this about the robbery:

> I wasn't aware of what was happening because I was in the drugstore, the Beasley Pharmacy, just across the way having a soda. And I looked out and I saw things happening, but, you know, busy people coming and going around the bank was not unusual, until Florie Oakley came into the little drugstore, and she was just quivering. And she said, "They made me lie on the floor." And I could not imagine Miss Florie ever being on the floor because she was such a prim and proper lady, so it turns out that some guys had just robbed the bank.[1]

Clint Smith recalled the words of another eyewitness, his friend Jimmy Nix:

> Well, my friend, Jimmy Nix, saw the bank robbers. He was working with his dad in the grocery store directly across the street, Nix's Grocery, and one of his tasks was to get their cash in a canvas bag and make deposits in the bank. So, Jimmy was walking across to the bank, and he

told me that when he got there he saw someone coming out the door, so he held the door open for him. Stood back like a kid with good manners, and these three men came out and got in the car and drove away in a big hurry. And Jimmy realized later they were the bank robbers.[2]

John Beasley likewise described what he saw after the robbery:

Mr. Reddin and I were sitting at one of those soda found tables, and it was in the morning. And we heard this clambering noise, and a person hollering real loud. . . . We saw Mr. Oakley, Mr. Walter F. Oakley Jr., who was president of the bank, came out on the sidewalk, and we got to the front of the drugstore and looked across and opened the door. He was yelling, "We've been cleaned out! We've been cleaned out!" And then he fainted on the sidewalk.[3]

John went south on Main Street, then made a hard left onto East Church Street and took it across the Chattahoochee River into Georgia. About five miles down the road the three found the spot where they had parked John's Ford Custom. They transferred the bags of cash and abandoned the stolen car.

The brothers worked their way south on less frequented roads, reaching Ruskin six hours later. Along the way, they counted the money, which totaled more than $19,000 (about $170,000 in today's dollars). They also listened on the radio for reports about the robbery. Other than a general description of the assailants and stolen car, nothing in the news reports connected the bank job to them.

The police arrived on the scene not long after the brothers made their getaway. They took statements from witnesses and collected as much evidence as they could, though the authorities had no idea at that time Alfred, John, and Clarence Anglin had committed the robbery, despite not wearing masks. The FBI was also notified and took over the investigation upon arrival.

When the three returned to Ruskin, the plan dictated they'd wait things out for a day, see what the radio reports said and if any roadblocks had been set up. If they hadn't been identified as the robbers, the brothers planned on packing up their things, collecting the girls, and meeting at the planned rendezvous spot in Ohio. John, however, had one other thing in mind.

He often felt bad about his mother never having the good things in life, and so he convinced his brothers to buy her a washer and dryer with some of the stolen money. She had cleaned and scrubbed by hand all her life. He thought she'd appreciate having something that would make her life a little easier.

The store delivered them both later that day, but when Rachel became aware her three sons had purchased the appliances, she refused to accept the washer and dryer. Though she had no idea about the bank robbery at that time, she also knew her boys and didn't want anything from them paid with what she called "bad money." In the meantime, John drove over to Helen's house. The time had come he told her about the robbery and his plan for leaving Ruskin the next day. Depending on how things went, he didn't know if he'd ever see home again.

What John didn't expect was seeing Jim there trying to convince Helen to give him another chance. John declared his love for her and said they needed to leave right away since he may never return.

After hearing the news reports earlier in the day, Jim put two and two together and figured out John's reason for wanting to leave in a hurry.

"Is that true?" she asked.

John found himself backed into a corner. "Afraid so. My brothers and me needed the money for buyin' a farm in Ohio. We plan on headin' out first thing tomorrow."

Helen hugged John. "I don't care what you did, I love you and I'm goin' with you."

"I'm sorry it has to be this way," John said to Jim, "but you heard her. We're in love. If you love Helen and want the best for her, you won't stop us."

Jim looked at Helen, then at John, but didn't respond.

"Maybe this will help." John pulled out two hundred dollars. "Take this. If we make it there safe, I'll send you some more. Do we have a deal?"

Jim looked at the money, then again at Helen, who remained at John's side. "Fine, we have a deal." He grabbed the bills. "Just promise me you'll keep her safe."

"I promise."

After Jim left, John told Helen the real reason they planned on going to Ohio was because of her father, who had moved there by this time, and the brothers thought it a good place to hide until the heat died down. She suggested calling first to let him know they were coming, but John talked her out of it. Best if they didn't let anyone know about their intentions until they arrived.

When John returned back home, he and Clarence grabbed their clothes and packed them in suitcases. Alfred had gone home with Jeanette, where he likewise told her about the robbery and getting out of Ruskin.

The brothers also stashed their guns in John's cars in case they might be needed. If the police somehow cornered them, both men knew it could quickly become a "shoot first and ask questions later" type of situation.

As the two packed, Robert suspected something was up and asked them what they were doing. John and Clarence replied with a vague comment about leaving town and didn't know when they'd be back. Though Robert hadn't yet heard anything about the robbery, he knew his brothers had gotten into some kind of trouble.

John took out five hundred dollars from his pocket and handed it to Robert. "Do me a favor, hang on to this in case we need it later, okay?"

"I will. What about Mama and Daddy? What should I tell them?"

"Tell 'em . . . tell 'em not to worry about us and we'll get in touch as soon as we can."

The next morning, John and Helen in his car, and Clarence in the car Cohen had given him, met up with Alfred and Jeanette at their house. After a brief discussion about the route they'd take, all three cars pulled out onto the road and headed north for Hamilton, Ohio.

When they arrived, Helen told her father the brothers were in a bit of trouble, and needed a place they could lay low for a while, though she omitted the part about the bank robbery. He didn't like them showing up unannounced, especially when they had apparently run afoul of the law, but he still let them stay at his home and at the nearby Cross-Roads Motel.

The next few days, news about the robbery blanketed the airwaves and newspapers. Helen felt bad about the way she left things with Jim. She had no intention of returning to him but thought she should at least let him know she was all right. Helen waited until everyone was asleep when she called. He told her she could still get herself out of this situation if she left now, and no one ever need know she had aided known fugitives. Helen appreciated his concern, but she hadn't changed her mind about John.

For Jim, that was the last straw. If she couldn't see the situation for what it was, then he'd make her. Under the guise of needing the name of the motel in case he needed to get ahold of her, Helen gave him the information. As soon as she hung up, he called the police.

Early morning on January 22, FBI agents burst through the door. "This is the FBI, get your hands up!" multiple agents shouted. "Get your hands up!"

Alfred awoke to Jeanette screaming next to him in bed. He looked about until the barrel of a machine gun inches from his face stopped him cold. Alfred put up his hands.

In the house nearby, similar FBI commands filled the air.

The *Tampa Morning Tribune* filed this report the day they were arrested:

HAMILTON, Ohio, Jan. 22 (AP)—The Federal Bureau of Investigation arrested three brothers wanted in connection with the $19,000 robbery of the Bank of Columbia, Ala., on Jan. 17.

Two of the men are escapees from the Florida State Prison at Raiford.

"Nearly all of the $19,000 was found either in the men's room or in their automobiles," Special agent in charge, Ed Mason, told a reporter.

Taken into custody were: John Anglin, 27, Ruskin, Fla., charged with bank robbery. Alfred Anglin, 29, Tampa, Fla., and Clarence Anglin, 26, Ruskin.

Helen Taylor McIntosh, 32, Tampa, girlfriend of John Anglin, Fern Taylor, about 60, of Hamilton, father of Mrs. McIntosh, and Jeanette Anglin, wife of Alfred Anglin, all charged with being accessories after the fact.

Mason said they learned last night that the Anglins were in Hamilton, and immediately put John Anglin under surveillance.

Early this morning the agents made their move. The arrests were made without a fight. John Anglin and Mrs. McIntosh were with Taylor, the woman's father, when the agents seized them.

Alfred Anglin was awakened with a machine gun resting against his chest. His wife was with him. Clarence Anglin was seized . . . without resistance.

The FBI seized pistol and shotgun ammunition, an electric drill, two pistols, and three automobiles, in addition to the money.[4]

Not mentioned in the story was the toy gun used in the robbery also captured in the raid.

In the *Montgomery Advertiser*'s version of the arrest, they added these details:

"We had had information this 3:30 a.m. that a girlfriend of one of the men might be visiting relatives in Hamilton," the agent said.

This tip led the federal agents to Hamilton about 7 a.m. where they surrounded the home of Taylor and a neighboring house. . . . Mason also said Alfred Anglin offered a bribe of a "trunk full of money" to one of the agents. . . . "There's a trunk loaded with money in there. Why don't you just take it and forget about the whole thing."

A toy gun used in the robbery
FBI

The article went on to say:

The first concrete lead to the suspects was discovery of an abandoned car at Hilton, Ga., about 5.5 miles from the Alabama border town where the hold-up was staged.

An Alabama FBI agent said the Anglins were "considered strong suspects" following the discovery of the abandoned 1952 Chevrolet at a fishing site on the Chattahoochee River.[5]

After they were taken into custody, Fern Taylor, Alfred, John, Clarence, and Helen were brought to Cincinnati and arraigned before U.S. Commissioner Graham P. Hunt. He set their bail at $20,000. Even though Jeanette was married to Alfred, because she was a minor she was turned over to the Butler County Youth Authorities.

When the authorities determined only the brothers had an active knowledge of the planning and execution of the robbery, the charges against the three of being accessories after the fact were dropped. Later that week the brothers were arraigned on formal charges of bank robbery before U.S. District Judge John H. Druffel.[6]

What took place next would set the course for the rest of the brothers' lives, but not before they experienced a profound miscarriage of justice.

Jeanette with Alfred (handcuffed) after being captured and the trunk with money beside him
CINCINNATI ENQUIRER, JANUARY 23, 1958

CHAPTER 11

The Trials

There is no such thing as justice—in or out of court.
—CLARENCE DARROW

WHEN ALFRED, JOHN, AND CLARENCE WERE ARRESTED ON JANUARY 22, the authorities wasted no time bringing their case against them. Many people in the South at that time had a particular hatred for bank robbers. With the Depression from the 1930s still strong in their collective memories and the thousands of bank failures that resulted during that tumultuous decade, anyone despicable enough to steal workers' hard-earned money deserved little mercy. Even though President Roosevelt created the FDIC (Federal Deposit Insurance Corporation) in 1933 as a means of instilling confidence in the solvency of the banking system, most people felt as though robbers like the Anglins had personally stolen from them.

Two days after they were arrested the three were formally charged with the crime of bank robbery, and because they had crossed state lines, this warranted a federal case.

The location for the trial had been set in Montgomery, Alabama, which the brothers initially accepted. But after further discussion, considering the public's sentiments toward the crime, they thought the better of it and opted for Cincinnati five states away, where they believed they'd have a better chance of receiving a fair trial. However, Judge John H. Druffel at the U.S. District Court in the Southern District of Ohio denied their request, and the federal trial took place in Montgomery. On February 10, 1958, Frank M. Johnson Jr. presided over the proceedings less than a month after the bank robbery.[1]

Their bond set at $20,000 each (about $180,000 in today's dollars) on January 25 by Judge Druffel, he might as well had made it a million. The brothers didn't have that kind of money, so they prepared their defense while in jail.

Born in 1918, Frank M. Johnson grew up in Haleyville, Alabama. He graduated from law school at the University of Alabama in 1943, where he befriended future Alabama governor George C. Wallace. Johnson served in Europe as a captain during World War II. After the war, he settled in Jasper, Alabama, in 1946 with his wife, Ruth, where Johnson joined the law firm of Curtis & Maddox. When the federal judge for Alabama's Middle District died unexpectedly, President Eisenhower named Johnson to succeed him. Johnson moved to Montgomery in 1955.[2]

Since the brothers didn't have the money for a private lawyer, the state assigned William B. Moore as their public defender. Unknown to the brothers at the time, he was friends with Judge Johnson, and before the trial the two discussed ways of getting the case settled as quickly as possible. Moore convinced the brothers if they pled guilty to the charges, rather than take their chances with a jury, Judge Johnson would give them a relatively light sentence of five years, less if they stayed out of trouble while serving their term. Believing the word of their lawyer, the brothers agreed.

The following figures show the charges and court transcript of the trial presided over by Judge Johnson.[3]

The Grand Jury of said County Charge that, before the finding of this Indictment
John William Anglin, Clarence Anglin and Alfred Ray Anglin, whose names are to the
Grand Jury otherwise unknown, feloniously took Eighteen Thousand Nine Hundred Eleven
and 65/100 Dollars, in the lawful currency of the United States of America, the
exact denominations of which, and a more accurate description of which, are to the
Grand Jury unknown, of the value of Eighteen Thousand Nine Hundred Eleven and 65/100
Dollars, the property of Bank of Columbia, a Corporation, from the person of, or in
the presence of, Walter F. Oakley, who was, at the time, President of Bank of Columbia,
a Corporation, and against his will, by violence to his person, or by putting him in
such fear as unwillingly to part with the same.

Count Two

The Grand Jury of said County further charges that, before the finding
of this Indictment, John William Anglin, Clarence Anglin and Alfred Ray Anglin,
whose names are to the Grand Jury otherwise unknown, feloniously took Eighteen
Thousand Nine Hundred Eleven and 65/100 Dollars, in the lawful currency of the
United States of America, the exact denominations of which, and a more accurate
description of which, are to the Grand Jury unknown, of the value of Eighteen
Thousand Nine Hundred Eleven and 65/100 Dollars, the property of Bank of Columbia,
a Corporation, from the person of, or in the presence of, Florrie Oakley, who was
at the time Bookkeeper of Bank of Columbia, a Corporation, and against her will, by
violence to her person, or by putting her in such fear as unwillingly to part with
the same.

Count Three

The Grand Jury of said County further charges that, before the finding
of this Indictment, John William Anglin, Clarence Anglin and Alfred Ray Anglin, whose
names are to the Grand Jury otherwise unknown, feloniously took Eighteen Thousand
Nine Hundred Eleven and 65/100 Dollars, in the lawful currency of the United States
of America, the exact denominations of which, and a more accurate description of
which, are to the Grand Jury unknown, of the value of Eighteen Thousand Nine
Hundred Eleven and 65/100 Dollars, the property of Bank of Columbia, a Corporation,
from the person of, or in the presence of, C. L. Williams, Junior, who was at the
time Cashier of Bank of Columbia, a Corporation, and against his will, by violence
to his person, or by putting him in such fear as unwillingly to part with the same,

Count Four

The Grand Jury of said County further charges that, before the finding
of this Indictment, John William Anglin, Clarence Anglin and Alfred Ray Anglin, whose
names are to the Grand Jury otherwise unknown, feloniously took Eighteen Thousand
Nine Hundred Eleven and 65/100 Dollars, in the lawful currency of the United States
of America, the exact denominations of which, and a more accurate description of
which, are to the Grand Jury unknown, of the value of Eighteen Thousand Nine Hundred
Eleven and 65/100 Dollars, the property of Walter F. Oakley, from his person, or
in his presence, and against his will, by violence to his person, or by putting
him in such fear as unwillingly to part with the same,

The formal charges

ALABAMA CIRCUIT COURT

IN THE DISTRICT COURT OF THE UNITED STATES
FOR THE MIDDLE DISTRICT OF ALABAMA
NORTHERN DIVISION
Before: Hon. Frank M. Johnson, Jr.
February 10, 1958.

United States of America)
)
vs) No. 1818-S.
)
John William Anglin,)
Clarence Anglin, and)
Alfred Ray Anglin)

FILED

FEB 1 2 1958

A. O. DOBSON, Clerk

BY_____
DEPUTY CLERK

THE COURT: United States against John William Anglin, Clarence Anglin,
Alfred Ray Anglin; those defendants in court. All right. Mr.
Moore --
W. B. MOORE, JR.: Yes, sir.
THE COURT: -- at the request of these defendants I entered an order,
as you know, appointing you to represent them.
W. B. MOORE, JR.: Yes, sir.
THE COURT: Have you had an opportunity to confer with them?
W. B. MOORE, JR.: Yes, sir.
THE COURT: In your judgment, do each of them understand the nature of
the proceedings here today?
W. B. MOORE, JR.: Yes, sir.
THE COURT: All right. Which of you is John William Anglin?
JOHN WILLIAM ANGLIN: I am.
THE COURT: All right. And which of you is Clarence Anglin?
CLARENCE ANGLIN: I am.
THE COURT: All right.
HARTWELL DAVIS: Mr. Moore. Let the record reflect Mr. Moore has been
furnished with a copy of the proposed charges against these men.
THE COURT: All right. Now, John William Anglin --
JOHN WILLIAM ANGLIN: Yes, sir.
THE COURT: -- you are here and held in custody for a proposed
prosecution for violating the bank robbery laws of the United
States.
JOHN WILLIAM ANGLIN: (Nodded to indicate affirmative reply)
THE COURT: The offense for which you are being prosecuted is alleged
to have taken place in the Southern Division of this District, that
is, the Dothan Division; you have a right to have all the proceedings
in your case take place in the Dothan Division of this court, and
unless you request otherwise, they will take place there. However,
you can consent to be proceeded against in this Division, which is
the Northern Division of this court, here at Montgomery, Alabama.
JOHN WILLIAM ANGLIN: (Nodded to indicate affirmative reply)
THE COURT: Do you understand your right, however, to have your
proceedings take place if you want to --
JOHN WILLIAM ANGLIN: Yes, sir.
THE COURT: -- in Dothan?
JOHN WILLIAM ANGLIN: That's right.
THE COURT: What is your desire in that respect?
JOHN WILLIAM ANGLIN: Here will be okey.
THE COURT: Well, is that what you want?
JOHN WILLIAM ANGLIN: That's right.
THE COURT: All right. Now, Clarence Anglin, the same applies to you;
the offense for which you are being prosecuted is the same offense,
as I understand it, and you have a right to have all the proceedings
in your case take place in the Dothan Division of this court, because
the offense for which you are being prosecuted is the same offense,
as I understand it, and you have a right to have all the proceedings
in your case take place in the Dothan Division of this court, because
that is where the Government says the offense took place. You can
waive that right, and consent to be proceeded against in this
Division, the Montgomery Division, if you wish. You understand your
right --
CLARENCE ANGLIN: Yes, sir.
THE COURT: -- as far as the venue of the case is concerned?
CLARENCE ANGLIN: Yeah.

THE COURT: Do you want your case and the proceedings if your case to
take place in Dothan or here in Montgomery?
CLARENCE ANGLIN: Here in Montgomery.
THE COURT: All right. Now, Alfred Ray Anglin, the same applies to
you. You have a right to have all the proceedings in your case
take place in the Dothan Division of this court, the Southern
Division, however, you can consent to be and request to be proceeded
against in this Division. Unless you do, then the proceedings
will take place in the Dothan Division of this court; you understand
that?
ALFRED RAY ANGLIN: Yes, sir.
THE COURT: What is your desire in that respect?
ALFRED RAY ANGLIN: To be tried here.
THE COURT: All right. Let each of them execute waiver of venue. That
waiver of venue -- now, I am speaking to each of you, and your attor-
ney may examine it if you haven't examined it already -- consents
for your proceedings to take place here instead of Dothan. All
right.
HARTWELL DAVIS: If your honor please, these are prepared for any
Division, that is, here or Opelika; you understand that, Mr. Moore,
it is agreeable for your clients to sign this paper now?
W. B. MOORE, JR.: Yes, sir.
HARTWELL DAVIS: All right. John William Anglin, that is your name?
JOHN WILLIAM ANGLIN: Yes, sir.
HARTWELL DAVIS: Will you sign your name right there on the top line.
That agrees that the proceedings may take place in any Division
of this District. Now, your name is Clarence Anglin?
CLARENCE ANGLIN: That's right.
HARTWELL DAVIS: If you wish to, you may sign that paper, which carries
just what I told you -- and what the Judge told you. Alfred Ray
Anglin, do you wish to sign this waiver?
ALFRED RAY ANGLIN: Yes, sir.
HARTWELL DAVIS: That will agree that your case be disposed of in any
Division of this District. All right. You might want to be
looking this over while the Judge tells them about that.
THE COURT: All right, have each of them executed a waiver of venue,
Mr. Clerk?
HARTWELL DAVIS: Yes, sir.
THE COURT: Has it been filed?
CLERK: Just the waiver of venue.
THE COURT: Yes, all right. John William Anglin, the offense for
which the Government is prosecuting you is a felony. That means
simply this: That it carries a punishment in the event you plead
guilty or in the event you are convicted, of a period greater
than one year. On a felony charge such as this one, your case would
ordinarily be presented to a Federal Grand Jury to be investigated
by them before you are prosecuted any further on it. You can,
however, request and consent, if you want to, to be proceeded
against by an information. Now, an information is not anything
except a statement of the charges filed by the District Attorney
under his oath of office, and an information, if you are proceeded
against by one, will charge the same offense or offenses that the
indictment would charge if the Grand Jury indict you; do you
understand that?
JOHN WILLIAM ANGLIN: Yes, sir.
THE COURT: Do you want your case to go to a Grand Jury, which will
convene in this District within the next week or so, or do you
want to be prosecuted on an information?
JOHN WILLIAM ANGLIN: Next week or so will be all right.
THE COURT: All right. You want your case to go to a Grand Jury.
W. B. MOORE, JR.: I don't think he understood full .
THE COURT: Have you conferred with them -- all right, Mr. Moore.
W. B. MOORE, JR.: The last three days.
THE COURT: Uh, huh, and --
W. B. MOORE, JR.: If it please the court, let me tell him what you just

got through saying.

THE COURT: I want to make sure he understands it.

(Mr. Moore conferred with the defendants)

W. B. MOORE, JR.: He misunderstood the court, and asked me to express a desire he intended to waive, and wants to proceed on an information.

THE COURT: All right. As I understand from your lawyer, you want to be prosecuted on an information?

JOHN WILLIAM ANGLIN: That's right.

THE COURT: Here today?

JOHN WILLIAM ANGLIN: Yes, sir.

THE COURT: And not have your case go to a Grand Jury?

JOHN WILLIAM ANGLIN: That's right.

THE COURT: Is that what you want?

JOHN WILLIAM ANGLIN: That's right.

THE COURT: All right. Now, Clarence Anglin, the same applies to you; the offense that the Government is prosecuting you on is a felony and would normally be presented to a Grand Jury to be investigated by them before the District Attorney prosecutes you any further or prosecutes you at all; do you understand that?

CLARENCE ANGLIN: Yes, sir.

THE COURT: You can waive that right and elect to be proceeded against by an information, and it is just exactly what I explained to John William Anglin, that is, that if you are prosecuted by an information it would charge the same offense or offenses that the indictment would charge if the Grand Jury indicted you; you understand that?

CLARENCE ANGLIN: Yes, sir.

THE COURT: You can have it to go to a Grand Jury, or you can waive that right; which do you want?

CLARENCE ANGLIN: I waive it.

THE COURT: You want to be prosecuted on an information?

CLARENCE ANGLIN: That's right.

THE COURT: All right. Now, Alfred Ray Anglin, the same applies to you. You are here on a proposed charge of a felony. It would ordinarily go to a Grand Jury; you understand that?

ALFRED RAY ANGLIN: Yes, sir.

THE COURT: You can waive that right and be proceeded against and prosecuted by an information, which will charge the same offense or offenses that the indictment would charge if the Grand Jury indicted you; you understand that?

ALFRED RAY ANGLIN: Yes, sir.

THE COURT: What do you want to do?

ALFRED RAY ANGLIN: I want to waive.

THE COURT: You want to waive it and be prosecuted by an information; is that correct?

ALFRED RAY ANGLIN: Yes, sir.

THE COURT: All right. Let each of them execute the waiver of indictment.

HARTWELL DAVIS: Sign your name as it is -- he can use this pen, it is a little easier sometime -- top line if you want to do what the Judge just said and what you just said, sign your name there. All right, you can do the same thing on this duplicate paper. Alfred Ray Anglin, you do the same thing there. We are now filing these waivers of indictment and ask the Clerk to witness them.

THE COURT: All right. File the information.

HARTWELL DAVIS: Filing the information; you have been furnished a copy of the information on behalf of the defendants, have you not?

W. B. MOORE, JR.: I have.

THE COURT: All right. Have you had an opportunity to examine it and study it, Mr. Moore?

W. B. MOORE, JR.: Yes, sir.

THE COURT: Have you conferred with your clients as to what it charges them --

W. B. MOORE, JR.: Yes, sir.

THE COURT: In your judgment, do they understand it?

W. B. MOORE, JR.: Yes, sir.

THE COURT: All right. John William Anglin, do you understand that you are charged in this information with -- this applies to each of you -- with on or about January 17 of this year in this District that you did by force and violence and intimidation take from the presence or person of Walter Oakley a sum of money approximating thirteen thousand, six hundred dollars, that was in his care and custody and control and management and possession in the Bank of Columbia at Columbia, Alabama; do you understand that, that you are charged with that, John William Anglin?

JOHN WILLIAM ANGLIN: Yes, sir.

THE COURT: And do you understand that, Clarence Anglin?

CLARENCE ANGLIN: Yes, sir.

THE COURT: And do you understand that, Alfred Ray Anglin?

ALFRED RAY ANGLIN: Yes, sir.

THE COURT: And do you understand that that Bank of Columbia was at that time insured by the Federal Deposit Insurance Corporation, and that the Government says in committing this offense that you did assault and put in jeopardy the life of Walter Oakley by the use of a dangerous weapon, that is, a thirty-two calibre pistol; do you understand what you are charged with, John William Anglin?

JOHN WILLIAM ANGLIN: Yes, sir.

THE COURT: And do you understand, Clarence Anglin, what you are charged with?

CLARENCE ANGLIN: Yes, sir.

THE COURT: And do you understand, Alfred Ray Anglin, what you are charged with?

ALFRED RAY ANGLIN: Yes, sir.

THE COURT: John William Anglin, are you guilty or not guilty?

JOHN WILLIAM ANGLIN: Guilty.

THE COURT: Clarence Anglin, are you guilty or not guilty?

CLARENCE ANGLIN: Guilty.

THE COURT: Alfred Ray Anglin, are you guilty or not guilty?

ALFRED RAY ANGLIN: Guilty.

THE COURT: All right. Now, I am not going to sentence you all now; I am going to come back to this case later on. I am going to, in the meantime, give each of you and your attorney or your attorney an opportunity to confer with me regarding any sentence that is to be imposed on these pleas of guilty. You all have a seat.

- -

THE COURT: John William Anglin, Clarence Anglin, Alfred Ray Anglin. John William Anglin?

JOHN WILLIAM ANGLIN: Yes, sir.

THE COURT: Do you have any statement that you would like to make to the court prior to the time I impose sentence on your plea of guilty in this case?

JOHN WILLIAM ANGLIN: No, sir.

THE COURT: Do you know of any reason why I should not sentence you at this time?

JOHN WILLIAM ANGLIN: No, sir.

THE COURT: Let me ask you this: How much of the time did you serve when you were convicted in the State of Florida in 1951 -- in 1951 for grand larceny, how much of that time did you serve?

JOHN WILLIAM ANGLIN: Twenty-two months, I believe.

THE COURT: Twenty-two of the twenty-four?

JOHN WILLIAM ANGLIN: Yes, sir.

THE COURT: Did you have any escapes during that time?

JOHN WILLIAM ANGLIN: No, sir.

THE COURT: Did you have any difficulty in the penitentiary?

JOHN WILLIAM ANGLIN: No, sir.

THE COURT: That is your only previous conviction, isn't it?

JOHN WILLIAM ANGLIN: Yes, sir.

THE COURT: Other than one when you were a juvenile.

and released to the custody of your parents?

JOHN WILLIAM ANGLIN: Yes, sir.

THE COURT: All right. Upon your plea of guilty in this case, John William Anglin, it is the order and judgment of this court that you be committed to the custody of the Attorney General for a period of ten years, to stand committed this date. You can stand in the hands of the marshall. Clarence Anglin?

CLARENCE ANGLIN: Yes, sir.

THE COURT: Do you have any statement that you would like to make to the court prior to the time I impose sentence on your plea of guilty

CLARENCE ANGLIN: No, sir.

THE COURT: Do you know of any reason why I should not sentence you at this time on your plea of guilty?

CLARENCE ANGLIN: No, sir.

THE COURT: How much of the last thirteen years have you spent in the penitentiary?

CLARENCE ANGLIN: About seven.

THE COURT: About half of it?

CLARENCE ANGLIN: Just about.

THE COURT: And all of them have been State penitentiaries, haven't they?

CLARENCE ANGLIN: Yes, sir.

THE COURT: And you have three or four convictions?

CLARENCE ANGLIN: Yes, sir.

THE COURT: For breaking and entering and burglary and larceny; is that correct?

CLARENCE ANGLIN: Yes, sir.

THE COURT: Do you have any commitments pending against you at this time, unserved time that has been imposed on you?

CLARENCE ANGLIN: Yes, sir; Florida.

THE COURT: How much?

CLARENCE ANGLIN: About six years.

THE COURT: Six years is pending against you now?

CLARENCE ANGLIN: Yes, sir.

THE COURT: Do you know whether or not they have placed a detainer against you?

CLARENCE ANGLIN: No, sir; no, sir; I don't.

W. B. MOORE, JR.: If it please the court, I might partially answer that.

THE COURT: I would like to know.

W. B. MOORE, JR.: There was a hold order out, the F B I had a pick up on unlawful flight, and when they were apprehended on this of course that was withdrawn, but I understand the time is still --

THE COURT: The time is still against him?

W. B. MOORE, JR.: Yes, sir.

THE COURT: Uh, huh. And that is for the offense that he was sentenced on and escaped from the penitentiary on in February of this year; is that right?

W. B. MOORE, JR.: That is my understanding.

THE COURT: Now, I've discussed this matter with your lawyer, Clarence Anglin, and gone into it with him. If you have nothing to say, it is the order and judgment of this court that you be committed to the custody of the Attorney General for a period of fifteen years, to stand committed this date. You can stand in the hands of the marshall. Alfred Ray Anglin, do you have any statement you would like to make prior to the time I impose sentence on your plea in this case?

ALFRED RAY ANGLIN: No, sir.

THE COURT: I have discussed this with your lawyer. Your record is practically the same as your brother Clarence's. Each time one of you was sent to the penitentiary, I believe, as far as I can tell the other one was; each time one of you escaped, the other one did; is that not correct?

ALFRED RAY ANGLIN: Yes, that's right.

-6-

W. B. MORE, JR.: If it please the court, he has been out since '53,
and quite a bit of Clarence's was after that time.
THE COURT: That's right, I see that now.
W. B. MORE, JR.: Last three or four convictions Clarence got he was
not a party to them.
THE COURT: That's right, I see that. He was convicted in '47 for
burglary and got two years probation; is that right?
ALFRED RAY ANGLIN: Yes, sir.
THE COURT: And you were convicted in '50 for burglary and got one to
two years in Georgia?
ALFRED RAY ANGLIN: That's right.
THE COURT: And in '51 for burglary, and you escaped?
ALFRED RAY ANGLIN: Yes, sir; that's right.
THE COURT: And then '51, breaking and entering with intent to commit
a felony, you got five years to run consecutive with the other time?
ALFRED RAY ANGLIN: That's right.
THE COURT: And then since then you have had larceny of a motor
vehicle, you received two years on that?
ALFRED RAY ANGLIN: That's right.
THE COURT: And another breaking and entering?
ALFRED RAY ANGLIN: (Nodded to indicate affirmative reply)
THE COURT: Upon your plea of guilty, it is the order and judgment
of this court that you be committed to the custody of the Attorney
General for a period of fifteen years, to stand committed this
date. You can stand in the hands of the marshall.

I hereby certify that the foregoing is
a full, true, and correct transcript of
notes taken by me in above matter the
10th day of February, 1958.

Glynn Henderson,
Official Court Reporter.

Charges and court transcript of the trial presided over by Judge Johnson
THE DISTRICT COURT OF THE UNITED STATES FOR THE DISTRICT OF ALABAMA

The Anglins were tried in federal court on February 10, a mere three weeks after the robbery. Their lawyer, having persuaded them to plead guilty, corrected John when he opted for a grand jury. This would never happen today, but in the 1950s, in the era of southern justice, the brothers didn't know what hit them, and they paid the price for trusting their lawyer.

In the end, John was sentenced to ten years in federal prison. Since Clarence and Alfred had been escapees from prison in Florida, they were given fifteen years each. Yes, the Anglin brothers deserved the appropriate sentence for the crime they committed, but that didn't mean the three should've been railroaded by the judicial system. However, since they had pled guilty at the behest of their lawyer, their fate was sealed. John, Clarence, and Alfred were sent to the United States Penitentiary in Atlanta, Georgia, on February 13.

When the brothers arrived at Atlanta, they ran into an old friend they had met years before at Raiford State Prison—Frank Morris. They also met someone else who would have a profound impact on their lives four years later at Alcatraz—James "Whitey" Bulger.

For the Anglins, the injustice they faced at their first trial didn't end there. In an unprecedented move by the court system, the state of Alabama also filed charges against them for the bank robbery and set a second trial one month later, which they considered patently unfair and vigorously opposed. On March 10, Circuit Judge Keener Baxley set the date of their state trial for March 14, a mere four days later, hardly enough time for the brothers to mount a meaningful defense. The *Tampa Daily Times* filed this story about the second trial:

> Dothan, Ala., March 14 (AP). Three Florida brothers already under federal prison terms for robbing a Columbia, Ala., bank, were called to trial in state court today for the $19,000 holdup.
>
> Alfred Anglin, 29, John Anglin, 27, Clarence Anglin, 26, are charged with first degree robbery under the state indictments despite the fact that they pleaded guilty last month to violating the Federal bank robbery laws.
>
> Robbery under Alabama law is punishable by death by the electric chair or a prison term up to life under the state charges, which Circuit Solicitor Forest Adams said constitute a separate offense altogether from the Federal complaints.[4]

As George Anglin walked the fields thinking about the upcoming planting season, he saw Rachel approach from the house. Except for drying wet laundry on lines, she rarely came out there since most of her time was spent cooking, cleaning, and doing other household chores, so he figured this must be important. When George saw the tears in her eyes, he knew for sure.

"Mama, what's wrong? Something happen?"

Rachel could hardly speak. "Oh, Daddy, they want to kill our boys!"

"Mama, settle down now. Nobody wants to kill our boys."

She handed George the newspaper delivered that day.

George read the article. "They can't do this. How can they do this?"

Rachel felt just as confused as George. "I don't know, but I can't let them go through this alone. I plan on bein' there with my boys."

After he returned from World War I, few things in life upset George Anglin. But realizing what they intended for his sons had crossed a line. "Mama, I'm comin' with you."

Tampan, Brothers Indicted for 'Bama Robbery

Dothan, Ala., Feb. 14 (AP). A Houston County grand jury indicted three Florida brothers, one from Tampa and two from Ruskin, yesterday for holding up a Columbia, Ala., bank last month. They are already under Federal sentence for the robbery.

First degree robbery indictments were returned against Alfred, Tampa, and Clarence and John Anglin, Ruskin, who were convicted of bank robbery charges in U. S. District Court last week.

Convictions under the state charges carry a possible death sentence.

Clarence 27, and Alfred Anglin 28, were sentenced to 15-year terms in the Federal penitentiary after they pleaded guilty to the charges. John, 26, drew a 10-year term.

The Anglins admitted staging the holdup Jan. 17 of the Bank of Columbia in which $19,000 was taken. When they were arrested in Hamilton, Ohio, five days later, FBI agents recovered $13,648 in cash and checks, and $5000 in traveler's checks.

Charges carry a possible death sentence.

"TAMPAN, BROTHERS INDICTED FOR 'BAMA ROBBERY," *TAMPA DAILY TIMES*, FEBRUARY 14, 1958

When George and Rachel arrived at the jailhouse, they waited for several hours before finally meeting with John, Clarence, and Alfred. Seeing them behind those bars, both knew in an instant the newspaper article hadn't lied. Their very lives were on the line, and it was more than Rachel could take. She started to cry.

George assured his boys he'd somehow find the money and get them a proper lawyer.

Then John remembered something. "I gave Robert five hundred dollars before we left. Told him to hang on to it just in case. Think he could bring it up?"

George had left the farm in Robert's care, and with them not having a phone he had no way of contacting him. This only left one avenue for retrieving the money before the trial.

Just as George was about to get into his car parked in front of the jailhouse, he saw a sign for a lawyer across the street. Happy about his good fortune, he immediately went into the office and talked with an attorney. George asked if he'd be willing to take the case for five hundred dollars. Hearing the desperation in his voice, the lawyer agreed to defend his sons. With the deal done, George drove all night to Ruskin and returned the next morning.

Now armed with an attorney actually committed to a proper defense, as this newspaper account shows, Alfred, John, and Clarence made the court work for a conviction:

DOTHAN (AP)—The three Anglin brothers, already convicted in Federal court of robbing a Columbia, Ala., bank pleaded innocent by reason of double jeopardy in state court here yesterday.

They were indicted recently by a Houston County Grand Jury on first degree robbery charges for the Jan. 17 holdup of the Bank of Columbia. Circuit Court Judge Keener Baxley scheduled their trial for Friday.

Under state and Federal law a person can't be prosecuted twice for the same offense. This is usually referred to double-jeopardy.

Circuit Solicitor Forest Adams said the state charge is altogether different from that which the Anglins faced in federal court.[5]

According to family history, the trial turned into more a carnival than a legal proceeding. The courtroom was filled with people from the town of Columbia who were more interested in seeing the brothers given the electric chair than have a fair trial. At one point during the proceedings, the prosecutor declared to the jury, "They came here from Florida to rob us good people. . . . They should be put to death. . . . This will teach people from Florida to stay out of our state."

In response, people in the gallery shouted, "Electrocute them! Electrocute them!"

John threw up at the thought of death by the electric chair, while his mother fainted and was carried out of the courtroom.

The jury foreman, W. Otis Mendheim, read the verdict. Not surprisingly, all three brothers were again convicted of the charges, but the vigorous defense offered by their attorney saved them from the electric chair, and instead they were sentenced to an additional twenty-five years in state prison after their stint in federal prison. However, the jury never saw the toy gun used in the robbery, a crucial piece of evidence that might have lessened their sentence, nor would they hear any statements made by the Anglin family.

Though Rachel couldn't have been happier her sons had been spared the death penalty, which she attributed to God answering her prayers, she also knew it would be a long time before she'd ever see her boys again.

Just before the bailiff took them away, George and Rachel overheard the prosecutor warn the three about returning to Alabama after their federal stint. "When you boys are sent back, you'll never leave Alabama alive," a threat they took seriously that sadly came true for one of the brothers.

A deep-seated feeling of anger arose within George, partially because he believed the judicial system took advantage of his sons simply because they were poor and uneducated, but also because he didn't like people threatening them. George stopped the three as they were being led out and looked them straight in the eyes. "You boys have never stayed put no matter where they put you. I want you to promise me and your mama somethin'."

"We will, Daddy," Alfred said for the three.

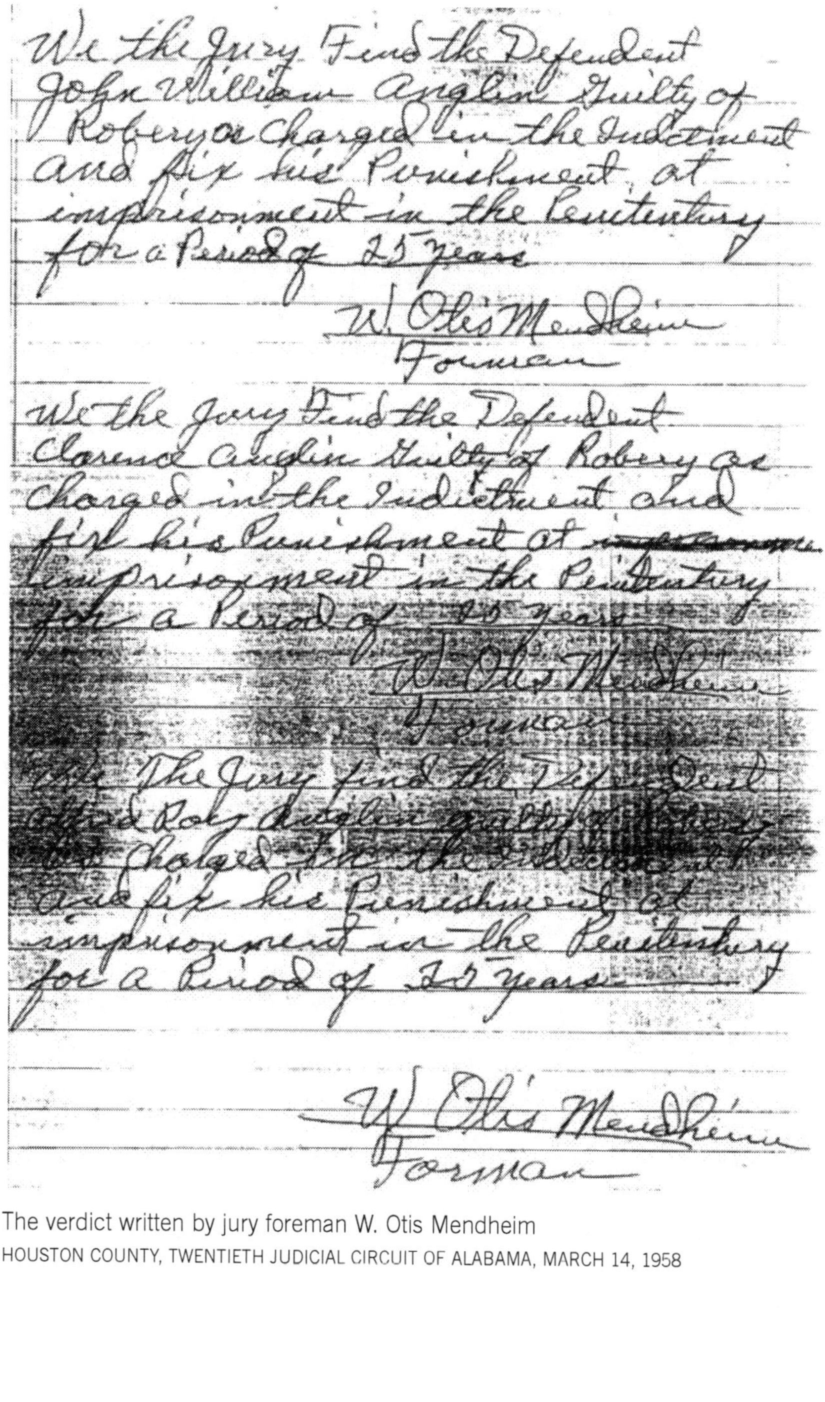

We the Jury Find the Defendent John William Anglin Guilty of Robery as Charged in the Indictment and fix his Punishment at imprisonment in the Penitentiary for a Period of 25 years

W Otis Mendheim
Foreman

We the Jury Find the Defendent Clarence Anglin Guilty of Robery as Charged in the Indictment and fix his Punishment at ~~imprisonment~~ imprisonment in the Penitentiary for a Period of 25 years

W Otis Mendheim
Foreman

We The Jury find the Defendent Alfred Roy Anglin guilty of Robery as Charged in the Indictment and fix his Punishment at imprisonment in the Penitentiary for a Period of 35 years

W Otis Mendheim
Foreman

The verdict written by jury foreman W. Otis Mendheim
HOUSTON COUNTY, TWENTIETH JUDICIAL CIRCUIT OF ALABAMA, MARCH 14, 1958

"If you can get out, then get out. Leave this place, and I mean this country, and never come back, you hear!"

All three nodded before being led out of the court.

Rather than incarcerate them together and risk an escape attempt like they had done multiple times in the past, Clarence was sent to Leavenworth on April 11, 1958. John and Alfred, on the other hand, were sent back to the United States Penitentiary in Atlanta and served their federal sentence there. John was later sent to the federal penitentiary in Lewisburg, Pennsylvania, on April 8, but before he was transferred Helen visited him at Atlanta.

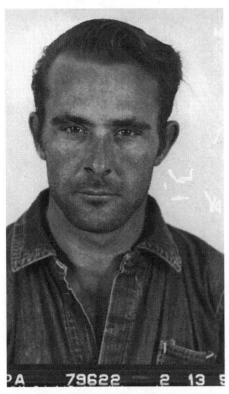

Clarence's 1958 mug shot
UNITED STATES PENITENTIARY, LEAVENWORTH

John's mug shot
UNITED STATES PENITENTIARY, LEWISBURG

Despite his best efforts to cheer her up, she feared she'd never see John again. He assured her there were different ways of getting out. When she asked him what he meant, John left it at that.

Helen promised John she'd wait for him no matter how long.

However, before John could act on his promise of escaping from the Atlanta penitentiary, he was sent to Lewisburg.

In a stunning breach of protocol not permitted today, evidence pertinent to the case was ordered destroyed on June 1, 1959. The duty of preserving trial evidence falls on the state's attorney general's office, which typically handles appeals and postconviction matters. Since the brothers were denied this opportunity in another effort to thwart their constitutional rights, the three had a much more difficult time appealing their two convictions.

John arrived at Lewisburg on April 4, 1958, and served his sentence there until he was sent to the U.S. federal penitentiary in Leavenworth,

The judge's order to destroy the state's evidence
TWENTIETH JUDICIAL CIRCUIT OF ALABAMA

Kansas, on January 20, 1960, after a planned escape had become known to the guards, most likely ratted out by a prison snitch. However, before his escape attempt, John wrote to his mother on October 25, 1958. As one would expect, Helen never lingered far from his thoughts. The figure is a portion of that letter, transcribed below for easier reading:

Hello Mom

Sure is nice to know that all of you are doing O.K. I got youre [sic] letter and the picture of Nell. I'm doing fine myself. I'm always thinking of everyone there. Say hello to everyone for me. Did any of you go to see Helen and the babby [sic]? If you haven't I wish some of you would drop by and see how she and the baby is doing. If there's anything you can do for them, I wish you would. She sure needs someone there to help out.

The question is, who was the father of Helen's baby, whom she named John? John or her husband, Jim? Unfortunately for both families, Helen never said before she died in 2010.

CHAPTER 12

United States Penitentiary, Leavenworth

Once again, John and Clarence found themselves incarcerated together in a United States federal penitentiary. But Leavenworth wasn't just any prison. The inmates there were hard-core prisoners convicted of murder, rape, and other heinous crimes. Worse yet, uncontrolled violence between prisoners, staff abuse, and medical neglect were common. Felons convicted of especially monstrous crimes were usually sent to Leavenworth.

United States Penitentiary, Leavenworth is the oldest of the three major prisons built on federal land in Leavenworth County, Kansas. Leavenworth also held the distinction of being the largest maximum-security federal prison in the United States from 1903 to 2005.

United States Penitentiary, Leavenworth, also known as the "Big House"
AMERICASROOF (WIKIMEDIA COMMONS)

The prison's walls are forty feet high and three thousand feet long. Its domed main building is nicknamed the "Big Top" or "Big House."

Considered one of the preeminent prisons in the federal judicial system, Leavenworth housed both notorious and high-profile criminals throughout the years, including "Machine Gun" Kelly, George "Bugs" Moran, James Earl Ray (who assassinated Martin Luther King Jr.), Robert Stroud (the Birdman of Alcatraz), and James "Whitey" Bulger, leader of the Winter Hill Gang.[1]

Though people often create romantic notions about a famous place like Leavenworth, especially after seeing a movie like *Birdman of Alcatraz*, life in a federal penitentiary was anything but romantic. In Pete Early's book *The Hot House: Life inside Leavenworth Prison*, he describes his experiences the year he spent there undercover:

> Entering a maximum security joint gets to you. The sights, smells, tastes, sounds, and dreariness of a prison envelope you even if you are an outside observer.
>
> Readers often ask me if I posed as a convict when I went into Leavenworth for what turned out to be a one year-long period, and the answer is no. Convicts survive by reading others, quickly identifying who they should be suspicious of and who can be preyed on. While Hollywood might think posing as a predator is possible, hard-core convicts can tell instantly if someone is faking it.
>
> Consider how Carl Bowles, a triple killer who has spent nearly all his life in prison, knew from asking a new convict just two questions that something was odd.
>
> "First time in a penitentiary?" Bowles asked.
>
> "Yeah."
>
> "Where you from?"
>
> "A state joint in Michigan."
>
> That was enough.
>
> "There are only two reasons why the federal prison system accepts a state prisoner," Bowles told me. "The guy is either such a mean son-of-a-bitch that the state joint can't handle him or the state has to get rid of him because he'll be killed by convicts if they put him in a state joint."[2]

In a documentary about Leavenworth, former inmate Harold Thompson said this about his experience while incarcerated at United States Penitentiary, Atlanta: "Fear. If you could put the fear of God in someone they'll stay away from you. As big as I was no one dared jump on me because they'd seen me whip a couple guys pretty bad. And so that was pretty much the element that kept me alive."[3]

When prisoners entered Leavenworth, they first went to the barbershop for a haircut and then received their institutional clothing. Inmates were then taken to the deputy warden's office and given a copy of the rule book. Prisoners were allowed showers twice a month, which could be doubled as a reward for good behavior. Enhanced privileges also meant first in the food line, first to the movies, getting your haircut before other prisoners, and mail up to four letters a week.[4] At the time of John and Clarence's incarceration, Leavenworth housed approximately two thousand inmates. Prisoners were also given the opportunity to earn money in the shoe shop, brush and broom factory, or barbershop as incentives for good behavior.[5]

Other ways of promoting positive behavior during an inmate's stay came in the form of earned privileges, such as checking out books from the library and access to cigarettes. Prison officials also appointed "trustworthy" inmates, also known as trusties, to positions of limited authority and responsibility.[6]

Maintaining control of rebellious inmates had always been a challenge at Leavenworth. As a way of channeling information toward the guards, experienced officers cultivated networks of informers (snitches), who let them know who was planning what.

John Mitchell, a former corrections officer at Leavenworth, echoed this truth in a 2018 documentary about Leavenworth:

Now these penitentiaries aren't run by somebody goin' out and lookin' and findin' somethin'. They're run by somebody whisperin' in their ear. And if you don't have snitches, well, you're in a world of trouble as far as I'm concerned in a penitentiary. You better have somebody tellin' you what's happenin' because there's no way in the world you can tell what's happenin'.[7]

The bitterness of the dual sentences still fresh on their minds, John and Clarence had no intention of completing their federal and state time. Upon Clarence's arrival in April 1958, he immediately began looking for a way of escape. As the weeks and months passed, he talked with fellow inmates about whom he could trust and whom he should avoid. And just as important, could the walls be scaled? Did they have work release programs? Who might help him on the outside? Anything and everything were considered.

Clarence also occupied his time with thoughts of home. Whenever possible he wrote his mother and let everyone know how he was, most especially that he was doing okay.

For inmates, correspondence from home was pretty much their only lifeline to family and friends, which meant every letter that arrived was highly prized and read a hundred times over. For inmates with nothing but time on their hands crammed into a small cell, simple words about the mundane things of life from loved ones meant everything, and it was no different for Clarence—news that everyone in Ruskin was okay, a recent letter from John, and memories of playing with Helen's baby. Clarence valued family above all else, and he felt pangs of guilt for causing them pain as a result of his many incarcerations.

Leavenworth, as with most federal prisons, housed two inmates per cell for the purpose of cost efficiency. The hours spent together each day sometimes resulted in bad blood between cellmates. As a way of promoting good behavior within the population, inmates could request a change with the prison administration from one cell to another. Clarence did just that in June 1959.

John was transferred to Leavenworth in January 1960 after a failed escape attempt at Lewisburg, and Clarence couldn't be happier to see his brother. They had a lot to discuss. One of the things the brothers learned in previous incarcerations was the importance of blending in and not drawing attention to oneself. If no one saw you, then no one hassled you.

When Whitey Bulger first met the brothers in 1958 while at Atlanta, he recognized those particular qualities in them: "The brothers Anglin were real nice guys—very quiet and real close to each other—resigned to want to just fade in and not stand out."

P. O. Box 1200
Leavenworth, Kansas
Clarence

this Letter is about
Clarence playing with
Helen's Baby

LEAVENWORTH KANS. NOV 24 '58
U.S. POSTAGE .04

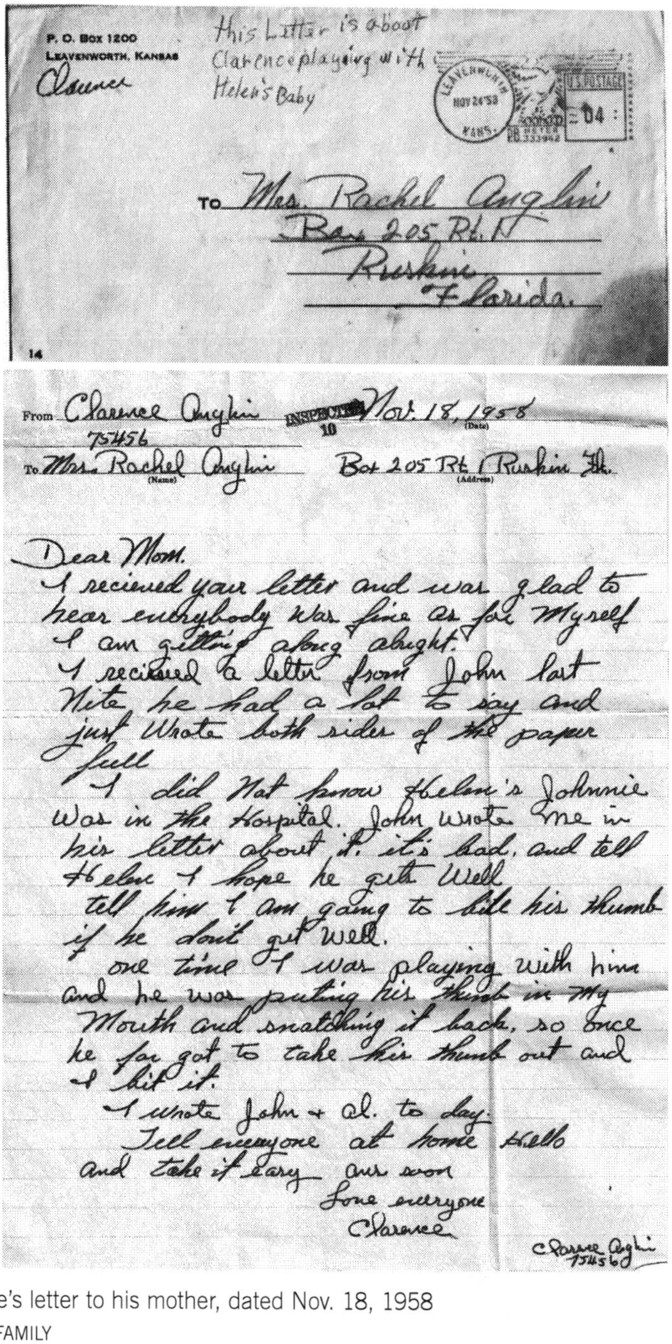

To Mrs. Rachel Anglin
Box 205 Rt. 1
Ruskin
Florida.

14

From Clarence Anglin INSPECTED 10 Nov. 18, 1958 (Date)
75456
To Mrs. Rachel Anglin (Name) Box 205 Rt 1 Ruskin Fla. (Address)

Dear Mom.
I recieved your letter and was glad to hear everybody was fine as for Myself I am getting along alright.
I recieved a letter from John last Nite he had a lot to say and just Wrote both sides of the paper full
I did Not know Helen's Johnnie Was in the Hospital. John wrote me in his letter about it. it's bad, and tell Helen I hope he gets Well
tell him I am going to bite his thumb if he don't get well.
one time I was playing with him and he was puting his thumb in My Mouth and snatching it back, so once he for got to take his thumb out and I bit it.
I wrote John + Al. to day.
Tell everyone at home Hello and take it easy our son
Love everyone
Clarence

Clarence Anglin
75456

Clarence's letter to his mother, dated Nov. 18, 1958
WIDNER FAMILY

UNITED STATES DEPARTMENT OF JUSTICE
BUREAU OF PRISONS

INMATE REQUEST TO STAFF MEMBER

Date _June 24, 1959_

To: _Mr. F. E. Aikens Associate Warden_
(Name and title of officer)

SUBJECT: State completely but briefly the problem on which you desire assistance. (Give details.)

Dear Sir:

I Would like to Move to B
Cell house With Jack Grier to B-
_287_

_OK by me_

_B-287_   _John R Green 76240_
(Use other side of page if more space is needed)

ACTION REQUESTED: (State exactly how you believe your request may be handled; that is, exactly what you think should be done, and how.)

Name: _Clarence Anglin_   No.: _75456_

Work assignment: _Dining Room_ Living quarters: _A-313_

Grade standing: (1st, 2nd, 3rd): _____

NOTE: If you follow instructions in preparing your request, it can be disposed of more promptly and intelligently. You will be interviewed, if necessary, in order to satisfactorily handle your request. Your failure to specifically state your problem may result in no action being taken.

DISPOSITION: (Do not write in this space)   Date: _____

_OK_   _Changed 6-30-59_

TO CENTRAL FILE

Date JUL 9 1959

BY _____

Officer

Clarence's cell change request
FBI

He provided me (Ken) with this insight in a letter he wrote me in 2015. Whitey was on the run from authorities from 1994 to 2011 after he had been tipped off by an FBI agent on his payroll about a pending arrest. When Bulger was finally apprehended in Santa Monica, California, he eventually landed at United States Penitentiary, Colman, Florida, in 2014. I had been doing research regarding my uncles and the Alcatraz escape and discovered he had been incarcerated there the same time as them. I decided to write Whitey in 2015 and see if he might provide me with any information about their stint on the Rock. Imagine my surprise when he actually wrote back and was willing to share firsthand accounts of my uncles, stories no one had ever heard before. Thus began a correspondence that lasted the next three years.

Whitey commented further on the importance of not signaling the guards or fellow inmates about an escape plan in the works in a letter he wrote me in 2017:

In Atlanta Pen. I worked out in the center of the yard track [which] circled us and prisoners would walk round and round single or in small groups—I could almost always pick out who was conspiring to do something illegal and I would see guard in the towers with binoculars watching the prisoners.

Men didn't realize that when they were conspiring and walking they had a tendency to lower their voice, heads closer together—real serious, no laughing or joking—super serious—and constantly watching [the] guard in [the] tower—later some men would run on the track preparing physically—men who never ran the track.

John and Clarence knew this as well, and so after the two were reunited they made sure whatever plan of escape they came up with stayed between them. A wise decision since they had no idea which inmate might rat them out as a way of currying favor with the guards.

As the weeks passed, John and Clarence continued looking for a way of escape. But the time apart from Helen had also been hard on John. A letter he wrote to his mother in February 1960 bears out his low state at the time:

From: John William Anglin   February 7, 1960
To: Mrs. Rachel Anglin

Hi Mom,
Just got your letter tonight.
     Sure was nice to hear from you, and to know that all of you are ok. Clarence and I are doing just fine.
     I think you should go up and visit Alfred as soon as you can, and find out why he isn't writing. We haven't heard from him in quite a while either.
     Helen is still on my mailing list and can write anytime she wants to, it would be nice to hear from her. I haven't wrote her in so long. She might not want to hear from me now. I stopped writing her for her own good. I would marry her today if I was free, and not ask any questions, but it's not that way, so I don't want her to try and string me along. I'm loaded with time and there's no room in it for any Woman. If I was free you would have a new Daughter-in-Law, whether any of the others liked it or not, you probably won't understand this, but she is my little Cinderella, you don't have to tell her any of this, because I think she already knows. You can give all the kids my Love, and tell everyone that I said hello, sure do miss all of you. You asked me if I liked it here, it isn't to bad here, and I think I'll make out ok. I like it better here than I did in Lewisburg. Well, it sure will be a Surprise to hear from Mearl after all this time. I thought she had forgotten me by now. I know there

From John William Anglin   Feb. 7-19-60.
                (Date)
To Mrs. Rachel Anglin Rt. Box 304.   Ruskin Florida.
  (Name)   (Address)

Hi Mom.
    Just got your letter tonight.
Sure was nice to hear from you, and to know that all
of you are ok. Clarence and I are doing just fine.
I think you should go up and visit Alfred as soon as
you can, and find out why he isn't writing we haven't
heard from him in quit a while either.
Helen is still on my mailing list and can write anytime
she wants to, it would be pretty nice to hear from her.
I haven't wrote her in solong she might not want
to hear from me now. I stoped writting her, for her own
good. I would marry her today if I was free, and not
ask any questions, but it's not that way, so I don't want
her to try to string me along. I'm loaded with time
and theres no sence in it for any Woman, off, I was
free, you would have a new Daughter-in-law, whether any
of the others liked it or not, you prubly won't understand this but, she is my little Sweetheart, you dont
have to tell her any of this, because I think she already
knows, you can give all the kids my Love, and tell
everyone that I said hello, sure do miss all of you.
you asked me if I liked it here, it isn't to bad here, and
I think I'll make out ok, I like it better here than I did
in Lewisburg, well. it sure will be a Surprise to
hear from Pearl after all this time. I thought she

had forgotten me by now. I know theres isn't enough
room on my mailing list for all of you, but any of you
can write once in a while, if you want to,
today is Sunday, and it's been a pretty nice day. it was
warm enough to get out in the yard, and get some fresh
air, everyone has to talk about something, sure talked about
all the good times, one thing led to another, and we
were back down in Florida. wound up with a good case
of the Blues, but that's the way it goes, your letter sure
did come in nice. I was beginning to think that you had
forgotten to answer my letter, I'll try to write as often
as I can, there isn't much to write about if your not
getting any Mail, and sometimes it's pretty hand then,
so I'd close for now, and I'll be looking to hear from
you real soon, dont forget to mention both of us in
all your letters, ok. take care. Love John.
                    John. W. Anglin.
                    77350

isn't enough room on my mailing list for all of you, but any of you can write once in a while, if you want to.

Today is Sunday, and it's been a pretty nice day. It was warm enough to get out in the yard, and get some fresh air, everyone has to talk about something, so we talked about <u>all the good times</u>, one thing led to another, <u>and we went back down in Florida</u>. Wound up with a good case of the <u>Blues</u>, but that's the way it goes, your letter sure did come in nice. I was beginning to think that you had forgotten to answer my letter, I'll try to write as often as I can. There isn't much to write about if your not getting any mail, and sometimes it's pretty hard then, so I'll close for now, and I'll be looking to hear from you real soon, don't forget to mention both of us in your letters, ok. Take care.

Love John
John W. Anglin
77350

In time, John's somber mood lifted, and he once again went about looking for a way out, but at the same time he continued writing home, letting everyone know he and Clarence were both fine. In fact, every letter Clarence wrote similarly focused on the positive. No matter what he might be experiencing in a dangerous place like Leavenworth, he never wanted his mother to worry about him or John. But what mother wouldn't?

From: Clarence Anglin   June 12, 1960
To: Mrs. Rachel Anglin

Dear Mom,
I received your letter and was glad to hear you was getting alright. As for myself I am getting along ok.

I was glad to hear you were planning on visiting Al. It's not very far up there to Atlanta the trip won't be to [*sic*] bad. But coming way out here would be rough. It's a long ways. If you are planning on coming anyway, the last of August would be about the best time to come. You mention selling the guitars you use the money on the trip if you sell them.

John is doing ok. And I just got a letter from Al the other day. He writes pretty often.

He says that he is still trying to do something about out time. And that he get a letter once in a while. Where is she staying now? I thought that he wrote once and said she was staying with Marie. I guess I close for now ans. Soon.

Love Clarence
Clarence Anglin 75456

In the hot July sun, Clarence walked the exercise yard as he had done a thousand times before. Despite their best efforts, neither he nor John had come up with a viable plan of escape, and he didn't know how much longer he could last.

John came running up to him. "Clarence, there you are. I've been lookin' for you all over."

"Well, you found me."

John's gaze darted about. When he felt confident prying ears didn't linger nearby, he walked alongside his brother as though the two didn't have a care in the world.

"I think I figured a way out of this place."

Clarence stopped in his tracks. "What? How?"

"The bakery," John replied.

"The bakery?" Clarence asked, a note of skepticism tinting his voice. "Don't see us gettin' out that way."

"I was talkin' with one of the other cons, and he told me two jobs opened up there after those guys were caught stealing food."

"That still don't tell me how baking bread gets us out."

"Simple," John replied, and he laid out his plan.

Not long after, their work request was approved. Though the brothers had never done this kind of work before, being more mechanically minded from working on the farm, along with hot-wiring cars, they took to the bakery more easily than expected. The two had certainly seen their mother bake enough bread growing up. Some of those skills must have rubbed off on them.

Both brothers quickly gained the trust of their supervisor and were soon given the coveted dinner shift, which meant fewer guards around. But more importantly, the night crew loaded the bread boxes onto delivery trucks and shipped them to the prison farm camp outside the walls. And best of all, each box was big enough for a grown man to fit inside.

On the evening of August 8, 1960, after the crew had left and the manager stepped out for a moment, John produced a box cutter he had stolen and cut through the top of one of the bins. He wished they didn't have to get in this way, but they didn't have much choice since the manager locked the boxes up when transporting the bread.

John jerked up the circle-shaped section he had cut and Clarence slipped inside.

"You okay in there?"

A couple of muted thumps sounded.

John glanced at the clock on the wall. They only had five minutes before the drivers came for the delivery. He started on the bin next to Clarence, but after only a few cuts the sounds of footsteps approached. John ducked into the storage room just as the supervisor appeared, but in his haste he dropped the cutter.

One by one the supervisor rolled the bread boxes toward the back door, until he grabbed the one with Clarence inside. His one hundred and seventy-five pounds made it more difficult to move than the others, something the two hadn't considered.

The supervisor stopped and looked the box over. John sucked in a short breath when a muffled noise came from inside. To John's disappointment, the supervisor took a step back when he discovered the cutter. He then examined Clarence's box more closely and discovered the top had been cut open.

"I want you to come out with your hands up," he ordered.

Silence.

"I know you're in there," the supervisor repeated himself. "You'll only make it worse for yourself if we come in and get you."

Another thump sounded, and then a hand pushed through the opening, followed by the other. Clarence slowly emerged as he stood, his expression denoting a mixture of defeat and disappointment.

An emergency call on the phone brought several guards into the bakery. They wrested Clarence out, and he was taken immediately to the Hole (solitary confinement).

As a result of Clarence's escape attempt, two years were added to his sentence. However, based on his history of previous attempts, Warden J. C. Taylor decided only one place existed that would put a stop to Clarence's troublesome ways—the end of the line, as he and other wardens called it. Located in the middle of San Francisco Bay, only twenty-two acres in size, it was of course Alcatraz Federal Penitentiary.

The *Ottawa Herald* filed this story about Clarence's capture:

> LEAVENWORTH, Kan. (AP)—Clarence Anglin tried unsuccessfully to escape in two large bread boxes while he was held at the Leavenworth Penitentiary.
>
> After that attempt was foiled by a suspicious food supervisor, Anglin was transferred to Alcatraz.
>
> Leavenworth officials said Anglin, with the help of his brother, John, hid in boxes destined for a prison farm camp outside the walls on Aug. 8, 1960.
>
> They said Clarence Anglin cut the top out of one box and the bottom out of another so he could hide among loaves of bread.
>
> A food supervisor sensed something was wrong before the boxes were taken out of the prison. He had rows of bread in the front parts of the boxes removed—and there was Anglin.[8]

John had been suspected as an accomplice, but an investigation by prison officials failed to connect him with the escape attempt. However, the warden decided both Anglin brothers were best gone, and so on October 24, 1960, John stepped off a transport boat that had shuttled him from Municipal Pier across San Francisco Bay and onto Alcatraz Island.

CHAPTER 13

Frank Morris and James "Whitey" Bulger

Childhood trauma does not come in one single package.
—ASA DON BROWN

IF THERE WAS EVER A PERSON WHO GOT A RAW DEAL IN LIFE, IT WAS Frank Morris. Even before he was born, the cards were stacked against him.

His mother, Thelma Marie Phillips, was only seventeen when she gave birth to Frank at Gallinger Hospital in Washington, DC, on September 1, 1926. At the height of the Jazz Age, she found herself drawn toward the glitz and glamour of that time and wasn't much interested in settling down into domestic life as a wife and mother.

Born into a middle-class home around 1909, Thelma's wild ways began at an early age. In 1920, she ran away from home. When the authorities finally tracked her down, they sent her to a school for wayward girls. Thelma found the place agreeable for a time, but at the age of seventeen she ran away again. It is not known if she became pregnant before leaving the school or after, but she gave birth to Frank Lee Morris in 1926, the father being Edward F. Morris (age thirty-six), whom she allegedly married two months before, though this is highly doubtful.

On her own with a child to take care of, Thelma didn't have the financial or emotional tools needed for such responsibilities, and so she placed him in a foster home. She figured if someone else took care of Frank for a while, she'd finally have the opportunity to get her life together.

She decided to enroll in a training school for girls, which she hoped would provide her the skills needed for a job. Thelma's progress at the beginning encouraged her as she looked forward to a better future for her and her son. One of her instructors echoed this same sentiment in a written evaluation of Frank's mother: "A good mixer, energetic and ambitious when she wants to be. . . . Makes a real effort to conquer her temper. . . . Does well in her nursing course."

Despite her success at school, Thelma missed her son, and so she left with him and found work at a Catholic orphanage, where she could earn a modest living and still be with Frank. The orphanage said of her, "She is bright, honest, devoted to her child, a leader among the other girls." However, the nuns also noticed a lack of a maternal instinct within her. Rather than nurture Frank, Thelma played with him like a toy and ignored the normal attention a child needs. The effect on him was noticeable, in that he cried more in her presence than in her absence.

Not long after, the county placed the two in a foster home in the hope it would be a more nurturing environment for them. But Thelma was more interested in spending time with friends than raising Frank. When he was four, she disappeared for several months so she could be with the latest man in her life, and returned as a chorus girl in a burlesque show. She disappeared again for two years, finally returning in January 1932. But after a brief visit, she left just as quickly as she had come.

As one might expect, being raised by foster parents wasn't an ideal environment for Frank, which was made worse by an ill-equipped mother who popped into his life unexpectedly, only to disappear again for long stretches.

Frank started acting out at the age of six when he stole some money from the teacher's desk at school. Said his teacher, "I really don't like to reprimand him because he's such a nice boy." His behavior worsened after sporadic visits from his mother, which often left him upset.

More foster homes followed, as did Thelma's coming and going. When Frank was about ten, his mother showed up out of the blue at Christmas, but he wanted nothing to do with her. She left again after a brief visit, most likely the last time the two saw each other.[1] He later said that his mother had died in 1936 at the age of twenty-seven. Not surprisingly, Frank turned to a life of crime not long after.

His first arrest took place in Clarksburg, West Virginia, in September 1939. He had been living in a foster home in Washington, DC, but ran away. A year later, he was convicted in juvenile court for theft and sentenced to the National Training School for Boys, a reform school in northeast DC, where he learned shoe repair.

Frank in juvenile custody
NATIONAL TRAINING SCHOOL FOR BOYS

He was given a sentence of six and a half years, but served less than a year. Freedom did not last long for Frank. He violated his parole within a year and was back in reform school at Chillicothe, Ohio, in 1943.

In 1945, Frank was again sent to the National Training School. According to his FBI file, other stints in prison followed: State

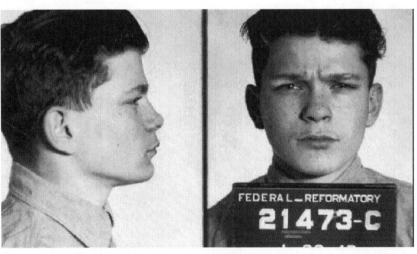

Frank's reformatory school mug shot
CHILLICOTHE FEDERAL REFORMATORY

Penitentiary, Angola, Louisiana (1945); Florida State Penitentiary for breaking and entering (1948); State Prison, Raiford, Florida (1949). He escaped from there in 1950 but was recaptured and sent back to Raiford.[2]

Morris was arrested again in 1952 for armed robbery and returned to Angola. While there he read books and worked various jobs, all the while looking for a way of escape. Finally, an opportunity presented itself:

> The spring harvest was in full swing at the Louisiana State Prison at Angola, about forty-five miles northwest of Baton Rouge, on a remote 18,000-acre tract in a blend of the Mississippi.
>
> Morris, doing ten years for robbery and possession of marijuana, and a fellow inmate, William Martin, were members of the work gang cutting sugar cane and hauling it to the prison mill. About four o'clock on a drowsy afternoon in late April, 1955, they disappeared.
>
> Warden Maurice Sigler said, "We don't know how they got away." Bloodhounds led searchers off the reservation to the shoulder of a road near the home of a black farmer, who returned that night to find the law waiting on his stoop. Yes, he had picked up two hitchhikers and let them out at an oil refinery on the outskirts of Baton Rouge.
>
> The fugitives spent a few months in New Orleans, cased the bank in the small town of Slidell across Lake Pontchartrain, then headed north to Kansas City where with a third partner, Earl Branci, they plotted the burglary. On Thanksgiving night they bored a hole in the rear wall of the bank, burned open two vaults, and lugged out $6165—a heavy haul, as it was all in coins. They had a fling for a month and a half, and then the FBI walked into the motor court southwest of Baton Rouge, where they were staying with three women.[3]

Frank was held in New Orleans while awaiting trial. Seems they held him a little too long. On September 13 he tried to escape. As expected, Morris was convicted of both robberies on September 23 and given fourteen years. The next day he arrived at United States Penitentiary, Atlanta.

Though Morris didn't know it at the time, waiting for him there was someone who not only became a good friend, but also change the course of his life. That man was James "Whitey" Bulger.

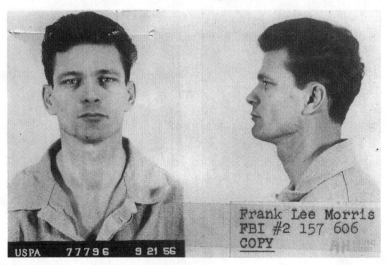

Morris's mug shot
UNITED STATES PENITENTIARY, ATLANTA

James Joseph Bulger Jr. was born on September 3, 1929, in Dorchester, Massachusetts, into a working-class immigrant Irish family. He grew up in a housing project in the neighborhood of South Boston. In his early years the police gave him the nickname "Whitey" on account of his whitish blond hair. As a youth he was arrested for larceny, forgery, assault and battery, and armed robbery and served five years in a juvenile reformatory. Upon his release in 1948, he enlisted in the U.S. Air Force. Despite a record of disciplinary problems, James was given an honorable discharge in 1952.[4] He returned to Boston and soon resumed his criminal activities.

Growing tired of arrests by the police for small-time crimes, Whitey aimed for a bigger score, a job that would not only make a name for himself but also provide him with the kind of money needed to launch a real criminal enterprise. And so, on May 17, 1955, he, Donald Dermody, and Carl Smith took part in the armed robbery of the Industrial National Bank in Pawtucket, Rhode Island. The three made off with $42,000. On November 18, he and William O'Brien robbed the Highland Branch of the Melrose Truck Company in Melrose, Massachusetts, where they stole $5,000. Lastly, in November 1955, Bulger and Richard Barchard participated in the holdup of the Hoosier State Bank in Hammond,

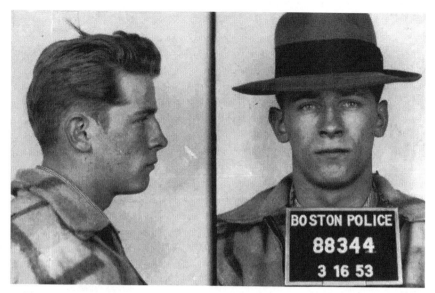

Bulger's 1953 mug shot
BOSTON POLICE DEPARTMENT

Indiana.[5] Bulger was caught soon after and tried for the string of bank robberies committed in all three states. In 1956, he was found guilty and sentenced to twenty years in federal prison at United States Penitentiary, Atlanta.

It is sometimes difficult to say how two people who grew up in different parts of the country with dissimilar backgrounds formed a close friendship. But in a prison as notorious as Atlanta Penitentiary, friendship meant protection, and protection meant survival. Whitey was outgoing and friendly. Morris, quiet and reserved. Both men were smart and had chosen a life of crime at early ages, eventually graduating to bank robberies. Perhaps the two saw in each other attributes they wished they had in themselves. Whatever the reason, Frank and Whitey became friends in the most unlikely of places.

Years later, Whitely Bulger still carried fond memories of Frank and often shared his admiration of him. In a letter he wrote me (Ken) in August 2017, Whitey said of Frank:

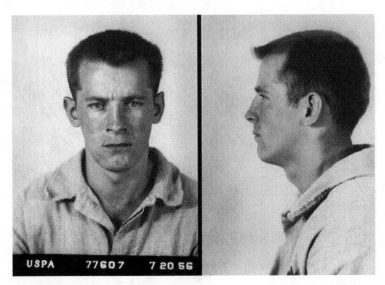

Bulger's 1956 mug shot

> Morris was a serious no nonsense guy—I was in cell opposite him in AD Seg in Atlanta—and prior can remember when he and partner arrived in Atlanta and in same cell house as I. Noticed him—intense and uptight because after Fed sentence for bank burglary—he was going back to Angola where he escaped from—and he would be the target of their wrath—for escaping. [*Note:* "Ad seg" is shorthand for administrative segregation. It's reserved for the worst prisoners who have attacked guards, other inmates, or ran prison gangs]

In a letter Whitey wrote me in March 2017, he also noted this about Frank: "I remember first seeing Morris and his partner older than Frank, obvious prison was no stranger to both—Very serious for young guy—not very friendly can understand once you learn about his past."

On a more positive note, Whitey also described his friend this way: "Morris was . . . a natural athlete. Well coordinated." A fair description since Frank played on the prison baseball team while at Atlanta.

Frank likewise possessed a superior intelligence. He took an IQ test during one of his stints in prison and scored 133, which put him in the top 2 percent of the population. Members of Mensa, the society for

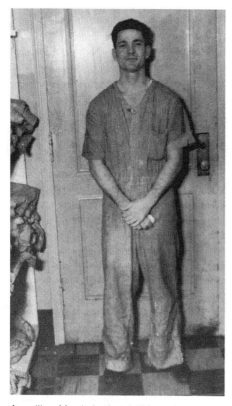

A smiling Morris in the clothing room
LOUISIANA STATE PENITENTIARY

high-IQ individuals, must score at least 132 on their tests to join. One can only wonder what Morris might have done with his life had he been raised in a stable, loving home.

Frank's intellect did not escape the prison staff either. Atlanta warden Fred T. Wilkinson said of him in a newspaper interview, "Morris [is] quiet and very intelligent. He's not given to rash violence. Above all, he's a planner. The whole operation seems typical of him."[6]

Morris was eager to break out of Atlanta at his first opportunity since he feared returning to the state penitentiary at Angola. His escape from there made the prison look bad, and so he feared the guards would administer "corrective measures" should they be given the opportunity. Morris said as much to Whitey more than once at Atlanta. In a letter he wrote in October 2015, Whitey shared this story: "Morris was motivated by fear of having to face Angola guards, having escaped from there. Feared being killed there if he were sent back." In the 1950s, such incidents in the South were not uncommon, which is why Morris had good reason not to go back.

In a letter Whitey wrote a few months later, he shared additional details of Morris's fears of returning to Angola.

Frankie mentioned to Jack Twinning he was escaping "Angola" Louisiana, at that time an infamous State Prison. Dog boys who hunted the
convicts with the armed guards—if you escaped from there, Frankie
Morris did, you would suffer badly when captured and returned—
working in the fields—chopping cotton—planting etc. Guards on
horseback would grab guys by the hair and try to throw them down
under the horse—those guards carried rifles and could kill you at a distance, which they would if a convict took a shotgun away from guards,
and if one escaped that way with shotgun he would pay with his life
upon return—I knew a friend in Atlanta Pen. Duke Dewan from Cam-
bridge Mass.—killed in Kilby—shot dead by guards trying to "Escape."
[*Note:* "Dog boy" is a pejorative term for fellow inmates who tracked
down escaped prisoners. They were considered traitors by their fellow
inmates and sometimes killed by them.]

It's little wonder Morris looked for ways of escaping from Atlanta. With
a fourteen-year stretch ahead of him, he knew they'd transferred him
back sooner or later. So Morris sought a way out before that happened.
But such attempts were not easy. The administration at Atlanta had
learned over the years ways of staying one step ahead of inmates, such
as having multiple head counts each day, surprise cell inspections, cell
rotations, interception of contraband, and fraternization between the
guards and prisoners kept at a minimum. They also employed a system of
snitches as a way of identifying those inmates planning an escape.

A snitch didn't get Frank, but time did. In late 1959 he received
news of his transfer before he executed a plan. Somehow, Whitey knew
that Frank wasn't returning to Angola but would instead be transferred
to Alcatraz and took great delight in telling him. "Told you're going to
Alcatraz! Angry—Morris was in cell opposite me."

Though Morris had no desire to go to Angola, he felt the same way
about Alcatraz. The prison had a reputation for being the toughest in
the criminal justice system; the end of the line for the worst prisoners.
Situated in the middle of the San Francisco Bay, it was considered by
most to be escape proof, including among the inmates. If Morris had
any chance of gaining his freedom, the news given him by Whitey dealt
a deadly blow.

Unknown to Frank at the time, Whitey had been planning an escape of his own. He had gotten a job in the prison hospital. With fewer guards around and the freedom to talk more openly, he and some of the other inmates in the hospital devised a way out. In a letter Whitey wrote in September 2017, he described what happened.

> I bribed guard to bring in two hacksaw blades—Louie, Charles Cat, Scotty, John Malone, Walter Splitt and Jesp were checked into hospital, worked there. Out window put out ladder. Snapped in middle then we got on roof—alarm—Warden and guards light on, then told come down—we said after we finish this last cigarette. We know this will be last for long time. All thrown in hole.
>
> Guy from Ohio "Darby" took two blades, he saw where they were hid to Warden—said give me parole I'll tell you who got these in. Warden said OK—Darby said "Bulger." Put in Hole—4 months sick—on concrete—naked—water in bucket ladle isolated—Wanted name of guard—said you will talk and I want name spare yourself lots of pain—Warden tried to convince me to name guard—I said you have the wrong guy I don't know anything . . . no one knew guard's name, lesson learnt—Secrecy—no one to this day heard guard's name.
>
> I spent four months in the hole then sent upstairs to AD Seg cells. Guys from roof sent to Rock right away. I'm in AD Seg cell across from Frankie Morris—Sunday and to left Santiago—after weeks they take Santiago—Sunday and Morris out in chains to Rock by bus.

When it became apparent to Warden Wilkinson that Bulger would never reveal the name of the guard who helped him and the others with the escape, he decided he didn't want a troublesome inmate giving other prisoners ideas, so he transferred him to Alcatraz.

Whitey continued the story in his letter:

> Later me alone to DC jail—then Marshals take me by car to Baltimore and tell me you're going to Alcatraz, we can fly in hours or week or so by TRAIN, only by plane if you give your word to not cause trouble in airliner jet—agreed so flew to Rock. Lodged me in city jail overnight

UNITED STATES

DEPARTMENT OF JUSTICE

WASHINGTON

October 21, 1959

To the   **Warden, United States Penitentiary, Atlanta, Georgia**

WHEREAS, in accordance with the authority contained in title 18, sections 4082, 4085, and 4125, U. S. Code, the Attorney General by the Director of the Bureau of Prisons has

ordered the transfer of   **James J. Bulger   #77607**

from the **United States Penitentiary, Atlanta, Georgia**

to the   **United States Penitentiary, Alcatraz, California**

Whitey Bulger's transfer to Alcatraz
U.S. DEPARTMENT OF JUSTICE

then in the AM the five marshals came and we went to dock—pier— and on prison boat to the Rock—I was put in new man's cell on Broadway then after time assigned job in clothing room and cell on 3rd tier in C Block #314. Two weeks later Morris—Sunday—Santiago get there. Shocked to see me in mess hall. Thought they left me in Atlanta.

In the thirteenth letter Whitey sent me, he added a humorous anecdote about what happened when he met Morris at Alcatraz. "When they see me they are shocked start to talk to me I make believe I don't know them to confuse them further! Then broke the ice—I had a fast trip on airliner good food and Marshals are pretty nice guys."

It should be noted the time line of Morris's arrival at Alcatraz two weeks after Whitey is not correct. According to his Alcatraz cell card, it shows Whitey's first day there as November 13, 1959, whereas Morris arrived at Alcatraz on January 18, 1960, a full two months later. But the idea of Whitey pretending to be someone else at first is still quite humorous.

John and Clarence were still at Leavenworth at this time, looking for a way of escape. When their plan of hiding in the bread boxes failed,

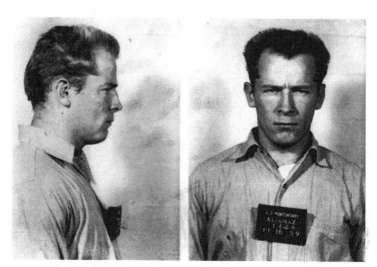

James "Whitey" Bulger's Alcatraz mugshot
UNITED STATES PENITENTIARY, ALCATRAZ

their future was set, and John arrived at Alcatraz on October 24, 1960, followed by Clarence on January 16, 1961. Four of the principal players in their famous escape had arrived, with two more left to include in the inner circle—Mickey Cohen and Allen West. They wouldn't have long to wait.

CHAPTER 14

Alcatraz

A low fog hung over the bay as a prison transport boat plowed through choppy waters toward Alcatraz Island. Inside, John held on to a pole, his hands handcuffed together. Across from him, a guard watched his every move. John paid him no mind, his attention instead fixed on a small porthole on his right. As the fog slowly dissipated, Alcatraz appeared in all its menacing glory. Above it, swarms of seagulls flew to and fro before a gray sky.

"There she is," the guard declared. "The Rock."

Alcatraz Prison
SAN FRANCISCO HISTORY CENTER, SAN FRANCISCO PUBLIC LIBRARY

A brief grin softened John's hardened features. "The Rock, huh. Cute."

The guard laughed in a condescending way. "Believe me, this place has seen your kind before."

"Yeah? How's that?"

"Young. Cocky. Think this prison's the same as the others."

This time it was John who laughed. "Like my brother says, all cages have doors."

Several minutes later the boat's engine powered down as they approached the dock on the southeast side of the island.

John gave the prison a long look. "I thought it would be bigger."

"It's good enough for you."

"Yeah, maybe, but there's one thing wrong."

The guard's eyes narrowed. "And what's that?"

"We're going the wrong way."

Two guards armed with 12-gauge shotguns, one taller than the other, waited on the dock as the boat came in nice and slow.

Transport boat pulling into the dock
BUREAU OF PRISONS

Escorted into prison
SAN FRANCISCO HISTORY CENTER, SAN FRANCISCO PUBLIC LIBRARY

When John stepped onto the pier both guards met him, their demeanor all business. He looked back over his shoulder at the hazy San Francisco Bay.

"Take a last look," the tall guard said. "You'll see the city every day from the yard, but it'll be a long time before you ever set foot outside these walls again."

John turned around and faced the guards, acting as though the taunt had no effect on him.

"This way."

"Where we goin'?" John asked.

"Processing."

The Alcatraz Federal Penitentiary, otherwise known as "the Rock," was a maximum-security federal prison situated in San Francisco Bay a little over a mile from the city. The main building was completed in 1912 as a U.S. Army military prison. The Department of Justice acquired the prison in 1933, and the island became part of the Federal Bureau of

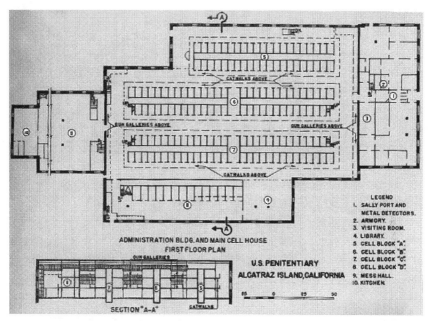

Layout of Alcatraz cellblocks
NATIONAL PARK SERVICE

Prisons in 1934. Given the island's remote location and cold bay waters, officials and politicians alike believed Alcatraz to be escape proof.

The three-story cell house included four main blocks—A, B, C, and D—the warden's office, visitation room, the library, and a barbershop. The cells measured nine feet long, five feet wide, and seven feet high, each one containing a bed, desk, washbasin, and toilet. As a policy, the prison kept African Americans segregated from other inmates because of racial abuse. D-Block, or solitary confinement, housed the worst troublemakers, with six of its cells designated by the inmates as the Hole, where the most egregious violators of prison rules found themselves locked in total darkness for several days or weeks of enhanced punishment, depending on the offense(s).

Cellblock corridors were named after famous streets: Park Ave, Broadway, and Michigan Ave. The dining hall and kitchen extended from the main building, where inmates ate their meals.

Working in the prison was considered a privilege for inmates, most of whom earned between five and twelve cents an hour in the Model Industries Building or New Industries Building, doing jobs such as sewing, woodworking, maintenance, and laundry.[1]

Clothing room

MICHELLE MAATMAN (UNSPLASH)

Upon John's arrival at the clothing room, he stripped down to his T-shirt and boxers. The guard on duty placed his clothes and other items in a box and put them in storage. In exchange, John received a pair of shoes, black and white pants, belt, blue chambray shirt, three pair of socks, two handkerchiefs, undershirt, slippers, heavy coat, knit beanie, and raincoat.

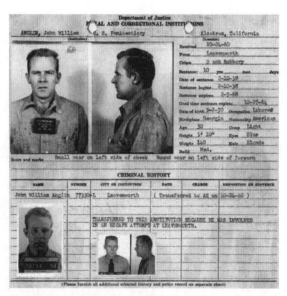

John's Alcatraz record card

UNITED STATES PENITENTIARY, ALCATRAZ

A different guard appeared from around the corner. "You finished with Anglin? Warden wants to see him."

The tall guard replied, "Two minutes. We gotta get him cleaned up first."

John did his best to maintain his dignity as he washed in the shower in front of the guards. He dried off and dressed in his new prison-issue clothes. John was then photographed and officially processed.

A large wooden desk sat on the far side of the room of Warden Olin G. Blackwell's office. Flanked by the American flag and the flag of California, a picture of President Eisenhower was prominently displayed on the wall behind him.

Born on February 15, 1915, Olin Guy Blackwell was the fourth and final warden of Alcatraz Federal Penitentiary. He served as warden at its most difficult time from 1961 to 1963. Blackwell was considered to have been Alcatraz's least strict warden, perhaps in part due to him being a heavy drinker and smoker.[2]

Warden Olin G. Blackwell in his office
BUREAU OF PRISONS

Sitting at his desk, Warden Blackwell, a stern-looking man with a piercing gaze, read a file. A knock on the door caught his attention. "Come in."

John entered the office, followed by both guards.

"Reform school at the age of nine," Blackwell said to no one in particular as he read John's record. "Breaking and entering, age fourteen. Car theft. A five-year prison sentence. Multiple escape attempts. Another two-year term for breaking and entering."

He looked up at John. "And your crowning achievement, a failed bank robbery." Blackwell set the file down. "Son, there's no doubt about it. You've lived a colorful life."

Based on his expression, the warden expected John to say something, but he didn't.

Blackwell's attention drifted toward the guards. "You can wait outside."

They nodded and left the office, closing the door behind them.

The warden sat back in his leather chair. "I trust you had a good trip."

"No complaints."

"Alcatraz Federal Penitentiary began operation in 1934. Before that it served as a military fortification and military prison. Do those facts say anything to you, Mr. Anglin?"

John's head cocked to one side and a slight smirk appeared. "It sounds like y'all have made a right nice home for me here. Nice 'n' cozy."

"There's no prison more secure than Alcatraz. If you follow the rules and don't cause any trouble, then things will go easy for you. If you don't . . ." Blackwell pointed at one of the windows facing the bay. "What do you see out there?"

John looked through the same window. "Water, and freedom."

Blackwell laughed. "Son, what you're looking at is death. Thirteen inmates have died trying to escape. Those cold waters out there will be your grave if my guards don't shoot you first."

"There's always a first time, Warden."

Blackwell's gaze bore into John. "Not on Alcatraz."

He picked up a piece of paper from his desk and held it in front of John.

"I have a letter from Warden Moore at Leavenworth. He expressed great concern regarding your proclivity for escaping prisons." Blackwell chuckled to himself. "Your botched escape attempt added two more years to your brother's sentence, and landed you here."

"Almost made it."

"Almost will get you killed. No one's escaped yet, and they never will."

His point made, Blackwell set the letter down.

"You've been assigned cell C-239. There'll be no trouble in my prison, do you understand?"

"Seems like you're the one holdin' all the cards."

"Of course I am." He pushed a button on his desk intercom. "Okay, you can come back in. We've finished our little chat."

The same two guards reentered the room.

"Take AZ1476 to his cell," Blackwell ordered.

As John walked the length of Cellblock C with the guards, various prisoners in their cells whistled and jeered.

"Lookie here," an inmate said, "seems we got us some fresh meat."

"Hey loverboy," another taunted him, "see you later tonight."

A third declared, "Welcome to the stink hole."

The shorter guard banged his nightstick against the bars. "Knock it off, or I'll put the lot of you on report."

The catcalls quickly subsided.

The tall guard looked back at the end of the cellblock. "Open up two-three-nine."

A couple of loud clanks echoed off the walls, followed by a rhythmic mechanical noise as the cell door slid open.

John looked both guards over, then stepped into his cell.

The door banged closed with an unmistakable finality.

The tall guard stepped up to the bars, a sinister grin pressed into his cheek. "Welcome to Alcatraz." He laughed, then walked away with the other guard.

Silence filled the cell as John stared through the bars. Drawing in a deep breath, he turned around and surveyed his new five-by-nine-foot home. On his left, sheets and a blanket lay folded on the mattress. To his right, two small shelves extended from the wall, several pieces of paper and pencils on top. Behind him, a pair of shelves lined the back wall. Beneath those, a sink and toilet. At the base of the wall, a small air vent covered by a metal grille.

Giving his mattress a couple of pushes, John sat on it. He looked up at the only source of illumination in his cell, a single light bulb. Looking down at the pillow next to him, John noticed a small pamphlet sitting on top. He picked it up and read the title: "Institution Rules and Regulations."

He flipped through a few pages, then threw the pamphlet onto his bunk. John noted the pencil and papers on the shelf next to his bed.

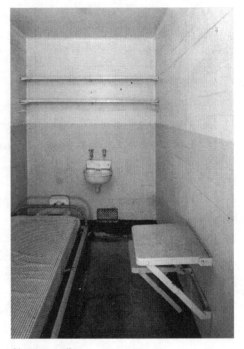

Alcatraz cell
LIBRARY OF CONGRESS

Though he was facing some serious prison time, his first order of business was to let his mother know he had made it there okay. She always appreciated a letter home. But perhaps tomorrow. It had been a long day and he felt tired. After a night's sleep, John figured, his thoughts would come much easier.

The letter has been transcribed for easier reading:

From: John William Anglin   October 25, 1960
To: Mrs. Rachel Anglin

Hello Mom,
Just thought I would write and let you know that I'm doing ok. Hope all of you are to. I hope all of you had a nice trip back to Fla. Let me know how everyone is. And I'll try to write as often as I can. I guess all

John W. Anglin

BOX NO. 1476
ALCATRAZ, CALIFORNIA

John
OFFICIAL NUMBER

Oct-25-60

TO Mrs. Rachel Anglin
RT.1 Box. 205
Ruskin
Florida

From John William Anglin October 25 19 60
(Date)

To Mrs. Rachel Anglin RT.1. Box 205. Ruskin. Florida.
(Name) (Address)

Hello Mom,

Just thought I would write and let you
know that I'm doing ok hope all of you are to
I hope all of you had a nice trip back to Fla.
let me know how everyone is, and I'll try to write
as often as I can I guess all of you will be surprised
to hear from me here in California but dont let it
worry you if you can help it, it's really a nice place
to build time and I like that part of it I also
enjoyed my trip out here, I came by train.
I sure did enjoy my visit with you, and Bill in
Leavenworth, and hope all of you got back home
without any trouble, you can tell everyone Hello
for me, and give my best to all the kids.
I'll be looking for those pictures you said you was
gona send me, pictures is something nice to have
around, specially in here. I'm a very long ways
from home now, and I want be expecting any
visits, so just write me, and keep me informed on
how all of you are. I'll make this letter short
because there isn't much to write about this time.
I'll be looking to hear from you real soon.
Love, John
John William Anglin
1476

of you will be surprised to hear from me here in California. But don't let it worry you, if you can help it. It's really a nice place to build time, and I like that part of it. I also enjoyed my trip out here. I came by train.

I sure did enjoy my visit with you, and Nell in Leavenworth. And hope all of you got back home without any trouble. You can tell everyone Hello for me. And give my best to all the kids.

I'll be looking for those pictures you said you were gonna send me, pictures is something nice to have around, specially [sic] in here. I'm a very long ways from home now. And I won't be expecting any visits. So just write me, and keep me informed on how all of you are. I'll make this letter short because there isn't much to write about this time. I'll be looking to hear from you real soon.

Love, John
John William Anglin
1476

Just like the letters Clarence wrote from Leavenworth, John kept his positive, almost suggesting he might enjoy his stay there, referring to Alcatraz as a "nice place." He also recounted his experience on the train that transported him across the country, though it must have been difficult for John to watch the miles go by, knowing that every town, every hillside took him farther away from home. To make the situation worse, he didn't expect anyone to come out for a visit. Too expensive. And a three-thousand-mile journey cross-country, none of them had attempted that before. Until Clarence arrived, he'd be a man alone.

Two weeks later on November 10, John had been assigned work duty in the dining hall, one of the privileges offered to inmates who hadn't caused any problems after they arrived. Having a job in the mornings and afternoons helped fill some of the long hours. John had also discovered an old friend he first met at Raiford years before, Frank Morris. On the weekends they chatted a couple of times in the exercise yard, mostly comparing notes between Alcatraz and other prisons. Other than that, his day pretty much consisted of working and passing the time away in his cell between 5:00 and 9:30 p.m., where inmates read or painted or played an instrument before lights-out, and of course wrote home.

From: John William Anglin   Nov. 8, 1960
Hello Mom,

Just got your letter tonight.
    Sure was nice to hear from you. And to know that all of you are ok down there. I'm getting along fine. I dig this Sea Breeze. It reminds me of home. It stays cool out here most of the time. I've been sitting here listening to the Election. And wondering how it was gonna come out. I don't think I would vote for either one of them. If I had the chance.
    I got those pictures you sent. And I also got a letter and a picture from Man and Billie, when you see them let them know that I got it, and I'll try to get them on my mailing list. Those kids sure are growing up fast. (Nell wanted to know if I enjoyed my boat ride out here.) (well—the ride was too short. And we were going the wrong way for me to enjoy it.) (Guess I caught the wrong boat.) Say—didn't that hurricane leave a place big enough for all of you to sleep in? Are you getting it fixed up ok?
    Nell was asking me about my things that Helen is keeping. I had a letter from her a few days ago. And she said that she was gonna keep them until I come home. But if she brings them to you I don't care what you do with them. You can tell Nell that she is wrong about me having a long time to stay here. Three years isn't such a long time. That's what I'll have if I get my good time back. I have a good chance to get it with a good record. I haven't heard from Clarence, or Al yet. Both of them has been taken off my mailing list. But I'm trying to get them back on it.
    Well I guess I'll close for now.

Love John
John W. Anglin
1476

In October 1955, radio jacks were installed in each cell on the occasion of the New York Yankees/Brooklyn Dodgers World Series. The Dodgers won the series four games to three, their only championship. After that, inmates' listening options expanded to several music stations. Though prisoners weren't usually provided with news from the outside, an exception was made on the night of November 8, 1960, when John F. Kennedy ran against Richard Nixon for the presidency of the United States.

John also mentioned receiving a letter from Helen. He must have missed her terribly. Ever hopeful, she continued believing they'd be reunited one day. He also seemed to suggest a rudimentary plan had already formed in his head about escaping from Alcatraz. The comment he made about Nell being wrong about him staying there for his whole sentence signaled to his brothers his true intentions about completing his term, part of the secret code they'd developed years earlier. Of course, John couldn't say that openly, so he suggested the idea of him being released early for good behavior, which the prison censors didn't catch. Little did they realize then what John and Clarence would accomplish a year and a half later.

Regarding the topic of John planning the escape, it should be noted that most documentaries and books covering this topic identify Frank Morris as the mastermind, no doubt a conclusion made by many because of his high IQ (133). Being uneducated men, John and Clarence are usually depicted as followers. Even the movie *Escape from Alcatraz* portrays Morris as the leader and mastermind. However, the FBI interviewed one of the inmates after the escape (his name has been redacted), in which he drew an important conclusion about John: "He thought that if the three had had a leader in planning the escape, it would have been the older ANGLIN brother who did the planning."[3]

Two weeks later, John sent his mother another letter:

From: John William Anglin   November 22, 1960
To: Mrs. Rachel Anglin

Hi Mom,

Just received your letter tonight.
    Sure is nice to hear from you. And to know that all of you are ok. Hope you aren't worrying about me. I'm getting along pretty fair myself. Hope all of you will have a big Thanksgiving this week. It will be a

holiday here also with a day off. Mom—you can thank Mrs. Buzbee for me when you see her. And I wish I could take her up on that paper from Ruskin. But we are not allowed to have papers here of any kind. And I can't receive any packages from home. But don't worry about it. I'm getting everything I need here, all those things would be nice. But we can't receive anything from home. You can send Xmas cards, photos, letters, that's just about it. Tell Mrs. Buzbee that I appreciate her concern very much. I'll try to send everyone a Christmas card this year. Tell everyone hello for me. And give my best to all the kids. Sure do miss all of you. And would like to be there to help Celebrate the big Holiday. There will be others, and I'll make up for all the ones I missed. Mom, I'm getting quite a few letters <u>from Helen</u>. And she said that she was gonna keep all of my things. Say, when you see Mrs. Buzbee, you can tell her that I would like to have some pictures of her, and Buddy. Getting pictures from home is almost like getting a visit. You said that you were gonna send me those pictures of Billie's family. I'll be looking for them.

When you write to Al and Clarence, give them my best. Say—what kind of work is Carson doing? There isn't much to write about from here, so I'll cut it short this time. Let me hear from you real soon. And take care.

Love, John
John William Anglin
1476

Now that he had been at Alcatraz for about a month, John had a better idea about the prison and how it ran, which he shared in the letter. Mostly, however, he thought about Christmas coming up next month and receiving cards and photos from home. As John put it, when you get a picture of family and friends, it's almost like actually visiting with them. And for men separated from their loved ones for years, that meant everything.

John wrote his next letter on December 8. In it, he conveyed the same idea about looking forward to Christmas, but then added a thought about the weather.

You should be proud of the cold weather your [sic] having down there. That goes with Christmas you know. It doesn't ever snow here. It gets pretty cold sometimes. It does snow on up in the mountains. But not here. I have never seen weather like we have here. It can be seventy degrees over in town, and on this island it's forty-five or fifty. We have to wear our coats year round here. Some days are pretty nice. But not many. I kinda like it myself, but I prefer Florida.

On January 2, 1961, John, still feeling the afterglow of the holidays, wrote home once again. Having received some Christmas cards helped him feel a little better during the holidays, and how the family did their best to be there for him.

From: John William Anglin   January 2, 1961

Hello Mom,

Received your letters, and cards.

Hope all of you had a big Christmas. And Happy New Year to all of you. I had a pretty good Christmas myself. I just didn't have the spirit to go with it. I got more Xmas cards than I expected. I got fifteen. So I guess someone out there knows where I am.

Well—I'll be on my fourth year next month. I know Alfred and Clarence is thinking the same thing. I wrote Clarence last week, so I'm expecting him to write me this week. I'll write Al this week too. You can tell everyone hello for me. I didn't have enough Xmas cards to send to all of you. And I hope it didn't hurt anyone's feelings. I don't like to send cards if I can't send one to all of you. But it just don't work out that way here. I got the pictures you sent. This one of Sue looks just like Marie, when she was small.

I didn't know Man's trailer was one of those big jobs. It sure looks like a nice one. But I don't think I would ever want to live in one myself. I had all I wanted in that one in Tampa. I won't ever forget that one.

I heard about all of that cold weather your [sic] having down there. Did you have everyone for Christmas this year but us there? I was thinking of everyone [sic] of you. And I know you were thinking of us. That was enough to make my Christmas a pretty fair one. I wish I could have been there with all of you. But it will have to be later. (I just might be down there in three more years). At last I'll be in Alabama. Well I guess I better close for now take care. And don't forget to write real soon.

Love—John
John William Anglin
1476

John conveyed a bittersweet moment in his letter when he realized he had been away for home for four years. In actuality, the bank robbery in Columbia, Alabama, took place on January 17, 1958, so his time away had only been three years, but he clearly missed everyone there. Though John didn't know it at the time, Clarence would arrive at Alcatraz in two weeks. And when that happened, everything changed.

After Clarence had been processed, a pair of guards walked him down Michigan Ave toward his cell assignment, B-140. With John now assigned C-205, the two were housed on different cellblocks, though he did catch a glimpse of an old friend on the third tier in B-356. Clarence nodded at Frank Morris, pleased to see a friendly face.

When the door to his cell slammed closed, Clarence set the things cradled in arms on the mattress and took in his new surroundings. On the back wall a shaving kit and roll of toilet paper caught his eye. He picked up the kit and looked inside. When he tried putting it back on the shelf, he caught the edge and the kit fell on the floor. When Clarence knelt down to pick it up, he noticed the air vent below the sink. Some of the paint had flaked off, exposing the concrete underneath. Scratching the surface with his fingernail, small bits broke off with relative ease. He picked up several granules and stared at them with great interest.

CHAPTER 15

Daily Life

How did I escape? With difficulty. How did I plan this moment?
With pleasure.
—*THE COUNT OF MONTE CRISTO*, ALEXANDRE DUMAS

ALCATRAZ EXISTED FOR ONE REASON—TO KEEP THE MOST TROUBLE-some prisoners in the federal penitentiary system from escaping. Administrators and staff alike had discovered long before the most effective way of achieving this goal was the implementation of strict discipline, and Alcatraz had earned the reputation of being the strictest prison in the federal penitentiary system.

As a way of maintaining discipline, each inmate received a copy of the "Institution Rules and Regulations" booklet upon arrival, which covered every aspect of a prisoner's life at Alcatraz. Written by Warden Madigan in 1955, the rule book was kept in an inmate's cell at all times, and they were expected to have a full understanding of it. Any infraction brought about immediate punishment by the guards, ranging from revocation of privileges to time spent in solitary confinement in D-Block, previously described as the Hole. Those cells had been set aside for the most severe discipline problems. The name was well earned since punishment sometimes included total darkness 24/7 and restricted meals. An inmate's time there usually lasted several days but could be longer if the warden deemed it necessary.

Institution Rules & Regulations booklet
UNITED STATES PENITENTIARY, ALCATRAZ

Beginning with the rule book's first paragraph, how an inmate conducted himself while serving his time at Alcatraz was presented in honest and frank terms: "This booklet is issued for the information and guidance of inmates of the U.S. Penitentiary, Alcatraz. It outlines the Institution's routines and explains what is expected of you in the matter of conduct and work. You are expected to learn and obey the rules and to perform your assigned work to the best of your ability."

In all, the pamphlet covered over fifty rules inmates were expected to follow from the moment they woke up in the morning to when they went to sleep at night. Just to give you an idea of how the guards and administration expected each inmate to conduct himself, the following are examples of some of the regulations listed in the booklet:

GOOD CONDUCT means conducting yourself in a quiet and orderly manner and keeping your cell neat, clean and free from contraband. It means obeying the rules of the Institution and displaying a co-operative attitude. It also means obeying orders of Officials and other employees without delay or argument.

STATUTORY GOOD TIME, MERITORIOUS GOOD TIME AND INDUSTRIAL GOOD TIME are types of reduction in sentence which can be earned only by inmates who establish and keep a good conduct record and a good work record.

PRIVILEGES. You are entitled to food, clothing, shelter and medical attention. Anything else that you get is a privilege. You earn your privileges by conducting yourself properly. "Good Standing" is a term applied to inmates who have a good conduct record and a good work record and who are not undergoing disciplinary restrictions.

DISCIPLINARY ACTION may result in loss of some or all of your privileges and/or confinement in the Treatment Unit.

TREATMENT UNIT is the segregation section of the Institution where privileges may be restricted to a minimum.

The booklet went on to discuss contraband, absence from work, cell house rules, threatening others, haircuts and shaves, visits, mail, and the like. Basically, other than the four rights outlined by the booklet (food, clothing, shelter, and medical attention), the guards doled out privileges to inmates as incentives for following the rules and good behavior. The moment anyone stepped out of line, punishment resulted.

As one would expect, prison regulations also covered how each inmate maintained his cell and what he could keep there. Any infraction of those rules also resulted in punishment.

An inmate's daily routine was also regulated by the administration and guards:

06:30 AM: Morning whistle. Prisoners arise, make beds, place all articles in prescribed order on shelf, clean wash basin and toilet bowl, wipe off bars, sweep cell floor, fold table and seat against the wall, wash themselves and dress.

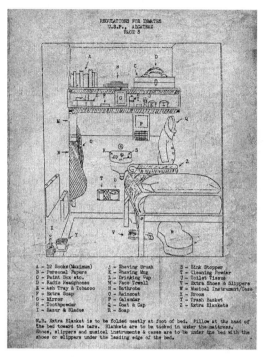

How inmates should maintain their cells
UNITED STATES PENITENTIARY, ALCATRAZ

06:45 AM: Detail guards assigned for mess hall duty; they take their positions so as to watch the prisoners coming out of the cells and prepare to march them into the mess hall. The guards supervise the serving and the seating of their details; give the signal to start eating, and the signal to rise after eating.

06:50 AM: Second morning whistle; the prisoners stand by the door facing out and remain there until the whistle signal, during which time the lieutenants and the cell house guards of both shifts make the count. When the count is found to be correct, the lieutenant orders the cells unlocked.

06:55 AM: Whistle signal given by Deputy Warden or Lieutenant; all inmates step out of their cells and stand facing the mess hall. Upon the second whistle, all inmates on each tier close up in a single file upon the head man.

07:00 AM: Third whistle signal; lower right tier of block three (C-Block), and lower left tier of block two (B-Block), move forward into the mess hall, each line is followed in turn by the second and third tiers, then by the lower tier on the opposite side of their block. The block three line moves into the mess hall, keeping to the left; block two goes forward, keeping to the right. Both lines proceed to the serving table. The left line occupies the tables on the left and the right line occupies the tables on the right. As each man is served he will sit erect, with his hands at his sides until the whistle is given for the first detail to begin eating. Twenty minutes are allowed for eating. Upon finishing, prisoners place their utensils in appropriate slot in trays, then return to table and sit down with their hands at their sides. Guard verifies utensils in the proper place.

07:20 AM: Upon signal from the Deputy Warden, the first detail in each line stands and proceeds to the rear entrance door of the cell house to the recreation yard. Inside detail, or those not assigned any detail, proceed to their work or cells.

07:25 AM: Guards and their details moved out in the following order through the gates:

1. Laundry, 2. Tailor Shop, 3. Cobblers Shop, 4. Model Shop, 5. All other shops, 6. Gardening and labor details

The guards go ahead through the rear gates and stand opposite the rear gate guard. There they count prisoners passing through the gate in single file and clear the count with the rear gate guard. Upon arrival in the front of the shops, the detail holds and faces the shop entrance.

07:30 AM: Shop foreman counts his detail as the line enters the shop and immediately phones the count to the lieutenant of the watch. He also signs the count slip and turns it over to lieutenant making his first round.

A guard watches the inmates as they prepare to eat.
GOLDEN GATE NATIONAL RECREATION AREA, PARK ARCHIVES (35178.007)

07:30 AM: Rear gate guard drafts detailed count slip, phones it to the lieutenant of the watch, signs it, and proceeds with it to the lieutenant's office.

09:30 AM: Rest period during which the men are allowed to smoke in places permitted, but are not allowed to crowd together.

09:38 AM: The guard gives whistle signal; all of the men on each floor of shops assemble at a given point and are counted, and return immediately to work. The count is written on a slip of paper, signed by the guard, and then turned over to the lieutenant making his next round.

11:30 AM: Prisoners stop work and assemble in front of the shops. The count is taken by the foreman or the guard. The foreman phones in the count and signs the count slip, turning it over to the guard, who proceeds to the rear gate and checks his detail in with the rear gate guard.

11:35 AM: In the recreation yard, the mess hall line is immediately formed in the same order as in the morning. The details proceed in the same lines to the mess hall.

11:40 AM: Lunch routine is the same as for breakfast, except at the completion of lunch prisoners proceed to cells.

12:00 PM: Noon lock-up cell count; the detail guards remain in front of cells until the prisoners are locked up and the count made.

12:20 PM: Unlock and prisoners marched in single file into the yard. Number three (C) cellblock first. Shop details again form in front of their guards.

12:25 PM: Details are checked out of the rear gate the same as in the morning.

12:30 PM: Details enter the shops and are counted by the foreman and the guard. Procedures are the same as 07:30 AM.

02:30 PM: Rest period; the procedure and count are the same as in the morning.

04:15 PM: Work stopped; the procedure and count are the same as 11:30 AM.

04:20 PM: Prisoners into the gate, with count.

04:25 PM: Prisoners marched into the mess hall, with count.

04:45 PM: Prisoners returned to their cells.

04:50 PM: Final lockup.

05:00 PM: Standing count in the cells by both shifts of the lieutenants and the cell house guards.

08:00 PM: Count in the cells.

09:30 PM: Lights out count.

12:01 AM: Count by lieutenants and the cell house men of both shifts.

03:00 AM: Count in the cells.

05:00 AM: Count in the cells.[1]

At 6:30 a.m., the day of multiple head counts and strictly regimented activities began once again. The reason for this was twofold. First, following the rules in a regimented and exacting way at precisely prescribed times reminded inmates every waking moment who controlled their lives. But if they did what they were told, when they were told, rewards in the form of privileges made their lives a little more pleasant. This ranged from working in the shops to receiving mail from home. But step out of line, and those privileges were taken away.

The second reason for monitoring the daily routine of each inmate was to deprive them opportunities for exacting revenge against a fellow inmate or guard, or forming a plan of escape. With every waking moment of an inmate's life at Alcatraz accounted for, prisoners enjoyed brief moments at best to form such a plan with a fellow prisoner. The constant monitoring by guards greatly limited their ability to acquire the tools necessary for revenge or escape. In a concrete cell measuring five feet by nine feet, few places existed they could hide such things even if a knife or saw blade had somehow been procured.

Alcatraz "snitch box"
BUREAU OF PRISONS

Another security measure employed by the guards was the use of metal detectors, or "snitch boxes" as the inmates called them. Some were portable, others fixed.

A guard operating the metal detector
SAN FRANCISCO HISTORY CENTER, SAN FRANCISCO PUBLIC LIBRARY

Prisoners walked through them at various locations. They were an effective way of finding hidden contraband or weapons. Even the prisoners' laundry wasn't spared the device.

The guards also monitored inmates' incoming and outgoing mail. Those in good standing could send two letters a week and receive seven letters a week from approved correspondents. Incoming letters were retyped on prison stationary to preclude any secret messages or forms of contraband from getting through.[2]

If a regulation violation was considered egregious enough, such as fighting or an escape attempt, the inmate went to the Hole in D-Block. Depending on the seriousness of the violation, inmates sometimes suffered the harsher punishment of being put into a pitch-black, windowless enclosure the same restrictive dimensions as their cells. Those inmates were limited to just one ten-minute shower and an hour of exercise in the yard a week. The first five cells that composed the Hole included a sink and toilet, whereas the last cell, nicknamed the "Strip Cell," didn't even have those, and prisoners would often be confined naked.[3]

Fear of being sent to D-Block proved an effective deterrent, considered an extremely harsh form of punishment by inmates and guards alike.

D-Block isolation cells
LIBRARY OF CONGRESS

Living in utter darkness in a small enclosure for days on end, with little food and water, no shoes, no bed, no mattress, and two blankets, did its work with great effectiveness, and few inmates repeated the experience.

As to the prison itself, the twenty-two-acre island situated in the middle of San Francisco Bay was not chosen by accident. Even though nearby Angel Island is only two miles distant and San Francisco one and a half miles away, the water is bitterly cold. Depending on the season, the temperature ranges from 53 to 60 degrees Fahrenheit. If desperate enough, someone might give the frigid waters a try and swim for shore, but he'd last about thirty minutes before hypothermia set in. The person's heart and respiratory system would eventually fail, leading to death. And with outgoing tides of up to six knots heading straight through the Golden Gate, even experienced swimmers couldn't overcome currents that strong. They'd be swept out into the Pacific Ocean, never to be seen again, which did happen for two escapees.

As an added deterrent for inmates thinking of making a swim for it, the guards warned them about different species of sharks that inhabited the bay, though they conveniently left out the detail that, except for an occasional great white, they were not dangerous to man. But the inherent fear we have of sharks did the trick, and most inmates didn't seriously consider escaping by swimming for fear they'd be eaten alive.

If sharks and frigid waters didn't get an escaping prisoner, the guards in the towers certainly would. They were trained marksmen with orders to shoot to kill. In all, seven inmates died at the guards' expert hands during escape attempts, which added that threat to the minds of every prisoner, including John, Clarence, and Frank.

On the positive side, Alcatraz did provide inmates with benefits not enjoyed in other federal prisons. The thinking was, if the privileges offered them made their time there preferable to Leavenworth or Atlanta, for example, they'd be less likely to jeopardize those privileges.

For example, the inmates valued single-occupancy cells at Alcatraz above all else. The reason for this was twofold. First, having one prisoner per cell kept them separated from one another. Experience taught the guards that inmates invariably formed plans of escape the more time they mixed with each other, or settled old scores. But keep them isolated, and many of those incidents seldom occurred. And second, having a cell to oneself meant enjoying a small measure of privacy not possible in other federal penitentiaries. This "perk" did not go unnoticed by former inmate Willie Radke, who served time in the cell next to George "Machine Gun" Kelly in the 1930s: "Having your own cell was a great advantage over other federal prisons. By having your own cell, it reduced the chances of being sexually violated and the privacy aspect was also a cherished

Guards doing target practice
BUREAU OF PRISONS

benefit."[4] The threat of being sent to a different federal prison, with their double-occupancy cells, hung over the heads of every inmate at Alcatraz if they became too troublesome, which acted as a powerful incentive.

Another benefit inmates enjoyed was the hot showers. In a concrete prison like Alcatraz, where the fog and cold winds kept the cellblock chilly most of the year, a hot shower twice a week helped make their time there a little more pleasant.

Also rated high on most prisoners' privileges list was the type of food served at mealtime. "The quality was reputed to be the best in the prison system—officials claimed they spent more money for food per inmate than other prisons did, and there was plenty to eat (prisoners could have as much as they wanted during each meal). The Alcatraz guards likewise ate the same food in their dining area. It was reported that, while Federal regulations stipulated a minimum allocation of 2,100 calories per day, Alcatraz inmates generally received 3,000 calories per day, per inmate."[5]

Keeping an eye on the inmates
SAN FRANCISCO HISTORY CENTER, SAN FRANCISCO PUBLIC LIBRARY

Prisoners enjoyed fresh milk, fruits and vegetables, butter, baked goods, ice cream, soups, coffee, and meat, hardly the fare inmates expected in a prison with Alcatraz's reputation.

But the benefits didn't end there. Inmates who behaved themselves watched a movie once a month and had access to over fifteen thousand books and seventy-five magazines from the prison library. In fact, some inmates considered the conditions inside Alcatraz more attractive than other federal prisons, and a number of them asked to be transferred there.

Preferred conditions aside, Alcatraz was still a prison, which closely regulated every aspect of inmates' lives. And no matter how "pleasant" conditions may have been for them, most people have an aversion to being locked up for years at a time. As previously discussed, Alcatraz existed to keep the most troublesome prisoners in the federal penitentiary system from escaping, and the guards and administration did everything within their power to keep that from happening. In effect, every member of the prison staff reinforced the same message every day: you have no hope of escape, so don't even try.

With all the measures put in place specifically designed for that purpose, it becomes all the more impressive that John Anglin, Clarence Anglin, Frank Morris, and Allen West not only risked punishment by discussing such a plan with each other, but actually set about pulling off the most famous prison escape in United States history.

CHAPTER 16

The Brothers Reunited

Everyone deserves not just to survive, but to live.
—STEVE MCQUEEN

CLARENCE HAD LITTLE TO DO OTHER THAN LIE ON HIS BED AND WAIT for dinner. More importantly, he wanted to know what John thought about the place. Despite the safeguards against escapes, had his three months here given him any ideas about getting off the island?

When the whistle blew and cell doors finally opened, Clarence was tempted to look up and see if he could find Frank, but a firm nudge from the prisoner behind him when he moved too close said otherwise. One thing Clarence learned in prison over the years was the importance of staying out of trouble, but he also learned not to show weakness in front of other inmates. A quick turnaround and the glare that followed told the guy it would best if he kept his distance, or else.

After the head count by the guards, the line slowly moved toward the dining hall. Clarence looked for John when he entered the hall. He found him right away at the far end serving food. His brother stood behind one of the metal tables, spooning something green onto trays. He also saw several guards standing nearby watching the kitchen workers close.

Clarence inched his way forward in the line until he finally reached John.

"Good to see you, John," he said in a low voice.

His brother glanced both ways before responding. "You too."

Alcatraz dining hall
BUREAU OF PRISONS

John slapped a spoon full of asparagus on Clarence's tray, then nodded. Clarence nodded back, and John slipped a small piece of paper in his hand.

Clarence hoped no one saw, especially one of the guards. But even if one of them had, he didn't worry much about what the note said. His brother was smart enough to use the code they had created years before.

In 2007 their brother Robert gave an interview to *New York Times* best-selling author Frank Ahearn in which he talked about the secret messages shared between the brothers:

> Man [Robert] told me that Clarence and JW [John] were thick as thieves, and since childhood they had a unique way of communicating between each other: secret destinations to meet up at, phone calls with certain number of hang-ups determined locations. JW received such a message and met up with Clarence when he escaped the Florida road gang and took him to stay with Alfred on the farm.[1]

Inmates waiting in line at mealtime
GOLDEN GATE NATIONAL RECREATION AREA, PARK ARCHIVES (3264)

As Clarence made his way toward the tables with his tray of food, a familiar sounding voice called out to him, "Hey Clarence! Is that you?"

He looked about the dining hall, finally zeroing in on a table where one of the inmates lifted his hand.

From the distance Clarence couldn't make the person out, but as he walked closer he finally recognized him—Frank Morris.

"Frank. Good to see ya."

The last time the two had been together was when they were housed in Atlanta with Alfred in 1958. They had talked of escape a few times, but nothing came of it since Clarence was sent to Leavenworth two months after he arrived. "Looks like they finally got you here."

"Yeah, they got me." Clarence took an open spot across from Frank. "So, how long you been at Alcatraz?"

"January 1960. Transferred from Atlanta."

"Atlanta. Then you must have seen my brother, Alfred."

"Sure," Frank replied. "We talked some. In fact, since I knew he was an escape guy I asked if he'd be interested in workin' on a plan together."

Clarence laughed. "I'm sure he was all over that."

"You'd think so, but no."

Surprise registered in Clarence's eyes. "No?"

"He was pretty ticked about getting that double sentence, so he figured he had a good chance on an appeal and get out early. Said he talked with a couple of lawyers from the ACLU."

"Really. That don't sound like Alfred."

"I told him he shouldn't waste his time on appeals that had no chance. Better if he took advantage of the opportunity right in front of him. But he didn't listen."

"If that was me, I'd have said yes in a heartbeat. My daddy always told us boys we should never squander anything good that fell into our lap."

"Didn't make much difference in the end," Frank added. "James here got busted for a prison break at Atlanta, sent to Alcatraz as a result. I followed a couple months later before I could execute my plan." Frank turned in Whitey's direction. "And speaking of James, this is James Bulger. Some people call him Whitey, but—"

"My friends call me James. Never did like that other name."

Bulger seemed affable enough to Clarence, clearly the opposite of Frank. "Got no problem with James." He reached across the table and the two shook.

Clarence looked out the barred windows. He was eager to become familiar with all of Alcatraz's ins and outs. "How far do you suppose it is to land?"

"What do ya think, James, a mile maybe?"

"More like a mile and a half."

Clarence laughed. "Heck, I've swam further than that back in Ruskin. I went about ten miles in Tampa Bay after I busted out of Raiford once."

Frank and James gave Clarence a particular look—San Francisco isn't Tampa Bay.

"Maybe so, but this water is much colder," he commented, "and the currents are strong. Don't matter how good a swimmer you are, the outgoing tide will pull you past the Golden Gate Bridge, where you become shark food."

"And with the currents and cold water," James added in an ominous tone, "you wouldn't last ten minutes without some kind of wetsuit or something to keep you from freezing."

"James is right," Frank said. "A person would have to be crazy if he tried swimming his way out of here. Besides, have you seen those guards up on the walk? Those ain't toy guns they're carryin'. I've watched them shoot targets in the water, if you're thinking of busting out, that is."

Clarence noticed a couple of inmates at the table across from him looking his way.

"Don't let them bother you," James said. "Everyone sizes up the new-bies to see what kind of people they are. As long as you sit with Paco and me you have nothing to worry about."

Clarence's eyebrows drew together. "Paco?"

Morris couldn't help but laugh. "James likes to call me that. It's Spanish for Little Frank."

"I see."

Some of the inmates behind them started to stir. When Clarence turned around, he caught sight of Warden Blackwell walking about the dining hall. He stopped at their table. The three tried not to make eye contact.

"Well, Clarence, I see you've made some new friends. I expect you're settling in okay."

"Fine, I guess. Not all that happy with my cell, though. Nothin' to look at."

"Well, I tell you what, you think about the job we talked about and maybe I'll allow for an early move. Alcatraz can always use a good barber."

"Like I said before, I'll keep that in mind, Warden."

"Good evening, gentlemen. Enjoy your meal." And with that Warden Blackwell left the dining hall.

James turned toward Clarence. "What was that all about? Sounds like the warden offered you a job."

"He talked with me about workin' in the barbershop when I arrived. Just not sure I want to keep doin' that. Got pretty old at other prisons."

Frank was quick to point out, "Think about this. You'll get out of that cell faster if you say yes. Besides, you never know what job might be useful one day."

"Don't know about being useful," James replied. "Unlessin', of course, you plan on makin' a wig and dressin' up like a woman."

All three laughed.

A guard's whistle sounded the end of mealtime.

As the inmates stood at their respective tables, Frank glanced in Clarence's direction. "Where did they put you?"

"B-140."

"Michigan Ave," James said. "I'm in C-314."

"Your brother's the next level down, C-219," Frank said.

Clarence nodded. He appreciated how much of a difference having a friend like Frank made in a place like this, and now James Bulger. The more friends you had the better protected you were, but it was nothing compared to family. Like their daddy told them growing up, "You can always count on family."

The guards returned the inmates to their cells when mealtime ended at 4:50 p.m. From 5:00 until 9:30, they occupied their time however they wished. Some of the inmates played their instruments, while others listened to music or baseball games on their cell radios. Clarence, on the other hand, stretched out on his cot and stared up at the ceiling. After a guard walked by on his rounds, he took out the piece of paper John gave him in the dining hall.

His brother had drawn three lines on the paper, the first two the same length, the third one shorter than the others, which translated, "Plan still in effect. Are you in? I know I can count on you." With that Clarence flushed the paper down the toilet. No use taking chances.

Clarence didn't relish the idea of being stuck in his cell for most of the day, so he figured he should take Frank's advice and accept Blackwell's offer about the barbershop job. But before he let the warden know, Clarence thought about his mother, and how she worried about her sons. He figured a letter from him, letting her know he made it okay, should ease her concerns, at least a little.

The letter has been transcribed for easier reading.

Clarence Anglin
Box No. 1485
ALCATRAZ, CALIFORNIA
OFFICIAL BUSINESS

POSTAGE AND FEES PAID
FBP

Jan. 61

To Mrs. Rachel Anglin
Box 205 Rte. 1
Ruskin,
Florida.

25

From Clarence Anglin   January 16, 1961
1485
To Mrs. Rachel Anglin Box 205 Rte 1 Ruskin, Fla.

Dear Mom.
I haven't recieved any answere from my last letter but I thought that I should write you any way. And let you know that I have been transfered here (Alcatraz). I have seen John and is alright.

I hope everyone there at home are getting along alright. I am making out here too. It sure is a long ways from home it took about thirty hours to come out here on the train. it would just about take a week to drive out here from there.

It will be hard on you all when you wont to visit, but I like it better so far then I did Leavenworth. And it's sure that as cold as it was there either I haven't been assigned any work yet, but there's nothing to worrie about I'll get along alright out here.

I wont write you much this time I just wanted to let you know I had been transfered. tell everyone Hello and ans. soon. Love always Clarence

Clarence Anglin 1485

From: Clarence Anglin 1485   January 16, 1961
To: Mrs. Rachel Anglin

Dear Mom,

I haven't received any answers from my last letter but I thought that I should write you anyway and let you know that I have been transferred here (Alcatraz). I have seen John and is alright.

I hope everyone there at home are getting along alright. I am making out here ok. It sure is a long way's [*sic*] from home it took about thirty hours to come out here on the train. It would just about take a week to drive out here from there.

It will be hard on you all when you want to visit. But I like it better so far than I did Leavenworth. And it's sure not as cold as it was there either. I haven't been assigned any work yet, but there's nothing to worry about I'll get along alright out here.

I won't write you much this time I just wanted to let you know I had been transferred. Tell everyone hello and ans. soon.

Love always Clarence
Clarence Anglin 1485

Writing home for Clarence had always been difficult. Doing so usually brought up memories about his family and how much he wanted to be home again. He knew his mother worried about him and John, and she needed to know that they were getting along okay. Clarence also knew she prayed for them as a way of combatting her fears. And in a place like this, they could use all the prayers they could get.

A few days later a guard told Clarence his transfer had been approved, no doubt expedited by asking for the barbershop job. On January 23, Clarence moved to cell C-227. However, the job given him wasn't cutting inmates' hair; rather, he had been assigned dining hall duties with John.

The following Saturday Clarence walked into the exercise yard for the first time. The cold, salty air met him the moment he exited the cellblock. Tightening his newly issued prison coat warmed him, along with his knit beanie. A strange feeling came over Clarence as he took in

1961		
DATE	DETAIL	CELL
1/16	Idle	B-140
1/23	Cul	C-227
2-23	"	C 217

Clarence's cell card
UNITED STATES PENITENTIARY, ALCATRAZ

1960		
DATE	DETAIL	CELL
10/24	Idle	C-299
11/4	C.H.Maint	B-35
11/10	Cul	C-205
1961		
1/21	"	C-219

John's cell card
UNITED STATES PENITENTIARY, ALCATRAZ

San Francisco across the bay, an amalgam of freedom and temptation. A gentle wind blew past him and with it the sound of music playing in the distance. So close to the city, and yet so far.

"Keep it moving," a guard standing nearby barked.

Walking down the cement steps into the main yard, he started taking mental notes of the prison, like where the guards stood on the walk above the walls, how many there were at any given time, had inmates found any blind spots, places the wall could be scaled, and the like.

He stopped and lit a cigarette.

"Hey Clarence," a voice called from behind.

Clarence turned around, and there he saw John walking toward him. "I got out of kitchen duty so you and me could talk."

"Yeah, we definitely have some things to discuss." Clarence looked about the yard. The last thing he wanted was prying ears nearby. In the

Exercise yard and baseball diamond
GOLDEN GATE NATIONAL RECREATION AREA, PARK ARCHIVES (3089 AND 19200.282)

distance, however, he spotted a pair of orange-colored towers stretching upward. He seemed transfixed by the sight. "Can you believe that we stood by that dang bridge just a few years ago lookin' at this place with Alfred? Seems like only yesterday."

John glanced at the Golden Gate then looked elsewhere. "Maybe we should have never robbed that bank."

The comment cut into Clarence, as he had been the one who had talked John into going along with the robbery.

"But if I had to do it all over again," John added, "there's no one else I'd want with me."

Clarence understood what John was trying to do, and it helped a little. Blood was thicker than water, after all.

As the two walked about the exercise yard, they eventually passed the baseball game. Far enough away from any guards in the back corner, Clarence finally asked John about the note he gave him. "So you been lookin' for a way out of here?"

"Lookin', yes, but nothin' workable yet. Just wanted to make sure you were still on board."

"You can count on me for sure."

Clarence caught sight of Frank and Whitey sitting on the cement steps.

"McQueen, up here!" Bulger called out.

John likewise turned to the sound of James's voice. Frank sat next to him. "Why don't we take a load off?"

Clarence took a spot next to the two. "Hey James, you got a nickname for me? I feel left out."

"Actually, I do. I was thinking you reminded me of Moses in the Bible."

"Moses? Why that name?"

"Well, your brother told us some swimming stories about you. I'd say that name fits you well."

Everyone laughed.

Then Frank spoke up, "If you're thinking of breaking out, maybe we can do it together."

Allen West and Mickey Cohen

AT THE END OF LUNCH MOST INMATES RETURNED TO THEIR JOBS.
Those who didn't work stayed in their cells. Once the doors closed, silence
descended on the cellblocks. Except for the guards who patrolled the
avenues or an occasional inmate who did maintenance work around the
prison, one of them being Allen West, the prison was like a ghost town
during the day.

Allen West and Mickey Cohen mug shots
UNITED STATES PENITENTIARY, ALCATRAZ

B-Block utility corridor
GRENDELKHAN (WIKIMEDIA COMMONS)

Plumbers had recently worked on some of the water pipes in the utility corridor separating B-Block. After they finished, West had been given the job of cleaning up the mess they left behind. Correctional Officer Charles Herman stood by as West lugged a bucket and broom through the three-foot-wide space, though the water pipes for each cell made the corridor even narrower.

"Don't take too long," Herman ordered. "I have rounds in twenty minutes."

"Yeah, yeah," West replied.

Dressed in coveralls and hat, he made his way down the dimly lit passage.

West came upon bits of rusted pipe and fittings and swept them into his bucket. He worked his way forward and found more pieces of pipe. Rolling up his sleeves, West knelt down and picked up the scraps by hand. As he grabbed each item, he noticed something bulky wrapped in paper tucked behind a cement support. He looked over his shoulder. Officer Herman stood at the end of the corridor with another guard, their backs to him. He reached down and wrested the package free from the crevasse, the items wrapped inside heavier than he expected.

When West opened the paper covering, several sawblades and files tumbled into his hand. Based on their rusted condition, he figured they must have been there for years, maybe decades, left behind by an unknown inmate who never had the chance to use them.

His first inclination, hide the files and blades in his bucket, but what if Herman searched him and his things when he emerged from the corridor? Then there were the snitch boxes. He'd never get past those. And if he somehow managed that feat, the threat of cell shakedowns hung over every inmate's head. Guards often showed up unannounced and went through prisoners' things, looking for contraband. If they found the blades, West knew he'd get two weeks in the Hole for sure, and probably a couple of years tacked onto his sentence.

He looked up and stared at the cellblock roof. Nine months before, he had been assigned the job of painting that part of the prison. Ventilator shafts above lined the cellblock ceiling. Most weren't used anymore, cemented up, except for one. Rather than seal the hole, steel bars had been welded across the opening. What he didn't have at the time were cutting tools, so he never did anything about it. But now, with these blades, everything had changed.

The question was, who could he trust with his discovery? A name immediately came to mind.

West rewrapped the blades and files and put everything back where he found them. Since no one had discovered the cutting tools after all these years, he figured they'd still be safe there. Not even the guards went into the utility corridor unless it was absolutely necessary.

When West finished his work, he reemerged from the narrow passageway. Herman checked his watch. "Just in time. I was about to come in after you."

West wiped the dirt off his clothes. "Believe me, that's not a place you want to go."[1]

The first chance West had he looked for John in the yard. The two first met in 1952 when they were both doing time at Raiford Prison in Florida. John may not have had much of a formal education, but he was street smart in West's opinion and planned things out before acting.

"Hey John," West said. "It's been a while."

John looked at him, and for a moment couldn't quite place him. "You're, um . . ."

"Allen. Allen West."

John's face lit up. "Oh yeah. Now I remember. Raiford."

"How you been doing since then?"

"You know. In and out."

"Yeah. Me too."

John turned toward Frank. "This here's Frank Morris. We did some time together in Atlanta."

Morris nodded.

"You got a minute?" West asked John, then glanced at Frank.

"I got a lot of 'em. Somethin' on your mind?"

West flashed a second glance in Morris's direction.

John picked up on his unease. "It's okay. You can trust him."

The two kept their eyes on each other a moment before West turned in John's direction. "When we were at Raiford, you talked about how your brothers broke out of there. I think you tried yourself."

"Yeah, so?"

"Have any thoughts about bustin' out of here?"

Morris's expression changed in an instant. "You don't talk about somethin' like that without makin' sure no one can hear you."

West's mood darkened. "I checked. You think I'm stupid?"

"I didn't say you were stupid. Just be careful about what you say."

John put up his hands. "Let's cool it. Don't want to get the attention of the guards." He checked for inmates listening in. "What do you have in mind?"

West leaned close, his voice low, "A few days ago, I was working in the utility corridor behind B-Block and found some saw blades and files stashed there."

"You sure?"

"Of course I'm sure. They're a bit rusted but still in good shape."

"They just may be what we need for the vents on top," Frank suggested to John.

Surprise registered in West's eyes. "You know about those?"

"Everybody at Alcatraz does. Clarence and me were talkin' about them the other day. If we could get on top of the cellblock and cut through, we'd be on the roof and out of here. But we don't have saws."

"You do now."

"Let me talk with Clarence and see what he thinks. If he says it's okay, we'll talk again."

"He'll say yes," West assured him.

"What makes you so sure?" Frank asked.

"Because without me you don't have the blades."

West turned and walked away. When he looked back at John and Frank, West inadvertently bumped into a black inmate. "Sorry, man," the man apologized.

A fiery hate filled Allen's eyes. "Watch where you're goin', boy." He shoved the inmate back and kept walking.

When another black inmate saw what happened he took an aggressive step toward West, but the first inmate stopped him. "It's cool. It's cool. Don't wanna mess with him out here and get shot by a guard. I'll talk with Bumpy. See what he says."

Allen Clayton West was born in New York City on March 25, 1929. He dropped out of school in the eighth grade and quickly fell into crime. Known for being a loud-mouth racist with an explosive temper, West found himself in and out of prison most of his adult life. Then in 1955 he was convicted of car theft and sent to Atlanta Penitentiary, then transferred to Florida State Prison. And like the Anglin brothers, West frequently tried to escape. This resulted in his transfer to Alcatraz in 1957.[2] Whitey Bulger knew West and, like many of the inmates who crossed his path, held a negative view of him. In one of the letters Whitey sent me, he wrote, "West was weak and had a big mouth and said something that upset the others." In another letter Whitey added, "West was a shifty character. Prisons are full of them. Seems they grew up behind bars and this was their natural environment."

The next time John saw Clarence was in the dining hall. As they readied their food stations, he told him what West had found. Clarence recognized his shortcomings as a potential problem, but he also understood the opportunity West offered them, along with his knowledge of the prison.

"Okay, he's in the group. Now, how do we get the blades and files? Who knows when West will get back into the corridor?"

"I think I might have an idea about that," Clarence said.

A guard opened the dining hall doors and let in the first group of inmates. The brothers separated.

With Morris's recent transfer to B-138, he came through the doors after C-Block. He looked both ways when he approached Clarence, who scooped up a large helping of eggs.

"Frank."

"After talking with West, I checked out the vent in back of my cell," he said in a low voice. "The concrete's soft. Worth looking into."

One of the guards took note of the impromptu conversation. "Keep it moving."

Clarence gave Frank a second scoop. "Same in my cell. Broke off some pieces my first day here. I'll see about doin' some diggin' tonight. Let you know how it goes."

Frank nodded and went to the next station.

Like clockwork, the prisoners returned to their cells at 4:50 p.m. When the head count accounted for every inmate, the cell doors slammed shut. For the next four and a half hours, they could do whatever they wanted in their cells—read, play an instrument, paint, work out—so long as they didn't violate the rules or cause a commotion.

Back of cell
LIBRARY OF CONGRESS

Clarence turned off the light in his cell after he made sure no guards were around. He took his regulations pamphlet off the back shelf and pulled out a spoon he had stolen from the kitchen.

He lay down on the concrete floor and gave the air vent a good, long look.

The cold air coming through the grate carried with it a damp, musty smell. He ran his fingers along the edges and found a couple of places where small bits of concrete had broken off. Clarence looked back over his shoulder and listened. No guard's footsteps. He used the end of his spoon to pick away at the concrete. Luckily for him, a nearby inmate played his guitar, which covered the sounds of his digging.

Small chunks of concrete broke off with relative ease. Clarence picked up one of the pieces and broke it up into smaller bits between his thumb and index finger. He smiled.

"John's gonna like hearin' about this."

As the first stages of their planned escape began to take shape, things couldn't have been worse for Mickey Cohen in Los Angeles. Rather than the heat from the Kennedy hearings cooling off as he had hoped, the pressure on him had actually gained steam over the months, no doubt the result of millions of Americans across the country watching the hearings on TV.

The United States Senate Select Committee on Improper Activities in Labor and Management (also known as the McClellan Committee) was created by the Senate on January 30, 1957. The committee had been directed to study the extent of criminal and other improper practices in the field of labor-management relations and to suggest changes in the law that provided protection against such practices in the future. The committee called Cohen to testify in November 1958, but despite vigorous and accusatory questions thrown at him he was not charged with any crimes.

Mickey Cohen at the courthouse with Candy Barr
KTTV-FOX 11 NEWS

Cohen may have avoided formal charges during the high-profile hearings, but he still remained fixed on the Kennedys' radar.

They first became aware of Cohen in 1950 when the U.S. Senate committee known as the Kefauver Commission investigated him and other underworld figures. As a result of that investigation, Cohen was convicted of tax evasion in June 1951 and sentenced to four years in federal prison. When he was released in October 1955, Cohen became a national celebrity. He ran floral shops, paint stores, nightclubs, casinos, gas stations, and a men's haberdashery as ways of rehabilitating his criminal image. In 1957, *Time* wrote an article about Cohen meeting with famous evangelist Billy Graham. "I am very high on the Christian way of life," he declared. "Billy came up, and before we had food, he said—What do you call it, that thing they say before food? Grace? Yeah, grace. Then we talked a lot about Christianity and stuff." However, when Cohen's lifestyle didn't really change, some of his Christian acquaintances discussed this with him. His response: "Christian football players, Christian cowboys, Christian politicians; why not a Christian gangster?"[3]

Though on the surface it appeared that Cohen had gotten on the straight and narrow, state and federal authorities had long suspected he had resumed his criminal activities upon his release in 1955 and kept the pressure on him, particularly investigating his business dealings. Cohen didn't help himself in 1957 when he did a television interview with Mike Wallace, later of *60 Minutes* fame. During the interview, Cohen admitted killing at least one man in self-defense and harshly attacked Los Angeles Police Chief William Parker's treatment of him.[4]

As expected, the LAPD closely monitored Cohen's movements. They arrested him multiple times for minor offenses, and in May 1958 the police bugged his house and investigated his personal and business records. Feeling personally persecuted by the authorities, Cohen had had enough and filed a lawsuit against the police, claiming his constitutional rights had been violated. In his mind, the war against him hadn't been initiated by local law enforcement; rather, they were taking orders from the Kennedy brothers, who he believed would stop at nothing to get him. His suspicions were confirmed in October 1958 when the Intelligence Division issued a subpoena against him in connection with his

alleged activities in the vending machine war between the Rowe Cigarette Service Company of Los Angeles and the Coast Vending Machine
Company.[5]

In March 1959, Cohen testified in Washington, DC, before Senator
John L. McClelland's Select Committee on Improper Activities in Labor
and Management, with a special focus on criminal corruption and infil-
tration of businesses by the mob. Senator Robert F. Kennedy had been
chosen as chief counsel for the committee. His brother, John Kennedy,
also sat in on the hearings.[6]

Robert Kennedy aggressively pressed Cohen about muscling in on
Los Angeles and Orange County labor rackets and his role in the feud
between two cigarette vending machine companies. Cohen repeatedly
invoked the Fifth Amendment, answering each question, "I respectfully
decline to answer on the grounds that it may tend to incriminate me."

Robert Kennedy changed his tactics and asked Cohen about his
knowledge of mob activity. "What does it mean to have someone's lights
put out?"

Cohen, always ready for a joke, replied, "Lookit, I dunno what you're
talking about. I'm not an electrician."

The Kennedy brothers during the televised hearings
NATIONAL ARCHIVES AND RECORDS ADMINISTRATION

Incensed by Cohen's mockery, Kennedy leaped toward Cohen as if to hit him, but Senator McClelland grabbed Kennedy by the arm and forced him to sit down.

By the time the hearings ended, Robert Kennedy had become a national figure. He had also created a personal enemies list of mob figures, Cohen being one of them.[7]

Though the hearings may have ended, that hadn't stopped Robert Kennedy's investigation of Cohen. When he believed he had sufficient evidence against him, Kennedy had Cohen arrested on September 16, 1960, for tax evasion. Federal authorities filed thirteen counts against Cohen, all of which focused on his business dealings.

During the trial, federal prosecutors called a number of witnesses who testified against Cohen, one of them being Candy Barr. Her cooperation with the authorities was especially hurtful to him. Cohen wanted to marry Candy, and when she fled to Mexico with her daughter in 1959, Cohen provided her with a safe house, fake IDs, and money. When she returned to the U.S. several months later, she was promptly arrested for a drug charge and later provided the prosecution with information that helped build a case against Cohen. At one point during the trial, Candy testified that he paid $15,000 to her attorneys and lavished gifts on her during their brief engagement.[8]

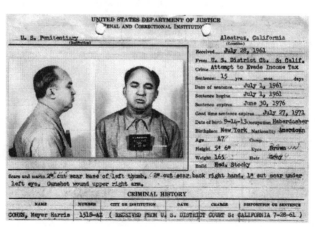

Mickey Cohen's Alcatraz record card
UNITED STATES PENITENTIARY, ALCATRAZ

Cohen was convicted on all thirteen charges of income tax evasion and given a fifteen-year sentence at Alcatraz, the only person in the prison's history sent there directly.

Cohen arrived on the island on July 28, 1961. Unknown to Mickey at the time, old friends would be there to greet him.

Though John and Clarence felt bad for Cohen, ratted out by Candy Barr no less, they were still glad to see him.

"Hey Mickey!" Clarence called out.

"John Anglin? Is that you?"

"And Clarence," his brother added.

He approached the two brothers. "John. Clarence. I can't believe it's you."

They shook Mickey's hand.

"Been a long time," Clarence declared.

"I guess I know now why you two disappeared after '58. What'd they get you for?"

"Bank robbery," John replied. "No-good feds sent us here for fifteen years. Then we got another twenty-five in Alabama."

Cohen laughed. "And I thought I got the short end of it. Fifteen sounds a lot better than forty."

The brothers assured Cohen they'd be gone long before that, to which he said the same for himself. His lawyers told him they thought his chances of bonding out were good as they appealed his conviction. John then clarified what he meant about getting out early.

Cohen got quiet and looked about the yard before he pressed close. "Are you talking about an escape?"

Both brothers nodded in reply.

"Been workin' on a plan. We got part of it figured out, but not everything."

"I only just got here, but from what I've seen this place will be a tough nut to crack."

A guard blew his whistle and started herding the inmates back into the cellblock.

"When you do figure it out," Cohen joked, "you let me know. I'll make a call to one of my boys and he'll have my yacht waiting for a nice cruise around the bay."

A week later, John, Frank, and Whitey walked into the exercise yard in the rain. During the weekdays, the only opportunities inmates had for talking with each other was at mealtime, or a quick conversation with someone while working in one of the shops. Only on the weekends or holidays were inmates permitted yard time, and no one squandered that opportunity. No matter the weather, be it freezing cold, foggy, or rainy, each prisoner prized every second outside the cell block.

Clarence would've normally been with them, but on July 19, 1961, a job in the barbershop finally opened up, and he took it.

Per prison regulation #34:

HAIRCUTS: Haircuts will be of regulation type. You will be placed on call for a haircut approximately every three weeks. You may be allowed to go to the Recreation Yard after your haircut if you are in good standing.[9]

When a stiff breeze blew off the bay, the three buttoned up their raincoats and made a beeline for the cement steps, the only place in the yard somewhat shielded from the elements.

"How ya doin', Paco?" Whitey asked.

"Little Frank. That doesn't get old."

John wrapped his raincoat a little tighter. "Is that what you do where you're from, come up with nicknames for people?"

Whitey laughed, then crossed his arms. "Yesterday it was sixty-five degrees and sunny. Today, it's freezing cold and raining. Not sure I'll ever get used to this crazy weather."

"What did Mark Twain say?" Frank asked rhetorically. "The coldest winter he ever spent was a summer in San Francisco."

The three turned their attention toward the bay.

John drew in a deep breath through his nose. "You smell that?"

Whitey sniffed the air. "Smells like hamburgers. Candlestick Park, maybe." He took another sniff. "What I wouldn't give for a beer and burger."

"Just another way for the warden to stick it to us," Frank groused. "They make that wall just right—too high to scale, but short enough for us to see the city."

"The sooner we're out of here the better."

"Got any ideas about that?" Frank asked. "The last time we talked Clarence told us about the concrete. So digging out the back shouldn't be a problem."

"He got four spoons out of the dining hall before being transferred to the barbershop."

"Even if we did start digging, what happens after that? We crawl out the back and make our way to the top of the cell block. It will take time cutting through the steel bars welded across the air vent, and every second we're doing that we're out of our cells. Best if we made that our staging area. Then we'll have the time for makin' everything we need for the escape."

"I've been doin' some thinkin' about that," John said. "First, West told me he painted a section of the cellblock roof last year. If he can get himself the job of painting the top of our cellblock, then we'll have all the time we need. And second, when we was kids, Clarence and me used to sneak out of the house usin' our sister's dummy heads."

Frank and Whitey looked at each other. Clearly, they didn't understand the reference.

"We dressed up our beds with her wigs and heads. Made it look like we were still asleep. Fooled Mama and Daddy every time."

"Where you gonna get a dummy head?" Whitey asked.

"Not get," John replied. "Make. I used to do a little painting some years back. All you need are a few colors for the face."

"Warden's always talkin' about filling our time with productive things. Easy ordering a paint set through the mail."

"Last time I checked, none of you are bald," Whitey observed.

"That's the easy part. Now that Clarence is workin' in the barbershop, he can start collecting hair for us."

"Fine," Frank said. "But we still haven't figured out how we get across the bay. It's a long swim, and I don't fancy the idea of becoming shark food."

The sound of a rifle shot brought the three to their feet.

"You don't think a prisoner busted out, do ya?" John asked.

Whitey scanned the yard. "In the daylight. Not a chance. Besides, no sirens. Target practice, I'd say."

"Do they have to do that while we're in the yard?"

Several more shots rang out.

"I think they wait until we're in the yard," John suggested. "Makes 'em think they're makin' a point about escapin'."

"Makes me think we better have everything figured right before we break out of here, or they'll be using us for target practice."

"That still don't solve the problem of getting across the bay."

"That water's freezing," Whitey declared. "You won't last long before hypothermia sets it."

Frank looked down at his raincoat and gave it a tug. "You know," he said. "Before they put me in the brush shop I worked in the library for a few months. A lot of time to read. Do ya know what vulcanized rubber is?"

Neither answered.

"You heat the rubber with a bonding agent so it forms a seal. It's how they make car tires."

"How does this help us?" John asked.

"We don't swim for it," Frank replied. "We make life vests or a kind of floating tube out of our raincoats. West told us about the water pipes behind the cell block. Cold ones for our cells. Hot ones for the showers. If those pipes are hot enough, we can fuse the rubber together."

"And paddle your way across the bay?" Whitey asked, disbelief tinting his voice.

"Shouldn't be too hard. It's only a mile or so to San Francisco."

"Not against those tides. You'll be pulled into the ocean no matter how strong you are."

A small boat moving past the island at a fast clip grabbed John's attention. Images of his youth filled his thoughts. In particular, when he and his brothers tied ropes to boats and stole rides on the Little Manatee River. "Maybe we don't have to worry about the tides," John stated. He then said to himself, "He'll have my yacht waiting for you." John faced Frank and Whitey. "Not paddle. We meet up with a boat waiting for us in the bay."

"What boat?" Frank asked.

John looked at the water and smiled. "I think I just figured out a way off the island."

CHAPTER 18

Overlooked

It was always better—safer—to be overlooked.

—MICHAEL SCOTT

BASED ON THEIR FAILED ESCAPES FROM PRISONS OVER THE YEARS, JOHN and Clarence had figured out that blending in was the key. If no one paid you any attention, whether it be a guard or an inmate, then you had a better chance of putting a plan in motion.

Whitey Bulger also took note of this characteristic about the two. In a letter from July 2017 he talked about the respect he felt toward John and Clarence: "The Anglin brothers were quiet easygoing men and always together attracted no attention. . . . No guard would think they were up to anything."

On August 8, 1961, Mickey Cohen was assigned a job in the clothing room, something of a surprise since he had only been at Alcatraz for two weeks.

Prisoners brought in their dirty clothes and towels on Tuesday afternoons and Saturday mornings and exchanged them for clean ones, compliments of the laundry facilities housed on the island. The work was divided into two areas: the cage, where the clean clothes and towels were kept. Most preferred that job. And the laundry room, where inmates toiled in hot and humid conditions.

When Cohen walked into the room, there waiting for him was John, who had been transferred there on April 27 four months before.

"Mickey, didn't expect to see you here."

"Hey, John. How are things moving along with your little project?"

In a place like this, where guards and snitches were always on the lookout for potential trouble, the brazenness of the question caught John off guard. He scanned the room before answering. "Good."

"Well, I expect I'll be getting out soon, so you'll have to take care of things without me."

John leaned in close. "About that. You mind talkin' with us in the yard on Saturday? Got something I want to run by you."

When Cohen walked into the exercise yard later that week, a stiff breeze slapped him in the face, he pulled his beanie down tight. As he looked about he saw his old friend Bumpy Johnson walking nearby.

USPLK- 70792-1-11-54

Bumpy Johnson's mug shot
UNITED STATES PENITENTIARY, LEAVENWORTH

Ellsworth Raymond "Bumpy" Johnson, later known as the Al Capone of Harlem, was born in Charleston, South Carolina, on October 31, 1905. Johnson's nickname "Bumpy" was given to him because of a bump on the back of his head.

As Johnson grew older, his parents worried about his short temper and insolence toward Whites, and in 1919 he was sent to live with his older sister in Harlem. Johnson dropped out of high school and began hanging out on the streets. Gangster William Hewett saw something in Johnson and started using him for small jobs. Over time, Johnson's criminal talents became evident, which sparked his rise up the underworld ladder. He later partnered with numbers queen Stephanie St. Clair, becoming her principal lieutenant in the 1930s. Johnson and St. Clair aimed to take over the territory controlled by New York mob boss Dutch Schultz. The war between them resulted in more than forty murders. Johnson was arrested in 1952 and sentenced to fifteen years for a drug conspiracy conviction, which Johnson served a majority of at Alactraz.[1]

Cohen's conversation with Bumpy caught the eye of several White prisoners. "You sure you wanna be seen talkin' with a Negro?" Bumpy asked. "Looks like your White friends ain't too happy."

"No friends of mine," Cohen replied in a dismissive tone. "I'll walk where I want and with who I want."

The two talked about happier days. After a while Bumpy told Cohen about the unfair treatment and outright prejudice experienced by Black inmates at Alcatraz. As someone who grew up Jewish, Cohen knew all too well about people hating you for no good reason.

As they talked, Cohen saw John and the others sitting at their usual spot on the concrete steps. "Tell you what, Bumpy. Things might be changing for all of us soon. Can't say much about it now, but we'll talk later."

"You planning on bustin' out, Mickey?"

"Me, no. I'm going through the front door."

"Yeah sure," Johnson joked and walked away laughing.

Cohen went straight for the concrete steps.

"Friend of yours?" Clarence asked when Cohen approached.

"Me and Bumpy go back a ways. He's done me some favors, and I've done some for him. Never keep people like him as an enemy, if you know what I mean."

"You didn't say anythin' about the escape plan, did you?" Frank asked.

"What do I look like? I can tell you this about your plan, there are more people in here that know about it than you think."

"Only the ones we let know."

Cohen shifted his attention back to John. "You can trust Bumpy. He'll keep his people quiet."

Clarence lit a cigarette. "So John tells us you think that bond hearing's gonna happen."

Cohen nodded. "From what my lawyers tell me, it's only a matter of time."

"Mickey, the boys in DC ain't gonna let you go without a fight," James countered. "You might get out on an appeal, but those Kennedys have it in for you, and right now they run the show."

"You're right, they do," Mickey replied, "but nothing lasts forever."

"If it was me," James declared, "I'd flee the country and never look back."

In the fourth letter Bulger sent me, he remembered telling Mickey the first thing he should do when he bonded out. "Mickey Cohen—Remember him well when he was bailed out of AZ he was talking to bunch of guys on the bleacher about should he jump bail or come back—everyone said Make a run for it—Go to Brazil father a child and they will never get you by extradition."

James tried to convince Cohen to head for South America if he had the chance, but John needed his assistance in another matter once on the outside.

"Clarence and me, we have a brother, Robert, and we were hopin' you'd go to Ruskin and meet with him. Let him know about the plan and how we're gonna need his help once we hit land."

"I suppose, though I've never seen your house. How am I supposed to find it?"

"Got that worked out. Clarence wrote home and asked my mama if she could send us pictures of the place under the guise of seein' the changes they done on it."

The following is an excerpt of the letter Clarence wrote on August 10, 1961, two days after Cohen met with John in the clothing room.

"John got a couple of photos of Helen and her sister a few weeks back after asking for them in a letter he wrote. They're needed for an import part of the plan."

This letter John wrote home on July 10, 1961:

I should write to Helen, I would like to write to her, but I just can't think of the right things to say to her. She doesn't know when to give up she still writes, I just got a letter and two very pretty pictures of her,

"You said a while back that you were going to send Me some pictures of the house just as soon as it was finished. Why don't you have some made and send them. I would kind of like to see what was going on around there."

she sure looks like a queen to me and I have too much time hanging on me to be Thinking of (queens).

Cohen appeared confused. "How do pictures of girls help you escape?"

"You know the air vents in the cells?" Frank asked.

"Yeah."

Clarence took a puff on his cigarette. "We're gonna dig out the back and escape through the cellblock roof. Then make our way to the water and paddle out of here in a raft."

Cohen whistled to himself. "That's the kind of plan that could get you killed."

"John's fixin' on paintin' pictures of the girls in his cell. We all ordered kits, which should get here in a couple of weeks."

"Paintings," Cohen said in a skeptical tone.

"That's just to fool the guards. We really need the paint for fake vents and dummy heads we plan on makin'. It's gonna take some time gettin' all the stuff we need, which we figure we can make on top of the cellblock after West gets permission to paint there. The dummy heads will make it look like we're asleep when we're really workin' on the escape."

Cohen laughed. "That's so simple it's brilliant. Can't see how your plan can fail, unless a guard takes a good look at one of your heads."

"We plan on using the buddy system," John said. "Clarence put in a request for the cell next to mine. When I dig, he watches for the guard. When he digs, I do the same for him."

"Frank just requested a move next to West's cell," Clarence added.

Cohen smiled. "You get me the address and picture of your house and I'll make sure someone talks with your brother."

"Good. Maybe you can also find out if Brizzi's been released yet. We might need him too."

"He has, about a year back. Have him working out of Mexico City."

A guard's whistle blew. "Back to your cells."

Everyone got up and started moving toward the cellblock. As they did, John came alongside Cohen. "You said before you had a yacht. Is that true?"

"Naw. Just joking with you."

John appeared disappointed. "Can you get one?"

"I suppose. Why you need a boat?"

When they reached the door John stopped him and said in a low voice, "That's how we're getting away."

In the end, the transfers worked out as they had hoped. Morris moved into cell B-138 next to West on September 10, 1961, and the following day Clarence moved into cell B-152 right next to John.

Despite the letter Warden Moore at Leavenworth sent to Blackwell, warning him about housing the brothers close together because of their propensity for escapes, he did so anyway. Now the brothers could discuss the plan whenever they wished without fear of being heard.

Clearly, Blackwell believed the security measures he had implemented were more than sufficient against any potential attempts made by the Anglins, or other inmates on the island for that matter, and so he didn't take the threat seriously. It was a decision he would later regret.

A rare photo of Alcatraz inmates in their cells
SAN FRANCISCO HISTORY CENTER, SAN FRANCISCO PUBLIC LIBRARY

The following day, as they had done the past few months, John, Clarence, Whitey, and Frank sat together for lunch. Before discussing each person's progress, they waited for West, who approached them with a tray of food. A couple of Black inmates stepped in front of him as they headed for another table, causing West to stop.

His jaw clenched tight, he set his tray down next to Whitey. "I'll be right back."

Looking both ways first, West went to the table where the two Black inmates sat, leaned close, and said something to them. One of the inmates said something in reply, which West didn't like, and he grew visibly angry. The first inmate got to his feet and balled his fist, as if to take a swing at West, but his friend sat him back down. West gave the table a shove and a parting comment before returning to the four.

"What was that about?" Clarence asked.

"Damn coloreds. This place would at least be tolerable if they weren't here."

Frank's eyes narrowed. "Every time you pick a fight it only draws attention our way. You keep your feelings in check or—"

"Or what?" West interrupted.

"Or nothin'," John intervened. "Y'all focus on the plan. Anythin' that pulls us in a different direction ain't nothin' but an unnecessary distraction." He glared at Frank and West.

"Fine," West replied between clenched teeth.

In October 1961, Mickey found out from his lawyers he would soon be a free man. After Cohen posted $100,000 for bail, U.S. Supreme Court Chief Justice Earl Warren signed his bond, which granted Cohen's release from Alcatraz. Once out, he could appeal his tax evasion conviction in earnest. For John and the others, they needed the boat situation nailed down, and soon.

When John arrived for his next shift in the clothing room, he approached Cohen. They discussed how he'd send word about meeting with Robert, maybe through one of his lawyers.

Cohen then brought up the boat. "So where are you planning on going when you get out. Mexico? Or somewhere north?"

"Neither," John replied. "Angel Island. Could you provide us with something for that?"

Though the location made sense to Cohen, he had conflicted feelings about John's idea since the island would be the first place the guards looked when they realized the four had escaped.

After a moment's thought, John offered San Francisco as another possibility, which is noted in the FBI's report regarding the Alcatraz escape:[2]

John had previously spoken with a fellow inmate and asked his thoughts about the probable success of heading for the dock once they

> During their conversations JOHN ANGLIN had indicated that it was a shorter route to go from the island to the mainland of San Francisco rather than toward Angel Island. At that time they were considering building the rafts and going with them to the docks near where the Alcatraz prison boat docked.

John talks about the prison boat option.
FBI FILES

got out and stealing one of the prison boats, the last one leaving at 11:15 p.m. each night.

After sharing that idea with Cohen, he suggested having their own boat would be less risky. No guard to subdue. Plus, they could instead focus on getting as far away from Alcatraz as possible, rather than aim for something close and risk getting picked up by local authorities.

"In that case," John said, "what do you think of Tijuana?"

A few days later the news came out: Cohen would be the first person ever to bond out of Alcatraz. And just as incredible, Warren was the first sitting Supreme Court justice ever to sign a bond order overriding a lower court.

BOAT SCHEDULE

EFFECTIVE OCTOBER 11, 19--

Leaving Alcatraz

Weekly	Saturday	Sunday	Holiday
A.M.	**A.M.**	**A.M.**	**A.M.**
12:10	12:10	12:10	12:10
6:40	7:05	7:05	7:05
7:20	8:10	8:10	8:10
8:10	9:00	9:00	9:00
10:00	10:00	10:00	10:00
	11:00	11:00	11:00
P.M.	**P.M.**	**P.M.**	**P.M.**
12:45	12:45	12:45	12:45
3:20	3:20	3:20	3:20
3:55	4:55	4:55	4:55
4:40	5:40	5:40	5:40
5:10	7:00	7:00	7:00
5:40	8:45	8:45	8:45
7:00	10:00	10:00	10:00
8:45	11:15	11:15	11:15
10:00			
11:15			

Alcatraz transport boat schedule
UNITED STATES PENITENTIARY, ALCATRAZ

Earl Warren served as the fourteenth chief justice of the United States from 1953 to 1969. The Warren Court presided over a major shift in American constitutional jurisprudence, which has been recognized by many as a "constitutional revolution" in the liberal direction, Warren himself writing the majority opinions in many landmark cases. The chief justice also headed the commission that investigated the 1963 assassination of President John F. Kennedy. Warren is considered to be one of the most influential Supreme Court justices in the history of the United States.[3]

No one is certain how Cohen's lawyer, Jack Dahlstrum, convinced a Supreme Court justice to rule in his favor, but whatever the

COHEN, Meyer Harris 1518-AZ

WORK ASSIGNMENT RECORD

UNITED STATES PENITENTIARY
(Institution)
ALCATRAZ, CALIFORNIA

DATE	ASSIGNED	QTRS	DATE	QTRS
7-28-61	IDLE	C-137		
8-5-61	"	B-256		
9-8-61	Clo. Room	B-256		
10-17-61	Released	on Appeal Bond		

Cohen's cell card showing his release
UNITED STATES PENITENTIARY, ALCATRAZ

reason, Mickey Cohen walked out of his cell on October 17, 1961, and waved goodbye to the guards and his fellow inmates.

Warden Blackwell stood by the boat as the guards escorted Cohen toward the dock. Just before stepping onto the transport, he told Blackwell, "No hard feelings, Warden. Enjoyed the stay."

Blackwell immediately replied, "Oh, I'm sure we'll be seeing you again, Mr. Cohen. I'll keep your cell open for you."

Even before Cohen's departure, the escape plan had been put into motion. But with him now gone John knew they had to speed things up so they'd be ready if Cohen contacted them sooner than expected. The first order of business was to dig out the six-by-nine-inch iron grate in the back of each cell. John had spoken with West about ways of removing the concrete. He told John he had once read a scientific essay about aggregate disintegrating between five hundred and nine hundred degrees, which might have worked, but after trying with two wires plugged into the electrical outlet in his cell, he couldn't get the wires hot enough to break up the concrete.

The electricity idea a failure, John figured he'd deal with the grate the old-fashioned way. Clarence had already provided everyone with spoons smuggled out of the dining hall before his transfer to the barbershop, which they filed down and used as digging tools.

With Clarence watching for guards, John laid his coat on the floor in front of the grate and started chipping away at the edges. When Clarence heard footsteps, he signaled John with a tap on the bar. John folded up his coat and jumped on his bed, reading a book by the time the guard went by. He looked down at John and kept walking without missing a beat.

"That was close," Clarence said.

"Guess it's safe to start up again."

"It won't be long before we'll need the fake grilles covering up your digging. We should also get started on those soon."

"I know. I know. But I can only do one thing at a time."

John unrolled his coat on the floor and started again on the grille.

As he and Clarence took turns digging, just down the way Frank and West did the same on their grilles. Each of them covered the chipped-away parts of the concrete as they went with toilet paper and soap and then touched up the area with paint so no one would notice it.[4] Even though they hadn't begun work on the raft yet, John knew they'd need a way of inflating it fast when they reached the water's edge. Frank said he had an idea about that. In the meantime, John and Clarence collected the materials needed for the fake vent covers and dummy heads between digging. They had ordered painting kits, which they'd start using upon their arrival. Of the skills the brothers possessed, art ranked near the top.

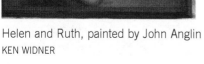

Helen and Ruth, painted by John Anglin
KEN WIDNER

John planned on doing a portrait of Ruth, Clarence a beach scene, the perfect cover for their clandestine activities.

As the days passed, John had dug out most of concrete around the grate, but the work was slow and tedious. Some of the aggregate and dust he flushed down the toilet, but he needed to be careful about that. Too much flushing might arouse the guards' suspicions. For the bigger chunks, he distributed them around the exercise yard using holes in his pants pockets.

But as Clarence had warned him, they didn't have the luxury of concentrating on one thing at a time. All the parts needed attending to simultaneously so they'd be ready when Cohen procured their boat. So they divvied up various areas of responsibility as a way of speeding up the work. For now, finishing the grates and dummy heads was their top priority. Then they'd focus on the raincoats needed for the raft and life preservers. Also needed were wood scraps for the paddles, along with the saw blades and files West had previously found in the utility corridor.

One night when John worked on his painting of Helen, one of the guards walked by, Officer Herman. Known as "Herman the German" by the inmates, he seemed to like John's work.

He stepped up to the bars and watched a moment. "Not too bad."

"I think it's turnin' out okay." John put a little more color on Helen's cheeks. "Not sure when I'll see her again, but this helps me remember what she looks like."

Overlooked by Herman was a piece of cardboard John hid behind the palette. The shade of green in her shawl closely matched the green in the cell; he was in the middle of painting both when Herman walked by.

Clarence's warning came just in time.

"Well, you keep out of trouble and time will pass by fast. Who knows, maybe I'll have you paint something for me."

"Yeah, maybe."

Officer Herman continued his rounds.

John had gotten the cardboard from a binder he kept on the back shelf. Per regulation #34, inmates were given two razor blades so they could shave in their cells, which they exchanged each Saturday with the evening watch officer. Without realizing it, the prison had given him and

Fake air vent grille
GOLDEN GATE NATIONAL RECREATION AREA, PARK ARCHIVES (356)

lower right hand corner and drilling small holes up the wall until
it hit the lower right hand corner of the metal grille. As ▓▓▓
completed each small hole, he plugged it with toilet paper and soap
and then touched the outside of it up with paint so no one would
notice it. The other three inmates were doing the same thing.

FBI REPORT

and painted them to match the walls in their cells and inserted
them after they had removed part of the wall. They hid their
working tools behind these false frames. JOHN ANGLIN got through
his hole first and got into the utility corridor containing the
plumbing fixtures which is located behind the cells. JOHN then
helped CLARENCE complete his hole.

John constructing his false grille cover
FBI REPORT

the others the perfect cutting tools. The blade made an easy job of the
cardboard, and with a bottle of cement provided by West, John glued the
pieces together into a replica grate, air holes and all.[5]

With the fake grille more or less ready, John figured another hour
or so of digging should do it. After lights-out he told Clarence to keep
watch as he made preparations for his last push.

John went around the edges and attacked those spots where concrete
still clung to the metal fasteners. One by one the chips dropped down
onto his coat, until a fateful hit knocked the grate out of its hole and
landed in the utility corridor with a metallic clank.

"What was that?" Clarence whispered from his cell.

"It's out," John replied. "Any guards hear?"

Clarence paused before replying. "Don't think so."

John reached through the opening and brought the grate back into his cell, setting it on his coat. He grabbed the fake vent and slipped it into the hole. John moved back a little and assessed the copy. In the dark, in his opinion, he thought the cardboard grille looked fairly convincing. Turning the light back on, he stood at the front of his cell and smiled. The vent was perfect. Put a couple of things in front of it and no one would ever tell the difference.[6]

John turned the light off again before anyone realized he had dug through. He then got down on his hands and knees and examined the hole. Looked big enough. He slipped his hands through the opening, followed by his head. When he got stuck, John knew the opening needed a little more work. He pushed himself out and started chipping away at the cement again.

John's heart stopped when he heard an unknown voice.

"Hey man, whatcha doin' over there?"

CHAPTER 19

Setbacks

Success is not a goal. It's a choice.

—SHARON PEARSON

HIS HEART POUNDING IN HIS CHEST, JOHN FROZE, HIS GAZE FIXED ON movement from the other side of the corridor. He grabbed the fake grate and slipped it into the hole before the unknown inmate realized what he had done.

"I heard somethin' bangin' over there."

He was one of the Black inmates who had been housed in C-Block with the others. Not surprisingly, a race divide existed at Alcatraz as it did with the country. Rather than say nothing John thought it best if he came up with an explanation for the noise.

"It's nothin'. Saw a rat in my cell. Tried to kill it."

"That didn't sound like no rat to me."

"You sayin' I'm lyin'?"

"Naw, man. Just wonderin' what that metal bang was. Didn't sound normal."

John got his drinking cup from the shelf. He did his best to replicate the noise made by the grate when it landed in the utility corridor.

"See. Tried gettin' it with this."

The inmate paused a moment. "So, did you kill it?"

"Nope. Got away."

"Next time you see that rat you let me know, okay? I hate rats."

"You'll be the first."

"Thanks, man."

John heard him lay down on his bunk, several squeaks of the springs a dead giveaway. Only then did he let out a long breath. Disaster averted.

When the prisoners lined up for breakfast the next morning, Clarence, Frank, West, James, and John sat together by the dining hall entrance. They knew some of the inmates didn't like the tables in the back of the dining hall. Even though each man could eat as much as he wanted, only twenty minutes were allotted for meals, and so if a prisoner hoped for seconds or possibly thirds, he had a better chance if he sat close to the food line, ate fast, and went back for more.

"I punched through the air vent last night," John declared. "Couldn't quite fit through the hole, but that shouldn't be too much of a problem. The concrete is softer on the back side."

"Leaks from the water pipes have been dripping down the walls for years," West surmised.

"I figure I'm about halfway through mine," Frank said in a low voice. "Another week should do it."

Inmates at mealtime
GOLDEN GATE NATIONAL RECREATION AREA, PARK ARCHIVES (35178D)

John took a bite of eggs. "Just be careful when you do. I almost got caught by the guy behind me. He heard the grate land in the corridor."

"How'd you explain it?" Clarence asked.

"Came up with a story about tryin' to kill a rat in my cell."

West shivered at the word "rat." "I can't stand those things. Disgusting creatures."

"Don't forget about the noise when you dig. Sound travels far when it's quiet."

Frank leaned forward. "I've been giving some thought about that. Some of the inmates in the prison band practice at night."

"They're called the Rock Islanders," James interjected.

"Right," Frank continued. "I ordered an accordion so I could join in with them." He turned toward West. "Should cover your digging when it's your turn on the grate."

"I don't play no instrument."

"As long as you keep an eye on the guards, I'll be fine."

John took a bite of his eggs, then looked at West. "What's the word with Herman about paintin' the top of the cellblock? We'll need to start workin' on the other stuff soon. Can't take the chance of the guards finding our things during a shakedown."

When a guard walked by the five fell silent.

Anger flashed in West's eyes and he leaned forward. "You sayin' I don't know that? I know what I need to do."

"Hey, keep it cool," James said in a calm tone. "No one's accusing anyone of anything."

West glanced over his shoulder. "I already talked with him about it. Let him know I done the top of C-Block a year ago. About time we should do the same for B-Block."

"What he say?" John asked.

"He'd talk with his lieutenant and get back to me."

"Ask him again. See if he got permission. Until we have a work area everything stops at the back of the cells."

They all looked at one another in silent agreement.

John shifted his attention toward Whitey. "You haven't said much about your progress. How's it goin' in your cell?"

Caught midbite, Whitey stopped and put his fork down. "I've been thinking about how I was gonna say this, but now is as good a time as any."

"Somethin' wrong?" Clarence asked.

"Yeah. Those tides in the bay. I know what those waters are like, and your chances aren't good. The raft could sink or you get picked off by one of the guards. Any way you look at it, either they tack on another two years or I'm dead. Don't wanna take that chance, so I'm not going."

The four looked at one another.

"No one can blame ya for feelin' the way you do," John finally said. "We know the odds are against us makin' it out alive."

"That don't mean I'm out. I'll still help you boys any way I can."

The four were understandably disappointed, but at least Bulger hadn't pulled out all the way. His years scuba diving taught him how the tides worked and the effect of the cold bay waters on their bodies. They'd need that knowledge if the four had any chance of success.

In a letter Whitey sent in July 2017, he brought up the point about being an experienced diver and how he likely addressed it with John and Clarence.

> I did lots of skin diving with SCUBA—double tanks used wet suit—also swimming if tide pulls you along try to move left or right gradually patiently don't panic—if tired float on back—deep breath for buoyancy arms out to side move hands will keep you afloat, relax stay calm deep breaths hold—swim breast stroke series and you will move at water level . . . Relax Don't Panic.

Because West hadn't yet been given permission to paint the top of the cellblock, the others focused their energies on digging through the back of their cells. If a guard came by, the partner on watch signaled the other, who stopped his work and jumped on the bed, book or magazine in hand.

One particular night three guards came around the corner and headed straight for Frank's cell. West tapped his cup on the bars, then jumped on his bunk, a pencil and pad of paper in his hands. The way the guards walked in cadenced step, West figured they had been found out and were coming for them. Whenever something big was in the works, the guards always showed up in numbers in case a confrontation took a bad turn.

As he wrote, their footsteps grew louder, until all three guards were right on top of his cell. West hoped Frank played it just as cool.

To his relief, they went right past him and kept on walking. The guards stopped at C-130.

"Open number one-three-zero," one of them yelled.

The metallic bang sounded from the end of the block, and the cell door slid open.

"Alright, out. Shakedown."

Though West couldn't see directly, he knew the drill. The inmate had been rousted from his bed and the guards started tossing everything in his cell. Susan Smith, who served as a guard in county and state facilities, shared this about her experiences:

Shakedown is basically a cell search where a prisoner's property is examined and thrown around by staff. Typically, prisoners are woken up in the middle of the night by a commotion of screaming, shouting and orders from the CO's. They are taken from their cell, strip searched, and the clothing they're wearing is also searched. Officers check everything. . . . They check clothing, bedding and what few personal items they are allowed to have. After an hour or so the inmate is allowed back in their . . . ransacked cell.[1]

When the guards had finished their work, they pushed the prisoner back into his cell.

"Close up one-three-zero."

The cell door banged close a moment later. The guards' footsteps faded into the distance.

West went to the front of his cell. "Hey, Frank."

"Yeah?"

"What do ya think?"

Morris replied without hesitation, "I start digging again."

Despite focusing their free time on the escape, Clarence made it a point to write home whenever he could. Not only did the practice maintain a connection with family despite being three thousand miles away, but doing so also presented the image he and John weren't involved in anything except doing their time as peaceably as possible.

CHAPTER 19

In a letter dated January 16, 1962, he wrote:

Dear Mom,

I thought I would write and ans. your last letter we received a few days ago. I haven't wrote since Christmas but everything is okay here with Me and John. Yes I know the weather is pretty cold down there I have been hearing it on the radio.

I hope everyone there at home had a good Christmas and holidays. I also hope that Daddy is up and around. And is feeling better.

You can tell everyone there at home. I couldn't send all of them Christmas cards because they only gave us five to send out.

Al wrote me about sending you fifty dollars for Christmas, I know that it came in handy. I forgot all about your birthday. I don't have any chance to get any birthday cards here anyway. I don't know if John wrote you about getting the money you sent or not. But we did and sent out and got a box of candy each. They also gave us some candy and cigars so it wasn't too bad a Christmas.

I guess Steve hasn't been around lately. What does he have to say where does he come. I guess you know that he picks the guitar and sings. I didn't know that the Windshur boy was in trouble. You say that he is home.

I guess I'll close for now, tell everybody hello and take it easy.

Ans. soon,

Love Clarence

Like he had done numerous times before, Clarence let everyone know he and John were doing fine but also hoped the family had a good Christmas. The holidays were always the worst. They served as stark reminders just how far from family they were, which made every inmate's sense of separation all the more real.

A week later, Frank's accordion arrived. He had never played one before, but it didn't take long before he learned the basics of pulling and pushing the bellows as he pressed the keys. But more importantly, under the guise of learning how to play, the "music" perfectly masked West's turn on his grate.

Though he had little musical talent, none of the inmates complained. They had heard equally bad music from those learning to play guitars, harmonicas, and the like.

West turned off his light, got down on his hands and knees, and started chipping away at the grate with the spoon Clarence had given him.

Like John, he had laid out a towel in front of the vent, which caught most of the concrete bits after each strike. When his hand tired, West took a breather and swept up the mess he had created. He then started on the grate again. Other times, he'd switch hands before continuing.

Wiping away a layer of sweat from his forehead, West didn't hear the sounds of two Black inmates being escorted from the kitchen to their cells after they finished cleaning up.

Despite Frank playing his accordion to cover up his digging, they saw him lying on the floor. The guard's attention set on the inmates in front of him, he walked right by West without noticing him.

As the two passed by Frank's cell one of the inmates said to the other, "Did you see West layin' there? Looked like he was diggin' or somethin'." The other replied, "Now we got that SOB."

West, Morris, and the Anglin Brothers knew they had a problem on their hands after several black inmates spotted them digging out the back of their cells. They probably figured it was only a matter of time before one of them ratted West out as payback for some of his violent outbursts against black prisoners. Frank Morris, who happened to work with some of these guys in the brush shop put a stop to that line of thinking. His idea was to talk to Bumpy Johnson.[2]

Normally, having inmates walk past a cell shouldn't have been a problem. The unwritten code for Alcatraz inmates was respecting others' privacy while in their cells. Whitey commented on this in the letter he wrote me in June 2016: "Considered bad manners for men walking past cells to look in—would get Remarks—Like 'What are you doing—the count!' or 'What do you want?' or 'Can I help you?'"

For whatever reason, the two Black inmates had violated the code, which meant Frank and the others were in danger of being exposed.

However, he became aware they had been found out and set about fixing the problem.

At his first opportunity, Frank sought out Bumpy Johnson. As the kingpin of the Black inmates at Alcatraz, he was a man well respected, and you didn't just go up to him and start talking. His lieutenants, who traveled with him outside their cells, made sure of that. Racist inmates were in abundant supply and wouldn't think twice about stabbing one of them with a shank if given the opportunity. (A shank is a homemade knife made out of scrap metal wrapped with a cloth as a handle.)

Frank found Johnson wandering about the yard in a group of about eight or so. As he approached Bumpy, the first lieutenant he ran into stopped him cold.

"Where you goin', cracker?"

"I need to talk with your boss. Something important."

The lieutenant looked back over his shoulder. Bumpy studied Frank and nodded.

"Don't you try nothin'," the lieutenant warned him, "or you'll be a dead cracker."

Frank smirked in reply, then made his way through the gauntlet of protectors until he reached Bumpy. Before Frank got a word out, Bumpy told him he already knew about their clandestine activities, courtesy of the inmates who saw West, and he feared they'd rat him out to the guards.

Bumpy assured Frank he'd keep their secret, but on one condition. "You tell West to back off on my boys. One day he's gonna push them too far, and there'll be a race riot."

A hot breath slipped past Frank's lips. "I'll make sure he doesn't mess with them again. You have my word."

Bumpy nodded and continued on his way.

The next night after lights-out John chipped away at the cement until he could finally slip through the hole and into the utility corridor. Without his dummy head started yet, he didn't want to stay in there for long. The first order of business, retrieve the blades and files West had found.

Staying as quiet as possible, John inched his way down the narrow passageway. Even though the walls and pipes pressed in on him, he enjoyed a brief surge of freedom he hadn't experienced since arriving at Alcatraz. John looked at the roof above. Only a thirty-foot climb. He was tempted to go up and check the top right then, but he didn't want to press his luck.

"Just get the blades," he told himself.

John got down low and patted the area West had indicated. Nothing. Perhaps he had been given the wrong location. Or worse yet, a guard had found them. Then his fingers brushed against something that felt like paper. "Must be it." Scooping up everything

Utility corridor
TOM.K (WIKIMEDIA COMMONS)

in his hand, the files and blades clinked together. Rather than examine his find in the corridor, John returned with them to his cell.

Slipping under the covers in his bed, John kept his prized find with him the entire night. However, before he fell asleep, he went over next steps in his head: distribute the files and blades, finish the fake grilles, then start on the dummy heads. The four had been tearing out pages from magazines for weeks, mostly ads no one cared about. Later, when the work area atop the cellblock had been set up, they'd start on the raft, paddles, and life vests. In the meantime, Clarence had been smuggling out bits of hair since getting the barbershop job, but not enough at this point where they'd look like real heads. They four would need more, a lot more.

The following Saturday, John, Clarence, and Frank met at the concrete steps in the exercise yard, as they typically did when discussing the status of their plan.

"I got my grate off last night," Clarence declared, more for Frank's benefit than for John's. "No one heard a thing."

"Good," Frank replied. "That makes three of us. West's shouldn't take too much longer."

Inmates relaxing in the exercise yard
BUREAU OF PRISONS

"I'll be startin' up on my dummy head tonight. Paper's been cut, and I saved some concrete dust for the plaster."

"My head's about halfway done," John said. "The paper hardens real good. Should be easy enough to paint once it's finished."

Frank's attention drifted toward the yard. In the distance he observed West talking with someone.

"The only thing that concerns me is Cohen," John commented. "We haven't heard from him since he got out. It's been months, and nothin'."

"No word from Man, either," Clarence added. "If he hasn't written, then they probably haven't met yet."

Morris kept his attention on West. "Never did like the idea of trusting Cohen with the most important part of the plan. If he doesn't get us that boat, then we're on our own. Might be smart if we start thinking about alternative ideas, just in case."

"What did you have in mind?"

"What I've been pushing for all along. Angel Island. It's only a couple of miles away, and the tides aren't as bad going in that direction."

"Cohen will come through for us," John assured them. "Don't you worry."

West finally finished his conversation and approached the three.

"Did I miss anything?" he asked.

"Just Frank and his usual fatalistic predictions about Cohen. Thinks we should go for Angel Island instead."

"Typical," West replied. "It's like you're a record with a scratch. Repeating the same part of the song over and over."

Frank sat upright. "Something wrong with a backup plan?" He stopped, then glanced at the inmate West had been chatting with moments before. "Who were you talking to over there?"

"No one. Just some guy I knew from Atlanta. I think he might be able to help with the escape."

John's and Clarence's heads turned in West's direction.

"What do you mean?" John asked.

"I mean I told him about the plan, and he wants in. He's good with mechanical things."

Morris grabbed West's shirt. "Are you really that stupid? We all agreed, no one but us knows about breaking out. What if he tells a guard?"

West broke free of Frank's grip and pushed him back. "You grab me like that again and I'll . . ."

"You'll what?" Frank asked in a dismissive tone.

John stepped between the two. "We'll talk about this later. Right now, I think you two should take a couple of laps around the yard and cool off."

Morris straightened his shirt. "From now on, you don't go anywhere without one of us with you," he ordered West. "When you eat, one of us is there. You spend time in the yard, you don't go alone. You get me?"

"And if I don't?"

"You talk with anyone about the escape again, and I'll kill you." Morris went down the steps and walked away.

Whitey didn't say how he knew about Morris's encounter with West, but he shared it with me in his fourteenth letter: "West talked about it and was told—threatened by Morris whenever out of cell you will be with one of us—also that Morris had got a kitchen knife . . . took it with him and if they were trapped by guards due to West he intended to knife West."

His recollection about the knife is confirmed in the FBI report: "The only weapons they could have . . . would have been a sharpened kitchen knife or a screw driver."[3]

John turned his attention back to the escape. "I'm going to take my chances tonight and check out the top of the cellblock. See what's up there."

"Let us know how it goes."

After lights-out John dressed up his bed so he appeared to be asleep. He then removed the false vent cover and crawled out the hole. Once in the corridor, John grabbed a water pipe and pulled himself up one careful step at a time. Most of the inmates had gone down for the night, but he wasn't taking any chances. One inadvertent sound, and he'd be caught for sure.

His hands finally reached the top and he pulled himself up. John scanned the area. The open space atop the cellblock having remained relatively untouched the past thirty years, a thick layer of dirt had collected during that time. John grinned. Cleaning that section of the prison first before painting meant they'd need additional time to complete the job, and the longer the four worked there the better their chances of making everything needed for the escape.

As John looked about, he also took note of the gunwalk behind him, which was at the same level as the cellblock. His heart sank at the sight. Gunwalks allowed guards to go the length of the building in relative safety behind hardened steel bars.

The sounds of footsteps approaching stopped John cold. He ducked into the shadows as a guard appeared in the gunwalk. He lingered there a few feet away, looked the area over with his flashlight, then continued on after several terrifying moments.

Only after the guard's footsteps faded did John pull himself up again. "That's gonna be a problem," he said to himself, then climbed back down.

Guard gun walk
SUPERCHILUM (WIKIMEDIA COMMONS)

CHAPTER 20

Headway

*Second chances don't always mean a happy ending. Sometimes, it's just
another chance to end things right.*

—UNKNOWN

NOW THAT JOHN COULD GET INTO THE UTILITY CORRIDOR AT WILL, HE
helped Clarence with his air vent. He didn't have as difficult a time after
John gave him one of the saws, and with them working on the concrete
from both sides, the two finished the job twice as fast.[1]

Clarence had likewise fabricated his own false cover, painting it the
same color green as his cell.

Despite the brothers' success, the situation between Morris and West
had worsened over time as both worked on their grilles. Morris had
managed to smooth things over with Johnson after the Black inmates
saw West digging in his cell. So far, West had behaved himself, but John,
Clarence, and Frank also knew he could erupt at any moment and destroy
the fragile truce that existed.

> JOHN ANGLIN had knocked his completely out by this
> time and one evening had crawled into the utility corridor.
> ANGLIN made a false cement back to cover the area he had knocked
> out of the wall leading into the utility corridor so it would
> not be noticed. JOHN then did work from the utility corridor
> side and assisted CLARENCE ANGLIN in completing his hole.

FBI FILES

Morris did his best to keep West on a short leash, making sure he stayed with them whenever they ate or walked about the exercise yard, but the three couldn't watch West every second. And that troubled them, especially Morris, who warned West if he so much as looked at an inmate the wrong way, he'd take out his shank and kill him on the spot. For now, at least, John and Clarence had access to the corridor, which necessitated the construction of the dummy heads. With cell shakedowns a constant threat, they couldn't take the chance of keeping the tools and other contraband in their cells. So John and Clarence hid everything in the corridor behind the false covers.

However, that created another problem—total darkness. The brothers could only work on the dummy heads at night, but they needed to see. But with no source of light in the utility corridor, a solution was needed. Fortunately for John and Clarence, they could make just about anything from nothing, and set about constructing a flashlight.[2]

As luck would have it, the different shops located in the prison industries building on the western side of the island provided John with most of what he needed. What he lacked, Whitey helped get.

The New Industries Building was constructed in 1939 near the water tower, power plant, store house, and officers' quarters. The ground floor contained a clothing factory, dry cleaning plant, furniture plant, and brush factory, where inmates earned about ten cents an hour for their work. They made items such as gloves, furniture mats, and army uniforms.[3]

The flashlight demonstrates the ingenuity of the prisoners in utilizing available material to accomplish their purpose. The housing for the two penlight batteries (one battery is a spare) is a small rectangular plastic box which has a hole in one end through which the bulb is screwed so that the base of the bulb contacts the center post of the battery. A fastener, similar to an Acco type file fastener, is employod as the means of carrying the electricity from the battery base to the side of the bulb and it also acts as the switch. There is no lens or other protection for the bulb.

Flashlight description
FBI FILES

Now equipped with a working flashlight, John and Clarence went to work on the dummy heads. Using the ads taken out of magazines and paper given each inmate for writing letters, the brothers used bits of concrete, dust, and soap and mixed it with water, creating a crude form of plaster that allowed them to fashion the paper any way they wished. Over time, a pair of faces slowly formed. Painting them wasn't a problem, but the lack of hair was. Without that, the guards would spot them as fakes in no time during one of their 9:30 p.m., 12:01 a.m., 3:00 a.m., or 5:00 a.m. bed checks.

With a steady stream of customers in the barbershop, Clarence stepped up his efforts after each haircut, making sure the strands he pocketed matched the four.

When Clarence finished with an inmate, he'd sweep the hair into the corner under the guard's watchful eye. As the day progressed Clarence scooped up the growing mound and dumped it into a garbage can. As he did, he slipped some into the cuff of his pants or in his pockets. After a week of transporting tufts of hair from the shop into his cell, adding to the stash he had already secreted out, the four had more than enough for the dummy heads.

At night after light's-out Clarence worked in the corridor on the head meant for John. He pasted on the ears and gave them a look. Clarence liked what he saw. He tapped the back of John's cell and out came a hand through the vent.

"You done?" John whispered.

Clarence bent low. "Here ya go," he whispered back. "Give Oink a nice paint job."

"Oink. Now that's funny, but it doesn't look like Alfred." The family referred to Alfred as "Oink" while he hid at the Pits as a way of protecting his true identity.

"Who would've thought the same trick we pulled on Mama and Daddy is now gonna be used on the guards?"

John painted Oink a convincing flesh-tone color. Then, using glue supplied by West, he stuck on patches of hair, even adding eyebrows and eyelashes for an extra measure of realism.

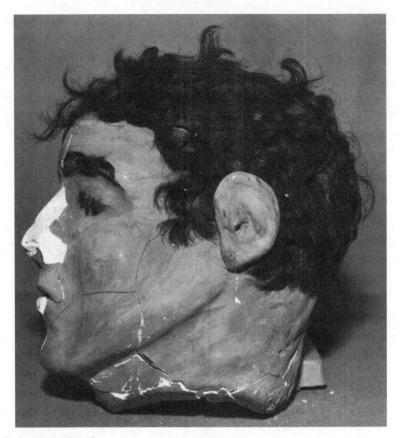

John's dummy head
FBI

Even though James no longer participated in the escape as a member of the inner circle, he still helped whenever he could. A couple of examples are found in one of his letters: "I was well aware of the planned escape and didn't want to put any heat on them. . . . At times we supplied rubber raincoats—glue and planned to create noise in C block to keep guards in that area and leave B block alone."

As John completed the work on Oink, Clarence decided to make a trip to the cellblock roof and see for himself what that part of the prison looked like. After what had happened with John when he checked out the same spot the week before, Clarence understood the dangers of showing himself without first checking the area. He reached into his pocket and took out a miniperiscope he had made and looked around. Footsteps from the gunwalk echoed off the ceiling. Clarence hid in the shadows until the guard passed by.

He then pulled himself onto the top. As John had reported, a thick layer of dirt covered everything. Clarence then looked up at the air vent. Out of reach eight feet above him, he checked for anything he might stand on. To his surprise, he found a bucket someone had left there from some job done years before. He flipped the bucket over and stepped onto it. A cool breeze wafted through the vent. Just three more feet and they'd be free. But stopping him were the steel bars welded across the opening. Clarence gave the bars a shake. They didn't budge.

He let out a long breath as he studied them.

Since there was nothing more he could do, and every second he delayed increased his chances of getting caught, Clarence climbed back down and returned to his cell.

"How did it go?" John asked.

"Not too good. The vent's just as you described."

John thought for a moment. "How about the bolts holdin' the vent in place? Be a lot easier cuttin' them than the bars."

"Should work," Clarence surmised. "Except the bars are pretty close together. Could be hard gettin' at the bolts."

"Guess we'll need to make a bar spreader. I'll start on that tomorrow."

"Okay."

John paused a moment. "I'm almost finished with Oink. Where you at with yours?"

"Should be done in a day or two."

"Good."

With that they called it a night.[4]

About this time, Clarence Anglin made a second dummy head of cement which was stored on top of the cell block next to the roof. This one was called "Oscar" and was to be given to Frank Morris.

Interview of West on June 13, 1962, by FBI agents
FBI FILES

Not long after, Frank finally broke through the back of his cell. And just in time. Clarence had finished putting Oscar together, a nickname given to him years before by his brother Robert, then gave the head to John, who painted the face and glued on hair. With two heads now ready for a test run, both men set them on their pillows after lights-out. Looked real enough to them. Of course, what the guards thought mattered the most.

As luck would have it, an interview of former FBI agent Don Eberle, who headed up the investigation, exists. In the interview, he spoke about the dummy heads and fooling the guards:

> So, you have very little light. So, when you walk down near those things, and all you could see in the cell that there's a bed in there and there's something in the bed. Because if you keep trying to wake the prisoners up all night long, well then you get problems, and they were in the bed and . . . one fellow would see somebody in that bunk or what appeared to be, then they'd go back up. . . . And then when they made those heads, you know, with the hair and all and you put that in the bed and you look in when it's obscure and really dark, why you'd swear there was somebody there.[5]

Once in the corridor, John and Clarence made their way to the top. Using the periscope like before, John looked the area over. The bucket was still where Clarence left it. This was a good sign since it meant no one had been there since his previous trip.

He took out the bar spreader John had made and used a wrench they had also fabricated.

The principle behind a bar spreader is remarkably simple: all one needs is a bolt and screw, or a bolt and threaded casing; slip them between the bars and turn with a wrench. As the bolt and casing expand, they exert enough force to push the bars apart.

After several turns, Clarence was able to slip his hand through the opening and reach the bolts holding the vent housing in place. He took out the saw John had given him and started going back and forth in a slow, steady manner. In the distance the sound of inmates playing their instruments filled the cellblock, just as Whitey had promised. He had no

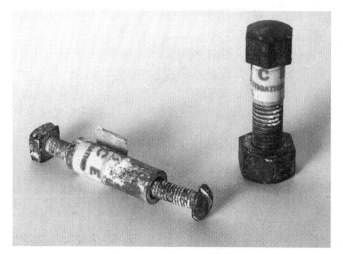

Bar spreader
GOLDEN GATE NATIONAL RECREATION AREA, PARK ARCHIVES (396, 397, 375)

Improvised wrench
GOLDEN GATE NATIONAL RECREATION AREA, PARK ARCHIVES (396, 397, 375)

idea how far the cutting sound traveled off the cement walls, floors, and ceiling, so Clarence worked the bolt as quietly as possible.

After a few minutes, his arms ached from being held in an upward position, so John took over. He lasted another five minutes before he tired as well.

John checked their progress. "I can feel a bit of a groove, but this will take time."

"Must be hardened steel. Didn't count on that."

"I say we give it five more minutes and then try again tomorrow."

The next night Clarence returned with Frank, except this time they brought a vacuum cleaner motor West had stolen.

By a stroke of good luck, West had recently learned that the prison's vacuum had broken. He was permitted to attempt a repair, and while inspecting the machine, he found that it had two motors. He carefully removed one, and was able to get the other working, thus deflecting suspicion. Morris and the Anglins were then able to use the vacuum motor for their drill.[6]

They tapped into an electrical source atop the cellblock and, with a drill bit an inmate named Carnes had smuggled out of one of the shops, fashioned a crude drill. The two waited until the "music hour," when inmates were allowed to play their instruments in their cells, which they hoped would mask the motor and cutting sounds.

A metallic grinding noise filled their air when Frank started on the vent housing bolt nearest him. After a minute he stopped.

"Well?" Clarence asked.

Frank touched the metal. "It's not even warm."

"Maybe if you made the motor go faster. Might cut through easier."

"It's as fast as it'll go, but I'll try."

Morris started up the motor again. Like before, grinding noises reverberated off the ceiling, but with the same result.

Dejected, Frank stepped off the bucket. "I don't think we can risk using the drill. In fact, we should get out of here in case the guards heard."

"Guess we do this the old-fashioned way."

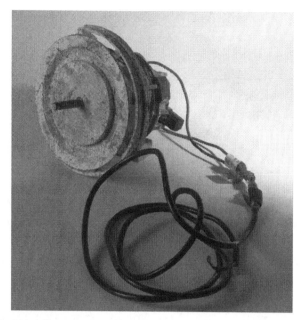

Actual fabricated drill
GOLDEN GATE NATIONAL RECREATION AREA, PARK ARCHIVES (372)

The two climbed back down and returned to their cells undetected.[7]

A few days later the group met at their normal spot on the steps. John let them know they were pretty much on track with the plan, with only one dummy head left to paint, though the drill didn't work out as they had hoped.

West felt the most disappointment about the setback since he had risked time in solitary getting that to them.

"So what's the next step in the plan?" James asked.

"That depends on him." John turned toward West. "Until you get permission to paint the top of the cellblock, we're at a stopping point."

> Clarence Anglin and Frank Morris went up the utility corridor next to the roof on about three evenings and they took the coupling out of the roof hole and from the ventilator. They put grease around it so it would slide out easily and replaced it so that no one would notice anything amiss.

Interview of West on June 13, 1962, by FBI agents
FBI FILES

"Don't blame me. I asked Herman the German yesterday, but nothing yet."

They all knew the entire escape plan hinged on being assigned that job, so West said he'd ask again.

Frank then shared his continued concerns about Cohen and his failure to contact them since getting out on bond. In his mind, no news was bad news. "He'll come through for us," Clarence assured Frank. "He's a man of his word."

"I know he's your friend and all, but we have to assume there's no boat so we're not caught flat-footed when we bust out."

Whitey agreed with Frank. Breakouts seldom went the way escapees expected, and a backup just might mean the difference between success and failure.

Frank took this opportunity to push for Angel Island once again.

When no one objected, he took it as the group finally seeing things his way.

Despite the makeshift drill not working on the bolts, it still proved useful for West. Digging out of the back of his cell took longer than they had expected, and so he hooked up the drill to his light socket and made a number of holes around the grate, speeding up his efforts.

Even better news, after several weeks of waiting, West was finally given permission to paint the top of B-Block. And best of all, they allowed him to pick his helpers.

West, John, Clarence, and Frank brought up the paint, tarps, and brushes for the job. They looked about the area and considered their options. With the gunwalk at the same level as the top of the cellblock, they'd have a difficult time working on the things the four needed for the escape without being seen. Then West had an idea.

Under the pretense of preparing for the job, he went to the edge of the cellblock with his broom and started sweeping dirt over the side when one of the guards walked by.

"Hey!" the guard yelled. "Whatcha doin' up there? You're making a mess."

"Sorry," West apologized. "Just following the warden's orders about cleaning up and painting the top of the cellblock."

"There's dirt all over the place. Can't you be more careful?"

West looked around. "I don't know how we can. There's a lot of dust and stuff up here."

The guard's voice grew louder. "I don't care how you do it, but you can't be getting dirt in the cellblock."

West reached down and picked up one of the tarps. "How about if we hang these on the bars? This way we can clean up without making a mess. John Anglin works in the clothing room." West pointed at him. "He can get us some blankets for the job."

John stepped up to the bars. "Yes, sir. About a dozen or so should be enough."

"Fine. Just be quick about it."

With that, the four now had the means of working atop the cellblock in absolute privacy, the guards none the wiser.

Whitey also knew about them working in plain sight and the circumstances behind that as they prepared for the escape, which he wrote about in one of his letters.

This 3 men with help of West who had job painting on top of B block barred lots of dusty ducts etc. he had job of cleaning and painting—guard on gun walk could look across that area—West flicked paint and dirt down on guard—pretty sure it was Lt. Double Tough—gruff comical looking guy who's whole life was AZ. He ordered West put blanket up there so paint and dirt doesn't rain down on humans! Yes Sir—that blocked off the gun walk's view on top of roof of cells.

John had no difficulty requisitioning the blankets from the clothing room, which he hung in short order. The four made it look as though they were busy working, first sweeping up the dirt, then getting started on the painting. In actuality, they did as little as possible as a way of extending their time atop the cellblock. And with John, Clarence, and Frank able to leave their cells at night, they set about acquiring as many raincoats as possible for the raft and life vests. The FBI noted West's activities at this time in their report.[8]

obtained an olive colored rubberized raincoat from one of the inmates who was transferred from this institution and over the next few days obtained a couple of more of such raincoats. In addition, over the next few days he would pick up a raincoat when it was placed down by another inmate and when this individual was not looking. In the evening he would take these raincoats and cut them up and paste them together with some glue which had possibly been obtained from the glove factory at the institution. He would also sew some of the material together.

FBI report

In fact, the theft of raincoats and requisitions for new ones became so prevalent the correctional officer who oversaw them grew concerned when he took inventory and discovered how few they had on hand. He had stated in the FBI report he hadn't ordered a replacement raincoat in about a year, but in the weeks before the escape he had ordered three dozen. In all, the four secured over fifty raincoats for their needs. And yet, despite this unexplained anomaly, the loss of so many in so short a time was never questioned by the guards or prison administration.

At night the three took turns cutting the coats up and gluing and sewing the pieces together. Unbeknownst to the guards, Frank's March 1962 edition of *Popular Mechanics* had arrived, and with it a how-to article of particular interest for the four.

Prison officials made it a practice to screen all reading material coming into the prison so inmates couldn't use the information for illicit purposes. Yet somehow a story about life vests—how one uses them and what they look like—had been approved for circulation.

When Clarence wasn't working in the barbershop or gluing pieces of raincoats together in the dead of night, his quiet moments often turned toward home. And in those quiet moments he typically wrote to his mother, hoping a few words from him provided her with a small measure of comfort. He wrote one such letter on April 2, 1962.

From: Clarence Anglin 1485   April 2, 1962

Dear Mom,

I received your letter and sure was glad to hear from you also to hear everyone at home was getting along alright. As for me and John we are doing ok.

March 1962 *Popular Mechanics* issue showing proper use of a life preserver

Whatever Al adds to your check you just keep because we don't have anything to buy here. Only at Christmastime I know that you need it anyway so don't worry about sending it.

Yes Al said that another lawyer was coming up to see him. It is the one that Marie met sometime or other at church. He has not wrote about Meeting him yet. But maybe he can do something for us.

I was a little surprised about Junior and his wife having a kid. Because it had been so long since I had seen him. And him still going to school and all back then it just surprised me a little. And I know that he was married too.

I suppose that you all have been up and visited Al by now. If you haven't I know that he is looking forward to seeing everybody.

I guess I'll close for now tell everybody at home hello and ans. Soon.

Clarence

With Clarence knowing full well prison staff inspected every letter mailed home, this only left family news and his general well-being as topics he wrote about pretty much every time. What he obviously couldn't say was that he and John had been busily working on their escape for a number of months and would hopefully implement their plan in the coming weeks, the reason he asked her not to send them money. How he must have wanted to tell them what they were really doing, but Clarence kept such desires in check and instead focused his letter on keeping his connections with his mother and family strong.

As the four continued their work, a growing sense of dread crept up on John. He had been told by guard and inmate alike the perils of the San Francisco waters. Hovering at a bone-chilling fifty-five degrees most of the year, it meant a swimmer wouldn't last long before hypothermia set in, and eventual death. Their odds of success were bad enough as it was. Why make them worse by ignoring obvious dangers? Fortunately for the four, they had an ace in the hole—James Bulger. He was a licensed scuba diver who understood the importance of preparation.

The following Saturday John found Whitey in the exercise yard watching a game of basketball. He approached him from behind. "Hey James."

Whitey turned around and smiled. "McQueen. How are things going?"

"Right on schedule. Mind if I grab a smoke?"

Whitey took out a cigarette and offered him one.

They wandered over to the steps and sat on the top level. In the distance, a seagull cried out as it flew overhead.

John took a puff from his cigarette. "I figure we should be ready in a few weeks, but that's got me thinkin' about that water. It's mighty cold out there, and the hot showers they give us keeps us from gettin' used to it."

James had already given that problem some thought and had come up with an idea he figured should work, which he shared in another of his letters:

I talked at length about how they should get themselves acclimated to shock of cold water—by running in place in their cells deep knee bends—cold wet thin towels on bare chest nights cell house was cold no heat—don't stay in hot shower soap up fast rinse and out experiment with glue on thick underwear then layer on each side of top tight against body and wristlets hoping for trapped air bubble for buoyancy and trapping heat "layer" of body heated water.

The solution for the cold bay waters had been in their cells the entire time. Warden Blackwell and everyone who served under him firmly believed the hot showers served as an effective deterrent for anyone thinking of swimming their way to freedom. What they didn't take into account was the sink and toilet water in each inmate's cell, neither heated. All the escapees need do was simple: soak down a towel, lay on the concrete floor and cover themselves with it. A shock to the system at first, the body would slowly acclimate to the cold as they employed this simple technique night after night.

But Whitey didn't stop there. He also told them the importance of having a kind of wetsuit under their clothes as a way of maintaining each person's core body temperature. The FBI corroborated Whitey's story when they interviewed an inmate who had been told certain details about their escape plan.[9]

```
                        They talked of wearing long under-
wear which they might dye or paint black and sweatshirts
similarly dyed or painted. This would be under their regular
prison clothing and they would discard their prison clothing on
the beach when they were ready to leave the island.
```
FBI FILES

On a rare warm day, John and Whitey sat on the cement steps in the exercise yard, not saying much as they enjoyed the sun. The four were making good progress on the raft and vests, and West had pretty much finished the paddles. As a reward, John gave himself a few carefree moments to not think about the hundreds of details that encompassed the plan. His moment of bliss didn't last long. The sounds of footsteps hurrying up the steps grabbed his attention. Clarence and Frank stood in front of him a bit out of breath. John saw on their faces something had happened.

"Clarence, something wrong?"

"No, except I just heard somethin' about Cohen."

A Friend Returns

Whenever a river reaches the ocean, it waits to go back.
—VELIKO TARNOVO

THE WAITRESS APPROACHED A MIDDLE-AGED MAN, WELL DRESSED, SITting at the table, his nose buried in a newspaper. A bit on the heavy side and his hair thinning, he took a sip of coffee before turning the page. When he looked up, the man noticed several people staring, as though they recognized him but weren't sure.

A woman mouthed to her friend, "Is that Mickey Cohen?"

Mickey smiled. He had already been something of a celebrity in Los Angeles as a result of the televised hearings in Washington, DC, where he squared off against the Kennedy brothers two years before. But when he bonded out of Alcatraz after his tax evasion conviction, the only person in the prison's history to do so, the media stuck with Cohen everywhere he went. And he enjoyed the attention.

But Cohen also knew his freedom could be taken away in short order. The charges brought against him were serious, and the witnesses sang like canaries. His lawyers, Jack Dahlstrum and A. L. Wirin, had done the near impossible and gotten him out, and the two remained confident they'd get his convictions overturned. As much as he appreciated their confidence, the trial didn't concern Cohen at the moment. Keeping a promise he made to John and Clarence did. He had flown down to LA just for this meeting and planned on returning to San Francisco on Monday, when the trial started up again.

No sooner had Cohen finished his eggs than a familiar face walked into the café—Fred Brizzi. He looked around until his searching gaze found Cohen.

"Glad you made it," Mickey said. "I know how busy you are these days."

Brizzi sat across from him. When he did, a waitress approached.

"Morning. Can I get you anything?" she asked.

"No, nothin' for me."

The waitress gave him a half smile and checked on a nearby table.

Fred shifted his attention back to Mickey. "I can't stay long. Got another shipment ready to pick up."

"Then I'll keep it short. Before I left Alcatraz, I talked with John and Clarence. They're planning an early release, and they asked for my help."

Fred let out a slow breath, visibly impressed. "From the Rock? That takes guts."

"I promised I'd have a boat there to pick them up when they busted out."

"So where do I fit in all this?"

Mickey showed his newspaper to Fred. "See this?"

He skimmed the article.

"A McDonnell Phantom II fighter set a low-altitude speed record, averaging nine hundred mile per hour."

"Yeah, so?"

"I've done a lot thinking since my release, and every way I look at it, having them go to Tijuana by boat won't work. The Coast Guard would catch up with them easy. What they need is someone who can fly them somewhere the feds won't ever think of looking."

Fred set the paper down. "And where might that be?"

"Someplace farther south. You know the farm outside Mexico City?"

"That's two thousand miles from San Francisco. No way you make it without stoppin' to refuel." (Years later, Brizzi was known as "Waterbed Fred" for using large bladders of fuel on his planes so he wouldn't have to refuel during drug runs.)

"But you can make it, right?"

"Yeah, I can make it, but it'll take time gettin' there."

"Not as long as you think?"

Fred's eyebrows furled together. "What do you mean?"

"I bought a new Beechcraft Baron last week. Top speed of two hundred and forty miles an hour. You think you can handle it?"

A broad smile stretched across Fred's face. "Do you even have to ask?"

"A couple of small airports in the vicinity of the prison might be suitable rendezvous points. I'll have one of my boys check them out. In the meantime, I have another job for you."

Fred parked his car in front of a simple house with a picket fence surrounding it. He turned off the lights and looked back over his shoulder. In the silence, the sounds of crickets filled the air. No headlights behind him. Fred had taken a circuitous route from his hotel to the Anglin house on the off chance he had been followed. Being in the business he was in, such precautions had become second nature to him.

The door swung open with a creak and Fred stepped out of the car. He gave the place a long look before walking up to the porch. Three soft knocks on the door produced a muffled noise inside, followed by footsteps.

After a moment the door opened. Standing there was the person who had brought Brizzi all the way across the country—Robert Anglin.

Cohen's tax evasion trial began on May 2, 1961, and finished on January 12, 1962. When he was released from Alcatraz on October 17, 1961, after Supreme Court Chief Justice Earl Warren signed off on his appeal, Cohen pursued a vigorous defense, claiming innocence of all thirteen counts. During the course of the trial,

> there were over 180 witnesses, and more than 8,000 pages of reporter's transcript. 947 government exhibits and 27 defense exhibits were produced. . . . Counts 2 and 3 involved unreported income. . . . Much of this evidence was also pertinent under count 4. It charged that appellant placed his assets in the name of others, deposited them with

others . . . and paid other creditors but not the government, all for the purpose of defeating the payment of his income tax liabilities.[1]

In the end, the witnesses who had testified against Cohen and the thousands of documents produced during the trial clearly indicating his guilt proved too daunting. Despite his lawyers' systematic attack against the credibility of witnesses and ensuing evidence, "Cohen was convicted under eight counts of a thirteen-count indictment, his motion for new trial was denied. . . . Thus, the total fines are $30,000 and the total prison terms are fifteen years."[2]

Cohen returned to Alcatraz on May 14, 1962, four weeks before the escape.

He had been assigned cell C-253 upon his arrival, which meant the four didn't see him over on B-Block. However, when he entered the dining hall that evening, John, Clarence, Frank, James, and West looked like they had seen a ghost. Their eyes widened at Cohen's unexpected arrival. It been seven months since his release, and not a single word from him about the boat in all that time. Even John was beginning to lose hope.

"Mickey," Clarence said, smiling. "As I live and breathe. Thought you were gone for good."

A tray of food in his hands, Mickey sat between James and West. "Hey boys. Good to see ya."

"So how was it on the outside?" John asked.

Mickey scooped up a mouthful of noodles. "Better than here, I can tell ya that. Los Angeles has some of the best restaurants around. And don't forget about the women."

The five laughed.

"Also been keeping up on business," Cohen added. "In fact, a friend of yours says hello."

"Brizzi?" Clarence asked in a low voice.

"Uh huh. Got a special job for him I think will interest you. But not here. In the yard."

Though Whitey was happy to see his friend again, he was also disappointed. Every inmate on Alcatraz spent much of their time thinking about getting off the Rock. But Mickey had actually done it. And what did he do with his golden opportunity? Came back. Before his release, Whitey had told Cohen he should head straight for Brazil the moment he stepped off the boat.

Extradition laws at that time made getting such a person back to the United States extremely difficult. Obviously, what he suggested made a big impact in John, Clarence, and Frank, which later played a key role in their lives.

Today, however, their collective attention focused on getting out. And the closer the day came, the more Clarence thought about what he'd leave behind, namely, his mother and the rest of the family. He couldn't just go and not say goodbye. Of course, he couldn't do so openly either, so a week before Mickey's return, he wrote another letter home. But this one was different from the others. Rather than talk about how much he missed home and family, Clarence said his goodbyes in a coded way, one that Robert and his siblings would understand.

From: Clarence Anglin 1485   May 6, 1962

Dear Mom,

I received your letter and sure was glad to hear from you also to hear everyone at home was getting along alright. As for Me and John we are making out ok.

We also received the birthday cards and Easter cards.

I guess that you all have visited Al by now. I just got a letter from him the other day. And he mentioned that you all were expected to be there on Saturday. I think that he may make parole back down there. He said that they asked him where he would like to go first if they did parole him and he said Alabama, but I think that he would have been better off to go back to Florida where he could be clost [sic] to home. I know that I would have anyway. Maybe he will get back to one or the other anyway. It would be something on the way to him getting out altogether. I don't know just how much chance there is of Me and John getting any closter [sic] to home. But we have heard they may close this place down and move us to a new place in Illinois it sure would be closter [sic] to visit. I don't know this for sure we will just have to wait and see.

Well tell everybody at home Hello and take it easy. Ans. soon.

Clarence

When Clarence penned these words to his mother—"I don't know just how much chance there is of Me and John getting any closter to home. But we have heard they may close this place down and move us to a new place"—there is only one way of understanding the truth behind them: they planned on breaking out soon and may never see each other again. For Clarence, such thoughts pained him, but he could also take comfort in knowing he had said his goodbyes.

As the four continued working on the paddles, raft, and life vests atop the cellblock, no real threat of "finish the paint job now or else" had been uttered by the guards, despite the slowness of their alleged work during the day. But the four also knew they shouldn't press their luck. With Cohen's timely return, they set about finishing up the last few things that needed doing and set a date for the escape.

Foremost on their minds, make sure the raft and vests didn't leak. Luckily for the four, Morris came across an article in the November 1960 edition of *Popular Mechanics* that discussed the process of vulcanizing rubber. Though it is commonly believed he had used the information

Morris's requests for magazines
UNITED STATES PENITENTIARY, ALCATRAZ

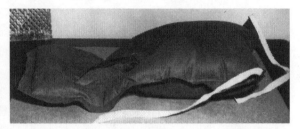

Mae West–style life vest
FBI

Paddle used for the raft

provided him from the prison's library, in fact Morris had paid his own money for that subscription and several others.

Part of the vulcanizing process required heat, of which they had in abundant supply from the hot water pipes used for the showers, which just happened to run along the top of B-Block.

Because of the raft's size and the number of raincoats needed to construct it, John, Clarence, and Frank focused their energies on that. They cut the coats into squares and set about sewing and gluing the pieces together, fusing the seams on the hot water pipes. West, on the other hand, had been tasked with making the life vests and paddles. Since they were quicker and easier to make than the raft, he worked on them as he "painted" the cellblock ceiling.

Withdrawals

On June 8, 1962, $15.00 to Guardsmen's Fund.

On April 1, 1962, he purchased a Concertina, cost $28.69, Catalog No. 7132*.

On March 14, 1962, for $11.65 purchased "Berlitz Self Teacher Spanish Books" and "Spanish Made Simple."

Record of Morris's purchases
FBI FILES

In anticipation of needing certain tools for their escape, Morris had also purchased a concertina the month before. A concertina is essentially the same as the accordion he had borrowed from the prison, except much smaller. It should also be noted that he had purchased two Spanish books in anticipation of hiding out in Mexico after the escape.[3]

Unlike the accordion, Morris didn't buy the concertina so he could play it. Rather, he needed the inside mechanism. A concertina consists of bellows that expands and contracts to push air through reeds, making different notes depending on which buttons or keys are pushed on both ends. For the escapees, the drawing in and pushing out of air would act as a pump for the raft when they reached the shore. With the guards given the orders of shoot to kill, the three needed the raft inflated as fast as possible and put into the water before being spotted.

Also as a way of maintaining the ruse about him learning to play the accordian, and later the concertina, Morris sometimes joined in with the inmate band, the Rock Islanders, who gave regular concerts on Sundays and holidays for the inmates.

Rock Islanders
GOLDEN GATE NATIONAL RECREATION AREA, PARK ARCHIVES (19200.288)

What the four still needed was a clear idea of what awaited them after their escape. Most important of all, had Cohen gotten the boat? He hadn't been willing to say either way when he returned a few days before, but Cohen said they'd talk in the exercise yard.

The sun shone bright on a rare cloudless day. John, Clarence, and Frank basked in the warmth the moment they stepped outside. Not far behind them, Cohen exited the cellblock. They called him toward the cement steps.

Cohen sat back against the step and stared out at the city. "Funny seeing San Francisco from this side. Just a few months ago during the trial, I'd go up to Coit Tower or down to Fort Point and look at the island, wondering if I was ever coming back."

John scanned the inmates nearest him. "So what do ya have for us?"

Cohen turned serious. "The boat's all set. All they need from me is the day. When do you figure you'll be ready?"

Inmates and guards milling about the exercise yard
GOLDEN GATE NATIONAL RECREATION AREA, PARK ARCHIVES (19200.340)

"We've been puttin' in some extra hours the last few nights," John said. "We figure we should be done the first or second week of June. The guards are gettin' a little antsy about the paint job, so we're tryin' to get things finished as soon as possible."

"Okay. I'll let my boys know."

"How?" Frank asked.

"Don't your worry about that. I got my ways. Though there is one other thing . . ."

Clarence took out a cigarette and lit it. "Yeah? What's that?"

"Tijuana won't work. The Coast Guard will be checking every boat up and down the coast after your escape. The only way of getting you safely away is if you fly out of here."

"Fly?" John asked.

"There's a small airport in San Rafael north of here, Marin Ranch. Been there since World War II. Perfect for your needs. You meet up with the boat in the bay, and they'll take you there, where a pilot will fly you to Mexico City. You remember the farm there? Should keep you safe for a while."

Frank glanced upward. "Who's flying us out?"

"You don't know him," Mickey replied. He turned toward John and Clarence. "But you two do."

"Fred Brizzi," John concluded.

"He's been outfitted with a new plane that will get you there fast."

"You trust him?" Frank asked.

"With our lives," Clarence replied without hesitation. "We've been friends since we was kids."

Frank appeared troubled. "It's a big bay out there. How are we gonna find the right boat?"

"It's been equipped with special lights. You know, the kind that fisherman use for attracting fish at night. They'll fire up the lights every ten minutes or so. You'll see it easy."

"That's perfect," John said. "Just make sure your people wait for us between Alcatraz and the Municipal Pier."

"Why that spot?" Mickey asked.

"Because that's the route the prison transports take. When we get near your boat we let go and paddle for it. Shouldn't be too hard."

Cohen appeared concerned. "You sure you boys can do this?"

Cigarette smoke came out of Clarence's mouth when he laughed. "Me and John have been pulled by lots of boats on the Manatee River growin' up. More fun than you'll ever know."

Mickey snapped his fingers. "Oh yeah. One more thing. Your sister Nell and a friend of hers, Floyd, are planning on being here just in case. Your brother Robert set it up."

"Floyd Stevens?" John asked.

"Yeah, that's the guy."

"They're comin' out here?" Clarence asked, incredulous. "But she's gettin' married soon."

"It's all set. Floyd's willing to drive her cross-country. All he needs is five days' notice and they'll be here."

Though there's no record of Nell and Floyd's trip to San Francisco in June 1962, an intriguing clue has surfaced that gives credence to the claim made by the family.

Author Frank Ahearn interviewed Robert in 2007 while doing research for a proposed television series about finding missing people. During the course of the interview, a friend of Robert had something interesting to say: "He told us what most people do not know is that one of the Anglin siblings was out in California during the escape and not far from the rock—information not in the FBI file."[4]

What is more interesting is the timing of Nell's arrival in San Francisco. In a letter written by John and Clarence's mother, Rachel, on June 11, 1962, the very day of the escape, she said this: "Also of Nell's wedding. She is getting married this Sat. nite, June 16, at the house. Jr and his wife will play and sing." According to family history, Nell and Floyd drove from Ruskin to San Francisco before her wedding, and then rushed back before Saturday. Why would their sister travel such a distance so close to her wedding day? Answer: the escape on Monday, June 11. Happily, Nell returned in time and married Wiley Greene on June 16.

There is additional evidence to suggest that Floyd and Nell knew about the escape ahead of time. In the same interview with Ahearn,

When he was committed to the USP-A or ▓▓▓▓▓▓▓▓▓▓
he resumed his friendship with ALFRED ANGLIN, and he felt, was
taken into his confidence. Shortly after his arrival, ANGLIN
informed him that his brothers, then confined at the USP, Alcatraz,
were planning an escape in the near future, but he did not feel
it could be done and did not place much stock in this prediction
until it happened about two months later.

FBI FILES

Robert described how John and Clarence communicated with each other for years using various secret codes. One of those methods could have easily been utilized when writing home from Alcatraz.[5] The FBI confirmed the brothers' method of communication when they interviewed an inmate at United States Penitentiary, Atlanta, who knew Alfred Anglin. While Alfred was serving time in Atlanta for the failed bank robbery, John and Clarence often wrote to him and informed him of their plans, which he shared with the inmate, whose name is redacted in the FBI report.[6] Clearly, Alfred knew about his brothers' escape plans ahead of time. The question is, how? The best possible answer is an encrypted message mailed to him by one or both brothers.

Now that John, Clarence, and Frank had gotten the information they needed from Cohen, they focused their collective energies on finishing up the few remaining tasks. Frank still didn't trust West, so he made sure the fourth member of the group remained in the dark as to their true destination. As far as West knew, once out, they'd head straight for Angel Island.

As the days passed, the guards pressed the four about the paint job and when they would be done. Yet, despite their growing impatience, never once did any of them check the top of the cellblock. In the meantime, Mickey returned to the clothing room on May 24, 1962, ten days after his return to Alcatraz. And as luck would have it, John still had that job. This gave the two ample opportunity to communicate with each other regarding the status of the plan without fear of being discovered.

With the boat Cohen had arranged soon on its way, and their final preparations just about completed, only one decision remained—which night?

Whenever books and documentaries discuss what happened to the three the night of the escape, most conclude the raft probably sank and they drowned, their bodies swept into the ocean by the tides. Or they tried to swim for Angel Island but succumbed to the cold and suffered the same fate. Ask former guards, law enforcement officers, and experts and most have drawn the same conclusion. But what if another option had been right in front of everyone all along, the roots of which can be found in the FBI report regarding the escape.

In a document written to J. Edgar Hoover on June 21, 1962, the head of the FBI at that time, an investigator made the following determination:

> It appears that the escape route at Alcatraz had been well cased and it must be assumed the three prisoners had rehearsed crawling through the vents to the roof in view of which they closely determined how much time was required to reach the selected location where they could be picked up by a row boat or a similar float at a given time. This would call for prearranged detail plans with an outside source. Naturally they would recognize the danger of trying to sneak such communication to outside contacts, therefore the safest and most logical method would be to verbally clear the entire project with a trusted prisoner scheduled for early release. This man would be in a position to furnish the complete outline with first hand information to outside assistance.

The letter concludes with this recommendation:

> I think it would be wise to learn the identity of prisoners released from Alcatraz during a given period and from that point trace possible contacts capable of engineering the escape assignment.[7]

The facts the FBI uncovered are startling. In a previous section of the report, it was confirmed that the escapees planned on making their way to the dock and using one of the transports to get off the island. This letter to Hoover builds on that idea, in which the escapees likely rendezvoused with a boat waiting to pick them up, made possible by an inmate who had been released and made the arrangements.

But the similarities between Mickey Cohen and this unknown person do not end there. The FBI investigation also uncovered this important fact:

He did state that ANGLIN did inform him that [name redacted] had informed him that who was then confined at Alcatraz, fixed the Subjects up with a "contract" in California, and that this "contract" had a small boat.[8]

The "he" in this report is Alfred Anglin, whose cellmate was interviewed by the FBI after his death in 1964. As we can see in this excerpt, Alfred stated that an inmate at Alcatraz acquired a boat for John, Clarence, and Frank.

Clearly, there is only one person this could be. Who at Alcatraz had been made aware of the escape plan, had access to a boat, had the money to hire one, had the right people who'd keep their mouths shut, and could arrange the boat's arrival at the exact time needed? Mickey Cohen had money, knowledge, motivation, and an underworld organization that could easily pull off an operation of this complexity.

But we don't have to guess or make arguments about the identity of this person. In October 2015, I emailed a U.S. Marshal familiar with the FBI report and asked him this question: "'Alfred informed him that [name redacted] who was then confined at Alcatraz, fixed the Subjects up with a Contract.' Who is this person in Alcatraz?"

His reply: "That is Mickey Cohen he is talking about." Mickey Cohen.

Once again, another piece of the puzzle has been set in place.

As the four finalized the last few details of their plan, the date of the escape quickly approached—June 11, 1962.

In an unintended coincidence, their mother, Rachel, wrote Clarence a letter on the exact same day. It is perhaps fitting she ended the letter, "Well I'm expecting to hear from John soon."

CHAPTER 22

The Escape

THE NIGHT OF MONDAY, JUNE 11, 1962—ABOUT SIX MONTHS AFTER fellow inmate Robert Schibline (1355-AZ) and other inmates first became aware of the four's intentions—Morris and the Anglins initiated their plan. Taking something of risk before then, he said the men spent Saturday and Sunday saying "goodbye" to friends in the prison.

A guard looks at one of the escape holes in the utility corridor.
FBI

Robert Schibline mug shot

UNITED STATES PENITENTIARY, ALCATRAZ

It was during mealtimes that Schibline first heard about the escape. . . . He said the men told him about their elaborate get-out-of-jail idea and shared details of their scheme of constructing a makeshift raft out of prison raincoats and use of a stolen electric drill powered by a vacuum cleaner motor and extension cord to drill through the cell wall. . . . "About half of the prison was working for them; they'd get them anything they needed or helped them with things they didn't know how to do. . . . I knew about the tides and currents. They didn't and they only had about an hour to make it out."[1]

Robert Schibline, bank robber, arrived at Alcatraz in June 1958 and was later assigned a work detail on the dock. Unknown to the correctional officers and fellow prisoners, he copied the tide tables from the daily newspapers tossed into the garbage by a guard. On June 11, 1962, Schibline handed off the morning tide table to John Anglin, helping give flight to the most famous prison break in American history.[2]

Schibline added,

You can't have a watch or calendar inside Alcatraz. So, I had to . . . see the current and tide activity all around the island while outside working my job. Then one day I noticed a guard reading a newspaper. Now, that was against the rules for him to bring that inside in his lunch pail, but I knew that the *San Francisco Chronicle* published the Tide Tables every day. So, I waited until he discarded the paper in the trash and got the tables.

I wrote them down on a piece of paper. Then I gave the paper to Clarence. . . . I sat with Clarence and Allen West at the same table in the dining hall. We had the opportunity to talk freely every day while we ate.[3]

Despite the precautions the four took, it's not surprising to discover many of their fellow inmates had become aware of the plan. Allen had already been observed by a couple of Black inmates digging in his cell, and they had undoubtedly told others. The four also needed tools and supplies from the shops, which inmates passed along to them. And then there was what might be considered the riskiest breach of security, asking inmates for their raincoats. It wouldn't have taken the general population long to figure out why they needed them. On top of that, James Bulger had brought others into his confidence about the plan, men carefully chosen who'd provide the four with anything they lacked. One example of this is shared by him in a letter:

> Ianelli knew and would cause noise to cover noise by blowing Charge on his trumpet or bugle in B block that would get a reaction every time! Guys would holler charge and lots of us would bang the bunks the 2 legs made loud noise and we would get a rhythm or cadence and wake up the whole island and mask any noise of bursting out the rear of their cells no easy task.

One can only imagine the thoughts that filled John's, Clarence's, Frank's, and West's minds on June 11. They had undoubtedly gone over the plan hundreds of times by then, and the only question remaining, perhaps the most pertinent of all: had they overlooked anything?

Since the exact date of their escape hadn't been determined until a few days before, Cohen made sure the boat positioned itself near the island at night that week, its lights going on and off every few minutes until the early morning.

With the means of their escape at hand and the raft, life vests, and paddles prepped and ready to go, there was no turning back.

All four of them were also fully aware of the possibility of being shot and killed by one of the guards in the towers. On the other hand, the brothers had no intention of spending the next forty years in prison. John and Clarence took to heart the prosecutor's threat in 1958—should they return to Alabama, they'd never make it out alive. Frank Morris similarly had his fears about returning to Angola State Prison, which he shared with James Bulger on more than one occasion. "Frank Morris said, 'I'm escaping going back to Angola Louisiana State Pen.!' Felt they would kill him for escaping there years ago."

At six o'clock that evening, inmates and guards alike enjoyed listing to a baseball game on the radio. Though the teams are not specifically mentioned in the FBI report, the most likely candidates are the St. Louis Cardinals and Philadelphia Phillies. The game started at 6:05 p.m. (Pacific Time) and finished at 9:22 p.m. Since the unnamed inmate said he turned off the broadcast at around 10:00 p.m., one can assume he also listened to the postgame show. The fact that a game was played the night of the escape is significant, as many of the inmates also likely listened to it (radios had been installed in the cells years before).[4]

> June 11, 1962. On that particular night he was listening to the baseball game through his radio earphones from approximately 6:00 p.m. until 10:00 p.m.

FBI REPORT

It is also interesting to note that the guard towers were likewise equipped with radios. Listening to music and sporting events helped pass the time a little more comfortably during the guards' shifts in the towers.

Whether the four chose the date of the escape because it coincided with a night game is not known, but the timing could not have been more perfect. With many of the inmates and guards distracted by the game, John, Clarence, Frank, and West made their final preparations. The first order of business: put on their makeshift wetsuits, the ones Whitey told them they'd need as protection against the cold water. All they could do after that was wait until lights-out. However, a small problem had arisen. The day before, Morris noticed an issue with the raft needed to be addressed. Rather than wait until lights-out, he took a chance of being discovered by a guard and slipped out of his cell at 7:00 p.m. that night. Morris set up his bed, then made his way to the top of the cellblock.

West gave this account to the FBI of what took place the night of the escape:

A guard on duty in the tower. (The radio is on the shelf.)
GOLDEN GATE NATIONAL RECREATION AREA, PARK ARCHIVES (18352E)

Monday night, June 11, 1962, MORRIS had told [West] that they still had to complete taking the top off of the ventilator leading to the roof and to separate the bars on the roof. In addition, he indicated there was a little work left to complete the raft. FRANK MORRIS said that the ANGLINs were talking about completing the work and breaking out that night. CLARENCE ANGLIN and FRANK MORRIS left their cells and went up the utility corridor to the roof about 7:00 p.m. on June 11, 1962.[5]

Unfortunately for West, he had stopped working on his air vent on April 25, figuring he'd complete the last of the digging the night of the escape. However, he had underestimated the amount of work still involved.

Morris came back down around 8:45 p.m. and told West the bars covering the air vent had been removed. The only thing stopping them from leaving was West. Though he had been steadily widening the hole in the back of his cell for more than an hour, West still couldn't fit through the narrow opening. He assured Morris he'd break through soon and continued working on the grille. Morris returned to the top of the cell-block and removed the bolts holding the air vent in place.[6]

In the meantime, Clarence had slipped out of his cell and helped Frank with the last of the work. He climbed down at 9:22 p.m. and checked on West's progress. He told him they could see the moon and were ready to leave. Either West got out now or he wasn't going. The FBI report states what happened next:

> [West] tried to kick the rest of the cement out of the hold at the back of his cell. He could not do it. ANGLIN tried to help for a minute or so, but could not do anything. He then went up and got MORRIS. MORRIS . . . got a two inch piece of pipe and handed it to [West]. He tried to push it out but could not do it without making too much noise.
>
> MORRIS left to get CLARENCE ANGLIN to help clear out [West's] hole. This happened at 9:37 p.m. that evening. This is the last [West] heard or saw of them.[7]

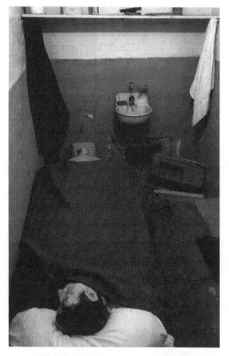

Frank Morris's cell with dummy head
SUPERCARWAAR (WIKIMEDIA COMMONS)

Knowing that precious minutes were ticking away, along with noise made by Clarence as he worked on West's grille from the utility corridor, Morris and the Anglins had no choice but to leave him behind, though they did promise to return after they had gotten everything on the cellblock roof. The three climbed up the pipes and readied the last of their things, including two black hundred-foot extension cords they had stolen.

Frank and Clarence boosted John up, where he bent back the

wagon-wheel bar stretched across the shaft, then scooted up the air vent. In their haste to get onto the roof, the three made more noise than they realized, which an inmate on the third tier heard. According to the FBI report:

> At about 9:35 p.m., just after the lights were dimmed out he heard someone walking or running on the roof of his cell, he thought it was guards on the roof. He volunteered that he would not tell anything about an attempted escape if he knew same since to do so was against the code of the underworld and not healthy.[8]

The lighthouse beam swept across Cellblock B's concrete roof, briefly illuminating the ventilator cover, before moving away in a different direction. When the roof fell dark again, the vent cover jerked up a few inches, then stopped when the beam briefly returned. After several moments the cover slowly moved up again, until a lone arm pushed it over the side and it landed hard on the roof with a heavy thud. The noise startled several dozen seagulls perched nearby, and they flew off, their high-pitched cries filling the air.

Down in the cellblock, those inmates who knew about the escape waited in dreadful anticipation. They knew something could go wrong at any moment and feared the worst. Whitey Bulger was no different. There was nothing he could do but sweat it out.

Then, without any warning, Bulger heard the ventilator cover land on the cellblock roof, which he recounted in his sixth letter:

> They left right after lights out—upon exiting cell house onto roof the heavy duct work when pushed up fell onto the flat roof with a loud thud—many of us were on edge hoping for a successful escape and wide awake—when the Thud noise—Very Loud to us—cell house quiet after Lights Out and guard making his rounds—fortunately it was a guard we called "Herman the German" younger and not as alert when "Thud" noise in flash of a second every seagull on the roof started squawking at once as they flew up.
> We leaped out of bed started banging bed up and down—2 legs hit the floor to distract the guard—hollered loud and banged tin cup on bars—then after few minutes stopped—Prison guard didn't

overreact—he was new unsure and older guard would have sounded alarm—our noise got his attention—distracted him.

In just about every account of the Alcatraz escape, whether it be a movie or documentary, Morris and the Anglins broke out of the prison in dead silence, none of the inmates aware of the escape. But in James's letters, he claimed a number of inmates actually did know about it, and when they heard the thud on the roof and the seagulls, they started making noise as a way of distracting the guards, in particular, the one James referred to as Herman the German.

Robert Schibline also heard the noise on the roof. But his reaction was quite different. "About 10:20 p.m., we heard a big 'thunk.' They went up in a vent and loosened the nuts to lower it and stepped out of there; it made a hell of a noise. I knew the job was in progress but I thought it was over. I thought they were busted."[9]

A small periscope appeared above the shaft's lip and scanned the area. The handmade device slipped back down when the searchlight swept across the roof a third time.

After several moments John pulled himself out of the shaft and crouched down next to it. Looking at the gulls flapping about, he watched as they disappeared into the night. The roof silent once again, John peered into the opening.

"All clear," he whispered.

Clarence appeared next. He handed John the bags, two hundred-foot extension cords, a blanket, rubber raft, life vests, and oars. Clarence lifted himself out next, followed by Frank.

"We did it," Clarence declared. "We actually made it out."

"We're not home yet," John shot back. "Get goin' before a searchlight catches us."

The three divvied up their things and made their way to the roof's edge. A bitter wind stung their faces as John scanned the bay. His eyes lit with recognition.

"I think that's it," he said, then pointed.

"You sure?" Morris asked.

He looked in the same direction.

"Must be. A white boat. And I saw some lights flash."

Clarence stepped between the two. "Let's not stand here arguin'. We'll know soon enough when we're in the water."

Locating the metal drainpipe, they lowered their things with one of the extension cords, then shinnied down to the bottom, their actions slow and measured so as not to make any noise.

Taking a quick look around, John, Clarence, and Frank stood before a twelve-foot-tall fence topped with barbed wire. Clarence climbed up with the blanket and laid it over the top, then tossed their things onto the other side. John went next, then Frank. The three grabbed their gear and started for the water. When one of the searchlights briefly illuminated the area, they ducked behind the water tower until the beam passed them by.

"That was close," John said between winded breaths.

The three headed for the water's edge, when another twelve-foot fence stopped them cold. This time, John draped the blanket over the barbed wire. Clarence and Frank threw him the raft, which he tossed onto the ground, followed by the other things they brought. After John landed on the other side, Clarence scaled the fence. When Frank climbed up he didn't see one of the barbed wires dangling from the top and sliced his leg.

"Damn!" he cried out in pain and landed hard on the ground.

The brothers rushed to him.

"What's wrong?" Clarence whispered. "You okay?"

"I cut my leg."

John looked up at the prison. To his relief he didn't see any guards running toward them.

"You think you can walk?"

Frank got up and tested the leg. A twinge of pain showed on his face. "I can make it."

"It's bleeding pretty bad."

"I'll worry about that later. Come on."

Morris pushed past the two and headed for the beach down the steep incline, the concertina and paddles in hand.

The three then came upon one of the paved roads. After looking both ways, they darted across and headed toward the lumber and debris area, the sounds of small waves hitting the water's edge growing louder after each step. They worked their way through some scraggily bushes until finally reaching the seawall just above the rocky shore.

Clarence dropped the oars and extension cord but kept the life vests. John laid out the rubber raft and Morris attached the concertina to it. After several pushes the raft began to fill with air.

"You sure this is gonna work?" Morris asked. "Angel Island's right there. Less risky."

"Keep your voice down," John snapped back. "The guards will pick us off for sure if they hear us. We stick with the plan."

Morris let out a hot breath but acquiesced.

As they slipped on their life vests, Clarence noticed how badly Frank's leg was still bleeding. "You should wrap that with something'."

"Like what?" Frank barked back.

John handed him a handkerchief. "Here. Use this."

Frank winced in pain when he tied the handkerchief around his leg and knotted it tight. "That should help."

Knowing every second they lingered at the water's edge increased their chances of getting caught, the three inflated their life vests, then threw the oars into the raft.

John stepped in the water and tested his wetsuit. "Not too bad. Should keep us warm enough."

Figuring their black wetsuits camouflaged them best, John, Clarence, and Frank left their prison clothes in their cells, which is not only corroborated by photographs taken after the escape but also by the FBI report: "They talked of wearing long underwear which they might dye or paint black and sweatshirts similarly dyed or painted.[10]

When Morris followed John's lead and likewise stepped in the water, he jerked back. "Are you crazy? It's freezing."

"Quit your complainin'," Clarence groused. "Cohen said they'll be waitin'. But that won't mean spit if we get to the dock and the boat's gone."

The three got into the raft and paddled to the south side of the island. With each push of their oars, the very real fear a guard might take a good look at one of the dummy heads never lingered far from their thoughts. Could they get to the transport in time if the alarm sounded?

Through the haze a faint outline appeared in the dim light: the boat pier. To the right of the dock, the guardhouse stood like a dark silhouette. Between the building and pier, a lone guard took a drag from a cigarette, the smoke from his lungs billowing into the brisk air when he exhaled. But a more immediate problem stretched upward fifty feet, the pier guard tower.

Pier guard tower
LIBRARY OF CONGRESS

"Didn't expect the tower to be that close to the dock," Clarence murmured. "Do ya think we can get by it?"

"Don't know," Morris replied. "Could be tricky."

"Shut up, you two," John barked back. "You want 'em to hear us? We go for the boat."

All three sank down like Navy Seals and faded into the darkness as they paddled their way toward the dock.

In the distance, a foghorn blared into the night, which momentarily masked the sounds of their oars. They slipped past the tower unseen and approached the transport. Using hand signals so as not to reveal themselves to the guard on the pier, their momentum carried them forward, until John grabbed one of the pilings.

The guard on the dock took a long drag of his cigarette and exhaled. The smell of smoke wafted down onto them. As the seconds passed John felt his heart pumping in his chest. One sound from them and it was over.

Just when it seemed they couldn't keep from making the slightest noise much longer, the guard flicked his cigarette into the water and disappeared.

The three let out soft breaths of relief, then started paddling once again toward the transport.

John had Clarence ready the second extension cord. But when he searched for it among their things, Clarence realized he had left it on the beach. Morris looked like he was fit to be tied, as did John. Their entire plan rested on that cord, and with it their best way of getting to Cohen's boat waiting for them in the bay.

"Maybe we can find some rope on the dock," Clarence whispered. "Must be something' there we can use."

John thought it over a moment, then nodded in agreement.

Clarence rose up and scanned the wharf. Fortunately for them the guard had gone into the guardhouse, presumably to warm himself.

"Don't take too long," John admonished Clarence. "The boat will be leavin' soon."

Clarence climbed onto the dock and looked around. His heart pounding in his chest, nothing ropelike showed itself. He decided to take a chance and approached the barracks used by the guards. Knowing he might be caught at any moment, he stopped when he saw something in the dark. Looked like a wheelbarrow. Inside the bucket he found power tools, gloves, and most important, another hundred-foot extension cord. He grabbed it and returned to the raft.

"Look what I got," Clarence declared in triumph.

"Perfect," John replied.

Clarence looped the extension cord around the boat's rudder and held on to both ends. The cord secured, the three pushed back a little and waited in the dark.

At about 11:15 p.m. a guard came out of the guardhouse. He untied the rope and jumped on board. After a quick check on deck, he went into the wheelhouse and started her up. Moments later the extension cord grew taut as he headed for Municipal Pier, located across the bay.

The three held on tight as the raft bounced off the wake created by the engines' propellers, the water's cold spray slapping their faces.

The transport made a sudden turn toward the right, then straightened out again when Municipal Pier came into view. At that moment another boat sitting on the water not far away flashed it lights, then went dark again.

"That's it!" John shouted above the engines.

Clarence let go of one end of the cord, which spun around the rudder in an instant and released them from the transport. The raft bobbed up and down several times until the waves slowly calmed. All three collectively turned their attention toward the transport. They watched and waited, but the vessel held its course straight for the pier.

"He's not coming back," Morris finally said.

They put their paddles in the water and went as fast as they could toward the white boat.

Several men spotted their approach and waved in reply. "Ahoy," one of them called out.

Their hearts pumping with excitement, the three finally made it to the boat. A rope ladder dropped into the water, and John, Clarence, and Morris climbed on board.

"Welcome to freedom," one of the men said, patting John on the shoulder.

John looked back at Alcatraz and smiled.

Meanwhile, West continued chipping away at the concrete. After waiting several hours for the three to return, he grew increasingly anxious and finally widened the hole sufficiently around 1:45 a.m. and slipped through. At the top of the cellblock he found the life preserver meant for him. He shinnied up the vent shaft and made it onto the roof. West hurried to the edge of the roof where the large black pipe leads to the ground. He searched the area below, but did not see the three. They had left him behind.[11]

The raft and escapees gone, West knew there was nothing more he could do, and so he returned to his cell. The realization of being left behind hit him all at once, and his tears came out like a flood. Neighboring prisoners later told the FBI they heard him sobbing that night.

During the investigation, agents interviewed West about his involvement in the escape, along with other inmates who had knowledge of the plan. In particular, an important piece of information came to light. The escapees planned on using one of the prison transports to take them into the middle of the bay and rendez-vous with a boat Cohen had gotten for them. If this is what actually happened, there should be a way of corroborating this part of the story, something that either proved or disproved their claim.

Turns out, evidence does exist in the form of eyewitnesses who recounted what they saw.

The first is Robert Checchi, an off-duty San Francisco police officer who happened to be sitting in his car at Marina Green near the water's edge the night of the escape. Years later, a TV reporter interviewed him about what he saw:

Officer Robert Checchi

SUSAN PASSANISI

Checchi was gazing out at the Bay when he noticed what he calls a "pristine white boat." He says he immediately felt like something was wrong because the boat had no lights on. He didn't see anybody on the boat and he couldn't hear any noise coming from the boat.

But after watching the boat intently for several minutes, Checchi said a light went on. He says somebody on the boat was shining a spotlight or a flashlight into the dark waters of the Bay. He told ABC7's I-Team it just didn't look right.

"I said this is really unusual," Checchi said.

He said, "It started moving out and the port and starboard lights came on. I couldn't tell whether it went north or south, it just disappeared into the dark."

The next day, when Checchi found out there had been an escape from Alcatraz, he . . . filed a report about what he had seen. The FBI questioned Checchi for days and days and sometimes the interrogations got somewhat nasty.

Checchi . . . explained . . . how the FBI agents asked him over and over again, "what did you see; where was it; what time was it" and even "How come you didn't swim out to check the boat out."

Checchi recalls one FBI agent said, "Let's make this go away. Let's bury it." . . .

"If I was on duty and had my police car, I would have called the Coast Guard as a suspicious boat sitting out there in the Bay. If they would have responded they would have caught everybody right there."[12]

However, based on Checchi's report to his superior and subsequent interview with the FBI, an *Oakland Tribune* interview of Checchi done on June 17, 1962, six days after the escape, touched off an intense boat-by-boat search throughout the Bay Area by the FBI. The reporter concluded in the article, "They could still be on the high seas or been transported to Mexico or Canada or other ports without being seen."[13]

The fact that a trained police officer like Checchi immediately became suspicious when he saw the boat sitting there is telling, especially when he thought the boat should be investigated, and it took the newspaper story for the FBI to do just that.

But the evidence doesn't end there. A man name John Leroy Kelly, in a 1993 deathbed confession, claimed to have been on the boat that picked up the escapees.

According to people who have seen and read the document, the deathbed confession was dictated to a nurse by a dying man who wanted to come clean about his role in the escape from Alcatraz.

The dying man told his nurse he and an accomplice helped Frank Morris and the Anglin brothers escape from Alcatraz.

The confession indicates the two men were waiting in a boat on the Bay near Alcatraz the night of the escape and they plucked the three convicts from the water and whisked them away.

The confession is very detailed and it says the men painted the boat white just days before they set out to assist in the prison break.[14]

The details of Kelly's account line up perfectly with Checchi's version, the two of them noting the boat being white, and with the FBI report on the escape.

But a third account of the boat exists that also corroborates details offered by Checchi and Kelly. This one is a tape-recording made in 1992 by the Anglin brothers' childhood friend Fred Brizzi with members of my (Ken's) family.

Brizzi claimed to have met with the brothers in South America in 1975, where they shared with him the particulars of their escape. In one part of the recording, he recounts some of those details: "And uh, [cross-talk] because we got a rope to tie around the motorboat . . . I said, 'I know how you got across there.' I said, 'You tell them [inaudible].' He said, 'You're the first one who ever thought [inaudible]' . . . they didn't swim."

Three different people, same story.

After Clarence climbed aboard the boat, he likewise looked back at Alcatraz, then turned toward the man who helped them out of the water. "You don't know how glad we are you're here. Not sure we would've made it if we had to paddle."

The man laughed. "If we missed each other, you'd be in the Pacific in about an hour. No way you'd beat those tides."

Frank hobbled over to the railing and sat on it, a trail of blood behind him.

"Is he okay?" the man asked.

"Not sure," Clarence replied. "He sliced his leg on some barbed wire."

The man turned around and got the attention of a nearby crewmember holding a rope. "Go get the medical kit."

The crewman disappeared below deck.

"What do you want to do with the raft?" the man asked.

"Cut her loose. In fact . . ." John went to Clarence, who gave him the life vests and paddles, which he threw in the water. "We won't be needin' those anymore."

"Why'd you do that?" the man asked.

"Looks like we drowned, don't it?"

The man smiled, then nodded at another crewman inside the cabin. He nodded back, and the boat's engines roared to life.

The FBI report likewise corroborates this particular detail: "He stated further that [name redacted] is telling that the subjects, as part of their plan before escaping, stated they were going to leave debris at some point strewn about so that it would appear they had wrecked and drowned."[15]

The boat set a course north for Marin Ranch Airport twenty miles away, just as Officer Checchi observed. Two hours later, the boat pulled into the mouth of Gallinas Creek near Buck's Landing in San Rafael. Except for a small dock, nothing but beach and scrub brush as far as the eye could see, the perfect drop-off spot for three escapees.

The driver powered down the engines and turned toward the dock. In the distance a man appeared with a flashlight in his hand. He turned it on and off twice, followed by a third flash. The boat brushed against the side of the dock.

"Hurry," the man with the flashlight said. "We don't have much time."

John turned toward their rescuers. "Thank you for everything."

Frank and Clarence nodded their thanks.

"You won't be feeling that way if you get caught. Get going while you can."

"Thank Mickey for us when you get the chance."

"Will do."

After the three had disembarked, the engines revved up and the boat backed away.

John spun around and faced the man on the pier whose face remained in the shadows. "I take it you're our ride."

He took a step closer. "Hello, John. It's been a while."

John recognized him in an instant. "Floyd. It's good to see ya."

The two shook hands.

"Hey Floyd," Clarence said with a wave.

"Can't think of anyone fool enough to drive all this way other than you, but we appreciate it."

"Wasn't so bad comin' out. Your sister told me some wild stories about y'all."

"Where is Nell? She here?"

Floyd pointed at a car parked not far away they hadn't noticed before. Sitting in the front seat, she waved from inside, her face beaming.

"Nell!" Clarence called out. He ran straight for the car.

She in turn jumped out and hugged her brother tight. "You don't know how long I waited to do that," she declared.

"Oh, Nell. It's so good to see ya. I feel better about this knowin' you're here."

She wiped away a tear. "You boys okay?"

"Right as rain," John said. They hugged.

"Save the reunion for later." Floyd tugged on John's arm. "Fred's waitin' for us at the airport."

Frank limped over to the car and sat in the back seat next to John and Clarence. Floyd sat in the driver's seat with Nell and darted off in a cloud of dust.

John patted Nell's shoulder. "I can't believe you drove all this way. How's Mama and Daddy, and everyone else?"

"They're good, though they miss y'all terribly. I wish there was a way you could tell them where you're goin'."

John looked at Clarence and Frank, whose stoic expressions let him know there was only one response. "I wish we could, but we can't take a chance of them sayin' somethin' to the police."

"They'll be the first ones they check," Clarence stated. "You know how Mama feels about lyin'. Don't want to put her in a difficult position."

Fred stood by the Beechcraft Baron twin-engine piston aircraft at the end of the runway when Floyd pulled up.

Nell turned around and hugged her brothers. "The two of you stay safe, okay?"

"You just take care of Mama and Daddy for us. We'll get word to you somehow."

"Come on." John pulled Clarence from Nell's embrace as Frank struggled out of the car.

"Hey boys," Fred said. "She's all gassed up and ready to go."

"Freddy, it's good to see ya too."

"We can talk on the plane. Long way to Mexico."

Fred met Frank when he reached the door. He grabbed his arm and helped him into the cabin. John and Clarence took the two seats in the back.

After slipping into the pilot's chair, Fred put on his headset and went through the safety check. Just before he started up the engines, he saw something in the distance. "Uh oh."

"What's wrong?" John asked.

"I see someone near the hangers. Might be a security guard."

A flashlight's beam momentarily illuminated the interior.

Clarence opened the door and got his sister's attention. "Nell. There's someone over that way. Try and hold him back until we take off." He closed the door and sat back down in his seat.

"Hold on," Fred said. "We're gonna do this quick and dirty."

He turned the engines over and throttled them up. At that moment Floyd met with the security guard walking toward the plane and the two became engaged in a heated discussion.

Fred stared down the runway and took his foot off the brakes. The plane lurched forward then began picking up speed. Both engines grew louder as Fred increased power, until all at once he pulled back on the control wheel and the plane lifted off the ground.

When he banked the plane over, John looked down at the airport. Floyd and the security guard were still engaged in a heated argument.

John smiled and sat back in his seat. "We made it. We actually made it."

CHAPTER 23

Heads Will Roll

Some people think that the truth can be hidden with a little cover-up and decoration. But as time goes by, what is true is revealed, and what is fake fades away.

—ISMAIL HANIYEH

ON THE MORNING OF JUNE 12, 1962, CORRECTIONAL OFFICER BILL Long started his day enjoying breakfast with his wife, Jean. Years later, the only shared memory both had of that morning was Bill complaining about the AM radio station that Jean listened to was playing Tommy Roe's hit single "Sheila" over and over again.

Carrying his steel thermos of fresh coffee, he made the hike up the steep hill with the other officers about to begin their shift. After a routine briefing, the guards prepared for the morning count. Senior Officer Lawrence Bartlett, known as Sarge, didn't show up at the desk as promptly as the others. Bill remembered Sarge in a panic:

> Bartlett was coming in my direction hot-foot'n it, and he's about twenty feet away and he starts yelling, Bill, Bill, Bill! I got a guy here who won't get up for the count! So, I went up to B-150, which was John Anglin's cell. I went up to the bars, knelt down, I reached in with my left hand to tap him on the head and it felt like it crumbled, and the head flopped off onto the floor. People who were observing me said that I jumped back about four feet. That's when all hell broke loose and the captain started ringing the bell.[1]

The FBI report described the guards finding out about the escape this way:

> During the 7:15 a.m. standup count . . . [name redacted] came running up to his desk at 7:20 a.m. and stated "We either have a dead man or a dummy in the cell block, I can't wake him up, I patted on the pillow and nothing happened." "I went to the B cell block, number 150 which is the cell of inmate JOHN ANGLIN. I reached in to tap him on the head and it felt like it crumbled. I immediately slapped at the head and it rolled on the floor. I shouted to the other guards, 'it is a dummy,' and I immediately threw off the blanket and stepped to cell 152 and slapped off the blanket noticing this was also a dummy. I immediately checked the cell of FRANK LEE MORRIS number 138 and noted it was a dummy also. I immediately sounded the escape alarm. . . . I noted the rear air vent partitions on both the ANGLINs cells had been kicked out. I then noticed MORRIS' cell to be the same. . . . I then returned to [name redacted] cell and [name redacted] was holding up a cardboard duplicate of the air vent and was beating it with his fist.[2]

Clearly, the inmate holding the cardboard vent cover was Allen West.

James Bulger also remembered the moment when the guards discovered the three gone, which he wrote about in his first letter.

> John Clarence and Frankie gave all of us a happy day on June 12 at 7:10 AM when "Sarge" to get Frankie up for stand up count pushed or slapped his head and it fell on the floor he leaped back in HORROR thought his head on floor guard in gun-walk kept hollering What's the matter—Sarge got his voice back and hollered "Morris is gone!" We erupted in cheers drowning out the cusses of the guards.

The Sarge's reaction is quite understandable. At 6:55 a.m. sharp, the deputy warden or lieutenant on duty sounded his whistle and the inmates stepped out of their cells, then faced the mess hall. On the second whistle, they closed up ranks in single file on each tier. However, the second whistle never sounded. In three cells no one came out. One of the guards angrily called for the men, most likely threatening them with a form of

punishment if they didn't coop-
erate. When they didn't comply,
Bartlett went to Morris's cell first.
He found him still "asleep" in his
bed. When he tried to roust him
awake, his dummy head fell onto
the floor. Believing someone had
cut Morris's head off during the
night, the Sarge jumped back
with a scream. He soon realized
something even worse had happened. When Bartlett checked
Clarence's cell, he also discovered
him missing, then John after.

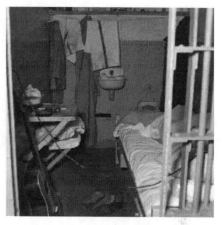

Clarence's empty cell after the escape
FBI

At that moment, according
to Bulger in another letter, "When 'Sarge' hollered to guard in the Gun
Walk 'Morris is Missing!' We all let out a cheer that lasted for 5 minutes.

"In less than fifteen minutes, the guards knew that the three inmates
were missing. In his cell, Allen West held up the vent from his wall,
which he'd painstakingly broken through, only to be left behind. He
banged on it and said to the guards, 'You may as well lock me up, too. I
planned the entire escape!'"[3]

In a stroke of luck for the escapees, Warden Blackwell happened
to be away at the time. His second-in-command, Acting Warden Art
Dollison, was notified and hurried out the door of his apartment a few
minutes after the sirens sounded. By 8:00 a.m., an all-points bulletin had
been issued for the escapees.[4]

A massive search machine was set in motion from the prison control
center, an office lined with bulletproof glass in the heart of the penitentiary's security system.

According to procedures, they notified the San Francisco Police, the
California Highway Patrol, the Coast Guard, and the Federal Bureau
of Prisons in Washington. A Coast Guard helicopter, two forty-foot
patrol boats, and a hundred-foot cutter manned with scuba-diving teams
immediately headed for the prison and assisted in the search.

Communication center

Control room

SAN FRANCISCO HISTORY CENTER, SAN FRAN-

NATHAN LYNCH

CISCO PUBLIC LIBRARY

With a field office located in San Francisco, the FBI dispatched agents to the island upon notification of the escape and took command. The 264 prisoners were brought into the dining room for breakfast and then locked in their cells for the rest of the day. Blackwell suspended normal work assignments and shut down the prison factories.

The rest of the guards were called at their homes in San Francisco and upon arrival formed into search squads. Not an inch of the island

Deploying the guards, weapons in hand
SAN FRANCISCO HISTORY CENTER, SAN FRANCISCO PUBLIC LIBRARY

went unexamined, including the old cells beneath the present prison structure.

Coastguardsmen in small boats, accompanied by prison guards, poked into the caves and recesses that lined the water's edge.

Coast Guard looking for the escapees
SAN FRANCISCO HISTORY CENTER, SAN FRANCISCO PUBLIC LIBRARY

Boats and helicopters working together.
SAN FRANCISCO HISTORY CENTER, SAN FRANCISCO PUBLIC LIBRARY

Warden Blackwell, who was on vacation at Lake Berryessa in Napa County at the time with his wife, Laveta, and son, Swayne, had been contacted by radio. He returned to Alcatraz and coordinated the search with the other agencies.

In the end, their combined efforts uncovered nothing on or around the island—the three had vanished without a trace.[5]

The night before, John had made certain the life vests, paddles, and raft had been cast adrift in the water after they had boarded the boat. Based on the information Schibline had provided him the day before the escape, he knew low tide that night occurred at 2:55 a.m., which pulled the debris toward the Golden Gate Bridge. But when the tides reversed at 8:43 a.m., they brought everything back into the bay. The raft, along with the other items, were carried in the direction of Angel Island. Sometime that morning, their raft came to rest on the beach.

At a distance of two and a half miles from Alcatraz, Angel Island figured to be a likely landing spot for the three. An initial interrogation of West by the guards confirmed that had indeed been their plan, which is noted in the FBI report:

Angel Island
NATHAN BARTEAU (UNSPLASH)

███████████████████████████, 561st M. P. Detachment, San Francisco Presidio, led a detachment of 35 Military Police and soldiers in a search of Angel Island on June 12, 1962. A small group of Military Police was left on this island overnight. On the following day, ██████████ made available 134 soldiers who worked with Special Agents of the FBI in a massive detailed search of Angel Island, including more than 100 deserted buildings. Coupled with this search was a search by Special Agents in small boats of the Angel Island beaches, some of which were inaccessible from the ground. No evidence was found to indicate the Escapees ever reached this island.

FBI FILES

Subjects possibly made good escape by utilizing home made raft. Confidential information from source in penitentiary indicated subjects would attempt to reach Angel Island located due north in San Francisco Bay from penitentiary and then cross Raccoon Strait to effect escape through Marin County, California. Source also indicated subjects would then attempt to steal automobile and perpetrate burglary or robbery of shopping center clothing store.[6]

Since the only way off Angel Island is by boat, the authorities surmised the escapees planned on stealing one after landing on shore, then heading for Marin. According to West, they then planned on stealing an automobile, robbing a clothing store so they'd blend in easier, and making their getaway to Oregon.

Losing no time, a military police detachment stationed at the Presidio in San Francisco was dispatched to Angel Island. But despite a thorough search by military police, they found nothing and left the island. No mention was made of any raft.[7]

Two days later, a Coast Guard cutter picked up a paddle floating about two hundred yards off the southern shore of Angel Island.

Later that day, a U.S. Army Corps of Engineers debris boat picked up two olive drab wallet-type pouches from the water a half mile east of Alcatraz. These pouches contained the names, addresses, letters, and photos of the Anglins' friends and relatives. And then on June 15, FBI agents found a Mae West–style life preserver, similar to one left behind on top of the cellblock, at Fort Cronkhite Beach on the Pacific Coast twenty miles away.[8]

And on June 22, one of the prison boats plucked a deflated life vest made of the same raincoat material out of the water fifty yards from the island, the last item found tied to the escape.

Recovered paddle
FBI

Recovered Mae West life vest
FBI

No additional debris was ever recovered, and no cars were reported stolen or businesses broken into. For the FBI, the collection of debris, along with no sign of their raft, told them and other authorities all they needed to know: the escapees most likely drowned in the middle of the bay, their bodies carried out with the tide past the Golden Gate Bridge, never to be seen again. But is that what actually happened?

The FBI, guards, and police certainly had enough evidence to suggest John, Clarence, and Frank hadn't survived. After all, the items retrieved from the water were telling clues. However, as we discussed in the previous chapter, John had planned on scattering debris in the bay as proof they had perished in the hopes authorities would call off the search.

And what of the raft? The FBI report makes no mention of it being found. The report also states that a search of Angel Island was made, with the military police finding nothing there connected with the escape. The FBI surmised the raft must have sunk, taking the three with it.

But what if evidence exists that shows the raft not only remained seaworthy but had been found by two Alcatraz guards, and that information had become known to the prison inmates, which Bulger makes mention of in a letter: "Next day after discovery, hours later heard that they found raft by a guard." Of course, this could've been nothing more than hopeful talk between inmates. No doubt, wild rumors flourished in the prison regarding the three's whereabouts days after their escape. But does any form of reliable information exist in regard to the raft's disposition? The answer is yes. In fact, three key pieces of evidence have been discovered.

Cliff Fish was first hired as a guard at Alcatraz back in 1938 and retired in 1963. Originally from Aubrey, Kansas, he moved to Oakland in 1936 with his wife. A friend suggested he apply for a job as a prison guard when a position opened up at the height of the Depression. Cliff leapt at the chance. His starting pay: $1,680 a year.[9]

Correctional Officer Clifford Fish had been a prison guard for twenty-four years when the escape occurred. During his tenure, he mixed with some of Alcatraz's most infamous inmates: George "Machine Gun" Kelly, Al Capone, Roy Gardner, and Alvin "Creep" Karpis. He also helped subdue the most violent prison escape attempt in 1946, in which two guards and three prisoners were killed. He had experienced much over the years, so it should be no surprise that he was asked to search for the escapees using one of the transport boats.

Years later, around 1999, Officer Fish was interviewed by Chuck Stucker, the son of an Alcatraz guard, about his participation in the search, a transcript of which was provided to us by Alcatraz expert and author Michael Esslinger in 2020.

Remembering the events as though they happened yesterday, he recalled with crystal clarity the moment the guards discovered the

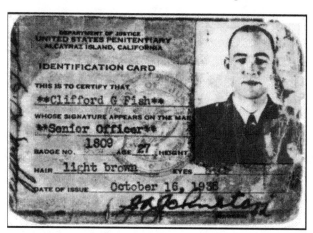

Clifford Fish Alcatraz identification card
UNITED STATES PENITENTIARY, ALCATRAZ

escape: "Guys [were] running all around looking at this and that trying to find out where they got out. . . . They knew they got on top of the cell block, but they didn't know where they went from there."

The guards combed every part of the island but found nothing. "They didn't know where they went from there. They just disappeared."

Realizing time was of the essence and with an eight-hour head start by John, Clarence, and Frank, the search area expanded beyond the island, and so Fish was paired with a fellow correctional officer and given the job of looking for the three on the bay. "They . . . told me . . . you go down and get Olaf. . . . He's the chief. You take the boat and go as long as you want, wherever you want. . . . So, they gave me a .30–06 and a .45 . . . and [we] walked down . . . under armed officers down to the dock to the boat. Got on the boat. . . . I know Olaf. . . . He'd been an old Swede fisherman all of his life. He knew those tides."

Of course, neither officer knew which way the escapees had gone, and they didn't really have an idea where they should look, so they took their boat out and went this way and that.

When their search didn't turn up anything, Olaf found a book on the transport that charted the tides. He said, "What time you figure those guys got out of there?"

"And I [Fish] said, 'Well I don't know, but I'd figure it was around so and so.'"

And he said, "Well, if that was about the time they got out . . . there was an incoming tide." Then he said, "They didn't head out the Golden Gate. But they wasn't blown out through the Golden Gate. . . . They're somewhere within this region." So he put the book back and thought for a while, then said, "Let me have that wheel."

Olaf took command of the transport and headed up through what's called Raccoon Straits, which is between the north strait of California and Angel Island. They went along at a slow speed looking for anything out of place or if the escapees' raft had beached somewhere. Then Olaf saw something. "Wait a minute. . . . Do you see what I see over there on that sandbar?"

Fish looked in the direction he indicated. "Well, there's something black over there, but I can't tell what it is."

"Oh no." He said, "I think that's raincoats."

Before the two had been assigned the search on the water, Fish had been told about the raft and how it was glued together from raincoats, no doubt information provided by West. So they decided to investigate. Their suspicions were confirmed not long after. It was the raft.

So Olaf said, "What do we do now?"

And I said, "Well, I gotta look. I'm supposed to. That's my job."

Olaf warned Fish about going on the island and searching for the escapees since they didn't know if the three were armed. Danger or not, Fish stepped off the boat and jumped onto the beach. He checked the raft first. To his surprise, he discovered it full of blood. As he described, "Looked like they had been sticking pigs. . . . You lift the boat and it'd run from one end to the other."

His senses heightened, he looked around but couldn't see any tracks. So he started making circles around the raft in the hope something out of place caught his eye. The wider the circle grew, the more Fish's attention focused on a line of trees about a quarter of a mile away. He searched the immediate area a little longer but didn't find anything. What he couldn't figure out was how the escapees could have run for those trees without leaving any tracks.

But with the raft on the beach, he figured they must be there. "Against my own will, scared to death, [I] started to go on through those trees looking for anything I could find."

Much to his frustration, and some relief, Fish didn't find a thing during his thorough search. With nothing left to do, he gave up and returned to the boat. Olaf had kept the engines running to keep it up on the sand.

He said, "What do we do now?"

"Well, we got two choices. Either leave the boat here for somebody else to find or for us to take it in."

"If you leave this boat here the next high tide's gonna take it some-place else," Olaf asserted. "The high tide swept in here. That boat went on the high tide up on the sand and it's sittin' there. . . . The next high tide is gonna wash it off. . . . I suggest we take it in."

So he gave Fish a rope and they tied the raft to the boat, then towed it back to the island.

Upon their return to Alcatraz, he noted how there didn't seem to be much commotion about the raft. The FBI examined it, along with the guards and prison bureau, but nothing more than that. Just a casual acceptance about the raft's retrieval, as though they hadn't been surprised it didn't sink.

When Fish returned the next day, the raft was gone. As he recalled,

> I've never seen nor heard of that boat since. And I don't know where it is. . . . And I don't know where the blood come from. I don't know whether they all got into a fight and killed one another or what . . . but whatever happened to that boat, whether it's in the bureau of prisons or inside a museum, or what, I Don't Know! And I don't know what happened to those three guys. They disappeared.

The story Cliff Fish tells is quite compelling. He and the officer named Olaf had been tasked with finding the missing men, though they had no idea where they might be. Just take a transport and search around the bay. It should also be noted the two guards hadn't been given the information West provided about Angel Island as a possible destination for the escapees. Even without this knowledge, Olaf's years of experience at sea helped him figure out where the raft might have gone after nine hours in the water, which led them to Angel Island.

Cliff and Olaf decided to take the raft back to Alcatraz, where it was examined by the FBI and prison staff. The way they brought the raft back is also quite telling. The two didn't put the raft into their boat. Rather, they towed it back, which meant the raft was still inflated. This then begs the question: how could John, Clarence, and Frank have drowned if the raft remained seaworthy? Fish also said he looked around Angel Island but found no footprints or any evidence the three had been there. What is more likely is that the raft had been carried by the tide to the island, just as Olaf had deduced, after the escapees left it in the water.

With the raft now safely back at Alcatraz, word spread quickly among the guards and prisoners it had been found, as Bulger indicated in his letter. The authorities also notified the police about the raft's discovery, which they sent as an APB.

Years after the release of the FBI files to the public in 2002, I acquired the very same APB through the Freedom of Information Act. There's no mistaking the information provided by the Marin County Sheriff's Office on June 12: "Raft believed used be escapees located on

Police APB stating the raft found
MARIN COUNTY SHERIFF'S OFFICE/FBI

Angel Island."

The discovery of the police APB raises questions in the FBI file regarding the raft's disposition. The report emphatically states: "No evidence was found to indicate the Escapees ever reached this island." Yet Cliff Fish, a twenty-four-year veteran at the time, claimed he discovered the raft on Angel Island with another guard and towed it back to Alcatraz. The police APB also claims the raft had been found on Angel Island. And lastly, James Bulger said in his letter the inmates knew the raft had been discovered after the escape. Put all the evidence together, and two possibilities emerge: either the FBI made a mistake when they claimed the raft hadn't been found on the island, or they lied.

But the evidence the three survived the escape doesn't end there. Take, for instance, the life vest found in the water on June 22.

The discovery of the jacket was made as a result of personnel stationed on Alcatraz in connection with their regular watch of the island, observing debris floating 100 years east of the island. Warden Blackwell utilizing a [*sic*] Alcatraz boat recovered the jacket and immediately telephoned the San Francisco Office. According to SAC Price, the jacket is similar in every respect to the one left behind on Alcatraz by the subjects and the other which was washed up on the Pacific shore not far from the Golden Gate Bridge June 15, 1962. Examination of the jacket . . . showed it had brown stains, possibly blood. The valve was open in a crimped condition, giving the appearance of having teeth marks. It is entirely possible that the escapee wearing this jacket attempted to prevent the air from escaping by squeezing this valve with his teeth.[10]

Teeth marks on the valve suggest it had been used. Later, the FBI detailed the results of their tests of the life vest:

The life preservers were tested for their ability to retain air. They were inflated until firm, and then weights were placed on them. It was necessary first to seal three punctures in Q5. Specimen Q3 appeared to be completely airtight, remaining firm for several hours. Specimens Q4 and Q5 lost most of their air in about an hour. However, the rate of deflation was slow, and pressure could no doubt be maintained by mouth.[11]

Of the vests the FBI recovered, they either held air outright or slowly leaked, though the report indicated the person wearing it could've easily reinflated the device as needed. In short, as long as the three wore their life vests, they had little chance of drowning.

Early on in the investigation, the authorities believed that finding family photos and addresses in the pouches was a clear sign something had gone wrong during the escape.

On June 14, debris boats searching the bay for any suspicious objects picked up two olive drab wallet-type pouches two or three feet below the surface of the water approximately half a mile east of Alcatraz Island. They contained pictures of John and Clarence, among others, as well as several letters and names and addresses of numerous individuals.[12]

The following is a partial list of what searchers found in the pouch two days after the escape:

- People's names and addresses
- A five-page handwritten letter signed, "You are my special angel"
- A photo inscribed, "Love Mother." Also says, "Son Clarence from MA"
- Photograph of child inscribed, "To my uncle"
- Family snapshot with notation on reverse, "This is the family at Thanksgiving dinner"
- Picture of young girl with notation on reverse, "To my Uncle John"
- Color photograph with the caption, "Your brothers, Alfred Anglin, Clarence Anglin"
- Photo of young boy with notation on reverse, "1961"
- Three colored snapshots of man bearing name "John Anglin"
- Picture of elderly woman
- Photo of woman next to car with notation, "This is Alfred"[13]

In all, over ninety items were retrieved from the pouches found in the water. When the family asked when those things would be sent home, the FBI said they were part of the investigation and could not be returned. Some sixty years later, the family has not received a single photograph or anything else found in the pouches, nor can the U.S. Marshals account for their whereabouts.

In regard to the five-page letter, I believe it's worth noting a certain fact I discovered years later. In the photo of John's cell the FBI took a day after escape, you can clearly see a group of letters under his foldable desk.

Before anything had been disturbed, the escapees' cells were photographed by the FBI for the purpose of collecting evidence. In the back of John's cell on the left, his shirt hangs on a hook. Below that are his pants and belt. Hanging on the sink pipe is his white shirt used for working in the kitchen. And on a hook on the far right, John's raincoat, the same type of things found in Clarence's and Frank's cells. But what differs from his cell compared to the other two is a large number of letters bound together. On top of the letters is a raincoat sleeve, just like the one found in the

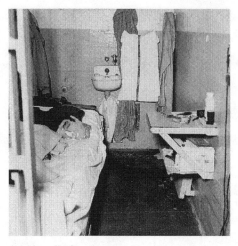

John's cell after the escape
FBI

bay. But how can this be? This photo was taken the morning of the escape. How could John lose the pouch filled with letters and photos if they were in his cell that morning? Was the embarrassment to the federal prison system so great that evidence was planted to make it appear the three men had drowned? Certainly, these discrepancies merit examination. If the FBI omitted the raft's discovery on Angel Island, one can conclude other parts of the report also contain errors, even possibly a cover-up.

Investigators and people alike have argued for years these were the most precious things to the escapees, which they'd never lose in the water, and so they're used this as proof the three must have drowned. Even today, sixty years later, you still hear these arguments being made.

Close-up of the letters
FBI

In the end, the combined search between the FBI, police, and prison guards found nothing except a few items floating in the water. The authorities concluded the three died during the escape, but new evidence provided in this book makes the case they did survive and were whisked away by their childhood friend, Fred Brizzi. But before the story of their escape shifts toward the next phase of their lives, one last piece of evidence necessitates inclusion.

Warden Blackwell received a postcard on June 18, six days after the escape. It was signed by Frank, John, and Clarence, which simply conveyed they sent it. The FBI examined the postcard, but fingerprint and handwriting analysis proved inconclusive. Was this a final taunt made by the escapees or someone else having fun with the warden?

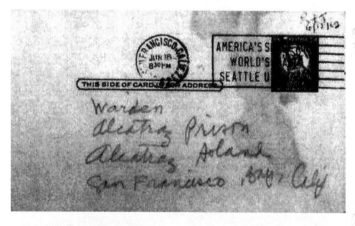

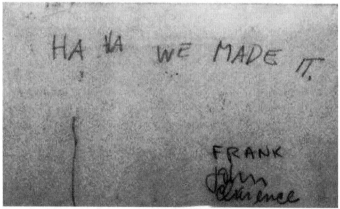

Did the escapees send this postcard to Warden Blackwell?
FBI

A guard inspects the escape hole.
FBI

B-Block staging area. Note the hanging blankets.
FBI

An air vent cover pushed onto the cellblock roof
FBI

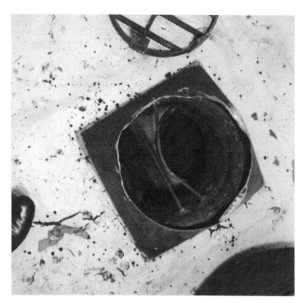

Bent bar to make room for escapees
FBI

The three's sooty footprints heading away from the cellblock
FBI

CHAPTER 24

Laying Low

It is a joy to be hidden, and disaster not to be found.
                                    —D. W. WINNICOTT

FRED LINED UP THE PLANE AS THE SUN HUNG LOW ON THE HORIZON.
Exhausted, John, Clarence, and Frank slept most of the flight, probably
the best night of sleep they had had in years. A farm with green fields
below appeared through the clouds. Not far away from the farm, a runway had been carved out of the dirt, not unlike the one in Tijuana.

His hands firm on the controls, Fred looked over his shoulder. "Hey
you sleepyheads, we're here. Wake up."

Frank stirred in his seat first, then John and Clarence.

"How long we been out?"

"A few hours," Fred replied.

They rubbed the sleep from their eyes and looked out the windows. A
scattering of farms dotted the landscape. From what John could tell from
the color of the crops, the farmers grew a mixture of fruits and vegetables,
and, of course, marijuana.

"Buckle up. It's gonna get bumpy real quick."

The three straightened in their seats and locked in tight.

Fred inched the control wheel forward. When the left wing dipped
left he leveled the plane out. The back wheels hit the ground hard, followed by the nose wheel. Vibrations rippled through the interior as Fred
powered the engines down and applied the brakes. The plane jostled

Brizzi at the controls
KEN WIDNER

somewhat on the uneven surface, finally stopping near the end of the runway.

"Are we in Mexico?" Clarence asked.

"Sí," Fred replied. "Bueno, ven a la granja."

Fred laughed.

"What he say?" John asked.

"Welcome to the farm," Frank translated.

Fred opened the side door and hopped onto the ground. He stretched his arms as he looked around.

Frank stepped off next, making sure he landed on his good leg, followed by Clarence and John. Still dressed in their wetsuits, the hot sun would roast them alive if they didn't change into cooler clothes.

In the distance a roof peaked above purple jacaranda trees. Around them, fields of marijuana plants stretched into the distance. Beyond that, armed security patrolled the edge of the property. Clarence let out a whistle. "That's a lot of money out there."

A reddish-brown dust cloud appeared not far from the farmhouse, moving toward them at a steady speed. Soon, a jeep materialized at the base of the cloud. "Right on time," Fred declared.

The jeep stopped hard in front of the four. John Kelly took off his sunglasses, the pilot who flew them to Tijuana with Mickey and Candy four years before.

"Hey guys. Welcome to Mexico." Kelly let out a yawn. "You hungry for some breakfast?"

"Starvin'," Clarence said without hesitation.

Frank hobbled to the jeep and sat in the front seat.

"We'll have to get that checked out. A lot of nasty bugs down here." Frank grunted his reply.

"So, what's the word on Alcatraz?" John asked.

"Get in," Kelly replied. "I'll tell you about it over some huevos rancheros."

At the farmhouse, Kelly pointed to a table in the corner of the kitchen and the five sat. Behind them, two women spoke in rapid-fire Spanish as they prepared breakfast.

Clarence breathed in the flavorful aromas. "Man, that smells good. I just might like stayin' in Mexico for a while."

Kelly handed each of them an envelope.

"What's this?" John asked.

"Some money, and fake passports. As long as you're here, you'll need those."

Frank flipped through the bills in his envelope. "Must be a thousand, easy."

"Compliments of Mickey Cohen. He did the same for Candy when she hid in Mexico a few years back."

The women plated the food and brought everything to the table.

Clarence scooped up some eggs, diced tomatoes and peppers mixed in, and savored the flavors on his tongue. "Umm, this is good."

Rather than eat, Frank crossed his arms.

"What's the matter?" Kelly asked. "You not hungry?"

"You said you'd tell us the news from Alcatraz."

"Yeah, right." Kelly looked back at the women. "Maria, alguna noticia sobre la fuga en la radio?"

"Sí. Sí." She spun around and turned on a radio next to her. A man's voice steadily grew in volume. To their surprise, he spoke perfect English.

" . . . though authorities haven't said yet if the escapees are armed, they are presumed to be very dangerous. If you see or encounter them, call the police immediately." The announcer took a breath. "To repeat our top story, authorities announced a half hour ago that John Anglin, his brother, Clarence, and Frank Morris, were discovered missing early this morning at Alcatraz Federal Penitentiary located in San Francisco. Though details of their escape have not been provided, a search has commenced on water, land, and sea on and around the island. Warden Blackwell is expected to make a statement within the hour."

In the recording Fred Brizzi made when he told the Anglin family about flying the three to Mexico, he gave the following account: "Well, they were in Mexico, just outside of Mexico City . . . up in an airplane the next morning about 10:30, something like that, 9:30 their time down there."

He went on to say the three were provided with money, IDs, and passports, things they'd need to start new lives.

John turned off the radio.

"Why'd you do that," Clarence asked.

"I heard all I needed to. They think we're still there somewhere since it's where they're searchin' . . . which means West didn't talk."

"You sayin' we made it?" Clarence asked rhetorically. "We're actually free?"

"We are," John replied, his voice somber. "But it also means we'll never see Mama or Daddy again, or anyone else we knows. Can't take the chance of them knowin' where we are. I'm sure the feds will be talkin' with them real soon, if they haven't already."

"You know," Clarence pondered after the took another bite of eggs. "West could be here with us right now enjoying this breakfast. So close, but he didn't make it."

"Oh yeah," Kelly replied, "The other guy. I almost forgot about him."

He had trouble gettin' out of his cell," John recounted. "We tried helpin' him, but he just stayed put. So we left without him."

Frank laughed. "Naw, he chickened out. Too scared to come with us."

Many have asked the same question about West over the years. Why didn't he go with the others? Did he underestimate the time it would take finish digging out the back of his cell, as he claimed in the FBI report, or might there have been another reason? Whitey certainly had his opinion. In a letter, he wrote, "Everyone felt he chickened out at the last minute." If true, what caused West to be afraid? One reason might have been Frank Morris. He had threatened to kill West more than once if he talked with the other inmates about the escape. Bulger shared this particular fact: "Morris made a knife from dinner knife from the mess hall . . . if we walk into a trap I'm doing West in." Or perhaps West feared Morris intended to finish him off at the water's edge before heading for the transport. We'll never know for sure. However, West said when interrogated by the FBI after the escape that he only participated in the planning so that he could bring his personal problems to the attention of the court and that he never intended to leave the penitentiary.[1]

If the West account is accurate, then that suggests he never intended to escape with the others. He went through the motions, but his real intention was to perhaps receive some form of leniency.

Or West had another reason for not going. When the lockdown finally ended and life at Alcatraz slowly returned to normal, Robert Schibline met up with West. According to Schibline, this was how the conversation went: "I asked why he didn't join them. He laughed and said, 'Cause they were gonna die! Look, I had two years and I was out. I was not gonna risk dying or getting more time in the hole. Look, I remember the loud boom, from the roof that night. I knew it was them; we all did. It was 10:20 p.m. and I just knew the guards heard what we did.'"[2]

A reasonable explanation, though the facts speak otherwise. West took a lot of risks the previous six months, things one wouldn't expect from someone afraid of getting caught. For example, he spent weeks digging out the back of his cell. He also smuggled the vacuum cleaner motor into his cell, which would've cost him big if it had been found by the guards. West also spent weeks on top of the cellblock making the oars and life vests. If a guard had gone up there and caught him in the act, they'd have thrown him into the Hole for an attempted escape and added two years to his sentence, if not longer.

Far more likely, West intended to escape with the other three, but as the day approached he thought better of it. This would account for stopping work on the back of his cell on April 25 when he could have easily finished before June 11. Also, inmates nearby heard him crying in his cell that night, strongly indicating his mental state about being left behind. Later, when prisoners accused him of "chickening out," West came up with a story about never intending to go so they'd think better of him. If this is what he hoped, it didn't work.

The prison was put in lockdown starting on June 12, which allowed the FBI to interview all 267 inmates. To a person, none of them claimed they knew anything about the escape until that morning. Lacking evidence to the contrary, Warden Blackwell had no choice but to lift the lockdown several days later.

In the second letter Bulger sent me, he recounted what happened after the inmates were let out:

> Warden Blackwell after we were off Dead Lock and out of our cells looked at Jack Twinning a good friend of Frankie Morris saw Jack Twinning smiling and remarked "Your real happy now!" Twinning said your Damn Right we all happy "They Made it" Blackwell . . . let out a mild growl.
>
> They shut the radio off—they didn't want us to hear any news of escape.
>
> When they finally put radio back on—we heard a song someone wrote about the escape—we cheered guards hated any mention—Song—A Mile and a quarter of treacherous water keeps men in Alcatraz is all I can remember—guard kept radio off at any mention some took it personal like the escape wasn't fair.
>
> On the yard 1st day over comes guard we called Herman the German—he was all upset.
>
> We egged him on when he said they blame me—Said well that's it you will never make acting Lt.—Report will follow most of your career the man who let the Escape happen.

Upon review of the escape, Blackwell suspended Charles German for twenty days. An investigation revealed he had not conducted the 11:30 p.m. head count required of him. German claimed he was behind schedule and didn't have enough time. Had he done so, the three might've been caught. None of the other guards were punished in any way.

One also cannot help but be amused by the song prison officials refused to let the inmates play on the radio, which had been inspired by the escape. Written by Sonny James, "A Mile and a Quarter" would understandably upset the guards and prison officials when they heard these opening lyrics:

A mile and a quarter of treacherous water keeps men in
Alcatraz
Three men did what folks have claimed for years could not
be done
Three men broke through prison walls and left there on the run
Tried to make a liar out of anyone who says
Once you're on the rock there's no escape from Alcatraz.[3]

As John had surmised, in the weeks and months that followed, FBI
agents interviewed anyone who might have heard from the three after

■■■■■■■■■■■■■■■■■■■■ was located in his cell by the
prison officers. It is noted that he had completed digging
in the vicinity of the ventilator area in his cell and he
could have left his cell and proceeded to the roof as did
the Escapees. In this regard he admits that he went to the

roof of the prison but found that they had left. He claimed
that he had just participated in the escape attempt so that
he could bring his personal problems to the attention of the
court and that he never intended to leave the penitentiary.

June 28, 1962

Correctional Officer Charles H. Herman, Jr.
United States Penitentiary
Alcatraz, California

Dear Mr. Herman:

    This is an advance notice, of at least 30 days of
proposed adverse action.

    It is proposed to suspend you from duty for twenty
(20) working days during period Monday, August 6, 1962
through Friday, August 31, 1962.

Warden Blackwell's reprimand of Charles Herman
GOLDEN GATE NATIONAL RECREATION AREA, PARK ARCHIVES

the escape. This included acquaintances, former coworkers, friends, and family. They talked with hundreds of people literally all over the country, from Albany, New York, to Seattle, Washington.[4] But at the top of the FBI's persons of interest list was the Anglin family.

Knowing how the brothers had a tendency of showing up at home after previous escapes, especially Clarence, they figured the family had made arrangements to rendezvous with them or provide the three with assistance in some way. With time of the essence, the FBI went to Ruskin first thing after the escape.

George Anglin sat in his chair listening to the radio, Rachel in the chair across from him knitting a sock.

The front door opened without any warning, and in walked two agents.

"What's the meanin' of this?" George asked as he rose from his chair. "Who are you people?"

Robert appeared from the back bedroom. "What's goin' on, Daddy?"

The taller of the two agents showed his ID. "My name's Agent Smith. And this is Agent Johnson. We're here to question you about your sons' escape."

"Don't know nothin' about that," George replied, "so you might as well turn around and go the way you came."

"You'll sit down and answer every question. If you don't, then we'll arrest you for obstructing a government investigation."

Rachel looked at Robert, then at George. "George, maybe it's best if we cooperated. This is a Christian home and we don't want no trouble."

"Fine." He sat down. "Ask your questions, but I already told you, we don't know where the boys are at. We haven't heard from them since Clarence mailed us his last letter."

"Would you mind showing me that?" Agent Smith asked.

Rachel put down her sewing. "I'll go get it."

"Make that all the letters John and Clarence sent," the second agent barked.

For the next several hours both agents asked the three the same questions over and over about what they knew of the escape. Had the brothers contacted them in advance? Were their siblings told anything?

Had they received any mysterious phone calls? George told them that wasn't possible since they didn't have a phone.

Both agents read the letters the brothers wrote during their incarceration, but none of them hinted at anything escape related.

Agents Smith and Johnson finally concluded their interrogation, but before they left the two warned the family about withholding information. If they heard from John and Clarence, they were to contact the FBI immediately. George assured them they would and then insisted the two leave.

After he closed the door, George turned around and faced his wife and son. "You don't say nothin' to nobody. You hear."

For the Anglins, the harassment by the FBI had only just begun. Members of the family often spotted a mysterious car outside their home, two men inside observing them. Their mail was also intercepted. The FBI tapped the phones of those members who lived elsewhere. The FBI was convinced the family knew more than what they had told them and attempted to get that information through a variety of means, some of it bordering on the illegal.

Several months later, the FBI returned to the Anglin home and questioned everyone again. And like before, George, Rachel. and their daughter, who happened to be there when the agents returned, insisted they hadn't heard from John and Clarence since the escape and had no idea where they might be.

When FBI agents interrogated the family a second time, they noted this interesting detail in their report: "She stated that her father and mother believed that if they were ever to hear from CLARENCE or JOHN ANGLIN again, that they would hear during the past Christmas season as they did not believe their sons would let Christmas go by without advising their parents that they were still alive."[5] Unbeknownst to the FBI, the daughter, whose name is redacted from the report, was more right than she knew about her brothers contacting the family at Christmas.

Their brother Robert had found out from Fred where he had taken John, Clarence, and Frank after he returned from Mexico. With the FBI hot on their trail, Robert wanted to make sure they were doing okay, plus remind them of the importance of not dropping their guard in Mexico. One little slip could tip off the authorities. So he had Fred fly him down to the farm. Robert also figured a visitor from home would help boost their spirits.

As Frank read a book in his room, John sat at the kitchen table with Clarence and finished lunch. Clarence scooped the last of the fried beans and washed it down with a beer.

The back door opened, and in came Fred, Robert close behind.

"Hey John, hey Clarence," Robert said in a casual manner.

"Man!" Clarence yelled. He jumped to his feet and gave his brother a heartfelt hug. "It's good to see ya. What are you doin' here?"

John shook his brother's hand. "Robert. I never expected to see you again."

"You can thank this guy." He pointed at Fred. "He agreed to let me see ya for a short visit. Can't stay too long or the feds might get suspicious."

"Sit down. Have a beer. You must be tired from the long flight."

"I'm not feeling too bad. Slept part of the way."

The three, along with Frank, spent the rest of the day talking about the escape and how things had gone for them since then. For the most part they were doing okay, but being stuck in the house 24/7 made for some long days. Only at night did they go outside and walk the property. Based on the newspaper stories and radio reports, the authorities hadn't let up on the search and showed no signs of slowing down. Robert also told them about the visits from the FBI and how the family had been followed and their mail intercepted. The three understood the chance Robert took coming down, but they appreciated him being there all the same.

Just before Robert and Fred left, Clarence pulled out a Christmas card from his pocket. "You give Mama this."

"We can't tell them where we are, but we can let 'em know we're okay and we're thinkin' about them."

Robert took the card. "I will, and I'll give it to them in a way they won't know I delivered it." He slipped the card into his pocket.

The brothers hugged each other, then Robert boarded the plane. Just before closing the door he said, "Fred here is gonna fly me up to Atlanta so I can let Alfred know you're safe. He's been powerful sad since you escaped. Thinks you didn't make it."

"Let him know there's room for one more in case he plans on joinin' us."

Robert laughed. "I'll give him the message."

Both engines turned over after Fred nodded at them from the pilot's seat. The plane barreled down the runway, then lifted into the sky.

Clarence patted his brother's shoulder and went back into the farmhouse.

Just as he promised, Robert visited Alfred at United States Penitentiary, Atlanta, and let him know the truth about the escape. He couldn't say so openly, of course, so both brothers employed the secret code they had developed years earlier. "Following the escape, when the newspapers were reporting the Subjects were presumed dead, ANGLIN was very morose and gloomy, but shortly thereafter, he received a visit from another brother, known as (name redacted) and from that point on ANGLIN was his normal, cheery self again."[6]

According to Alfred's cellmate, his disposition changed after Robert's visit. He went from sullen to happy in an instant. Only one reason that makes sense: he knew his brothers were alive.

The FBI report went on to say that Alfred told his cellmate on several occasions his brothers were alive and well. He, however, never mentioned where they were hiding out, though the cellmate's impression based on his knowledge of the brothers was that they were probably in Mexico.[7]

It is interesting to note the cellmate shared his belief the three were living in Mexico at that time. Apparently, Robert didn't tell Alfred the three's location, just that they were alive and well. This was most likely done for the escapees' protection. Though well intentioned, Alfred might have let it slip where his brothers were hiding if interrogated by the FBI, aggressively or otherwise.

Robert visited Alfred again, this time at Kilby Prison in Montgomery, Alabama. On September 18, 1963, Alfred had been transferred from Atlanta and started serving his state time for the bank robbery. Though he had been given fifteen years in federal prison, he had only done five and a half years of it.

According to family history, Robert and Alfred went to the restroom and Alfred told him that he had gotten word from John and Clarence and planned on reuniting with them after his release.

As the Christmas season approached, Robert kept the other promise he made to his brothers. He went to his parent's house and slipped the card into their mailbox unobserved.

Since people's signatures are like fingerprints, different from one another's, it is a simple matter of comparing Clarence's signature on the card with the letters he wrote from Alcatraz.

Even a superficial examination shows the way he wrote his name and "Mom" are exactly alike.

Though never admitted outside the family, they knew in December 1962 that John and Clarence hadn't died during the escape.

More Christmas cards followed the next three years, just as the parents believed would happen if they were alive. The following are two examples of Christmas cards signed by Clarence and John.

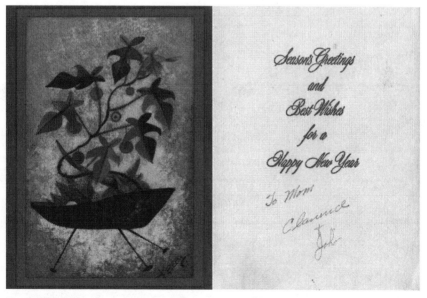

The 1962 Christmas card
KEN WIDNER

In 2015, handwriting experts concluded that Clarence's and John's writing styles on the Christmas cards matched their letters.

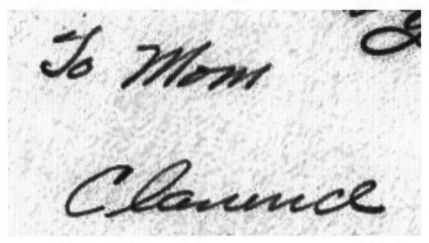

Close-up of Christmas card signature

June 1961 Alcatraz letter

May 1962 Alcatraz letter

March 1961 Alcatraz letter

Note John's signature and use of dots after the words on the Christmas card.

John writes "Christmas" a certain way.

November 1960—John's Alcatraz signature and dots

December 1960—John writes "Christmas" in his Alcatraz letter the same as the card.

CHAPTER 25

The Deaths

There is no such thing as freedom, only prison walls that forever change shape.

—CAROLYN CRANE

THE FIRST DEATH, MARCH 21, 1963

"Do ya hear that?"

John listened a moment and looked up. "Sounds like a plane." Clarence and John had been out riding on the farm when Fred flew overhead. He buzzed the field, then banked to the right.

It had been months since they had last seen him; the brothers hoped he brought with him news from home. Stories about the escape in the local papers had dwindled over time, so Fred had become an even more important lifeline. But with attention toward Alcatraz fading, the three felt safe going about the property during the day, and even went to Mexico City on occasion and enjoyed a bit of nightlife.

Fred pulled up near the farmhouse, where John and Clarence met him.

"Hey Fred, good to see you again."

"How are the crops lookin' this go-around?"

"Is that all you got to say?" Clarence gave him a big bear hug. "Doin' well. Should be a good harvest. How are things back in Ruskin?"

"Everyone's fine. Let's go inside and grab a beer and I'll bring you up to speed. By the way, where's Frank?"

"Went into town a couple of hours ago. Said he was picking up something, but John and me think he's seein' some señorita."

Fred's smile flattened. "I hope he doesn't do anything stupid, like get caught."

As the three grabbed some beers from the fridge, John heard another Jeep in the distance. "That must be Frank. Told ya he'd be back."

Fred pulled out a newspaper from his travel bag after Frank entered. "I thought you'd wanna see this."

All three men's eyes doubled in size when they read the headline.

"They closed the Rock? I don't believe it."

"Hit the papers all over the place. Wasn't sure if the news made it down this far. But it's true, and to think it happened because of you three."

On March 21, 1963, United States Penitentiary, Alcatraz, closed after twenty-nine years of operation. The prison didn't shut down because of Morris and the Anglins, which many believed—even Whitey Bulger

Inmates led out
GOLDEN GATE NATIONAL RECREATION AREA, PARK ARCHIVES (3264)

subscribed to this idea, which he shared more than once in his letters. In reality, that decision was made long before the escape. When compared to housing inmates at other federal prisons, Alcatraz was deemed too expensive to continue operating. The facility was three times more expensive than every other federal prison (the daily per capita cost at Alcatraz was ten dollars, compared with three dollars at Atlanta). The increased expense was caused by the island's location—food, supplies, fuel, and so on all had to be transported by boat, including one million gallons of water each week. The federal government decided it was more cost-effective to redistribute the prison population than keep Alcatraz open.[1]

For everyone associated with Alcatraz, March 21, 1963, was the day the prison died.

"With Alcatraz closed," Clarence declared, "maybe they'll stop lookin' for us."

"I wouldn't count on it," Fred stated matter-of-factly. "Right now, their ledgers show three men missing, and they want everything to add up. That's when Alcatraz is really closed for them."

"Any word on our friends there?" John asked.

A melancholy Warden Blackwell leaves the island for the last time.
GOLDEN GATE NATIONAL RECREATION AREA, PARK ARCHIVES (17975.0273)

"If you mean Cohen and Bulger, nothing that I've heard, though I did read in the paper most were transferred to Leavenworth, Lewisburg, and Atlanta."

Clarence sat back in his chair and gulped down his beer. "Poor devils."

Later that evening John and Clarence found Fred on the porch as the sun hung low in the sky.

"Sure is a sight," Fred commented.

"Uh huh."

Clarence sat in the chair next to him. "Hey, I forgot to ask you earlier, did Man say anythin' about Alfred?"

"Only that he saw him last Christmas and let him know you was okay. He said the ACLU was still trying to get his case heard, but they weren't having much luck."

"I told Alfred that was a lost cause. Those people in Alabama want our blood and nothin' will satisfy 'em until they get it."

The ACLU is a nonprofit organization founded in 1920 for the purpose of defending and preserving "the individual rights and liberties

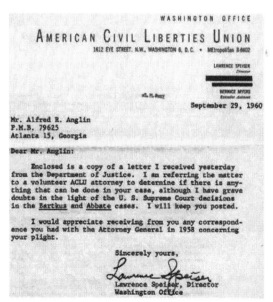

Response from the ACLU to Alfred
KEN WIDNER

guaranteed to every person in this country by the Constitution and laws of the United States."[2] Alfred believed his case merited their help.

The response Alfred received wasn't the news he had hoped for, but it also didn't discourage him either. The ACLU agreed to forward his request to an attorney but also warned of a case that had already gone before the U.S. Supreme Court on this very issue. Much to his disappointment, Alfred later found out the brothers' case did indeed fall under the previous ruling. "Abbate v. United States, 359 U.S. 187 (1959), is a decision of the U.S. Supreme Court. The decision held that the double jeopardy Clause of the Fifth Amendment to the U.S. Constitution does not prohibit the prosecution of a conspiracy in federal court under federal law when that same conspiracy has already resulted in a conviction in state court under state law."[3]

Loading up their latest harvest onto the plane, John helped Fred close the side door.

"I almost forgot to ask you about the roses. Were you able to get them to Mama?"

Fred put on his sunglasses. "Yep, just like you asked. Two dozen, and I left the card unsigned."

"Thanks for handlin' that for us. It means a lot to Clarence and me she gets somethin' special on her birthday."

The brothers never forgot their mother's birthday. They made sure she received roses every year until her death in 1973.

Fred climbed aboard the plane. "You boys stay safe. I'll see y'all in a few months."

Both engines sputtered to life, and the Beechcraft rolled down the runway. The plane angled upward and became airborne. After a soft turn away from the mountains, Fred faded out of sight.

Later that August, he returned as promised, but he also brought with him some bad news. Mickey Cohen had been badly beaten in prison.

Unfortunately for Mickey, he didn't have someone like Whitey or the brothers watching his back when he was transferred to Atlanta. On August 14, 1963, Burl Estes McDonald escaped a secure prison compound, entered an electronics repair training facility, and bludgeoned an unsuspecting Cohen into unconsciousness with an iron pipe. He underwent extensive neurosurgery, and following a two-week coma, doctors inserted a steel plate to replace the mangled bone fragments in the rear skull region. Though Cohen survived his attack, he was permanently disabled and walked with a cane for the rest of his life.[4]

The next day, Fred readied his plane for departure. John and Clarence stood at the edge of the runway.

"Guess I'll see you boys when I'm down this way again."

"Tell Mickey we're thinkin' about him."

"I will, which reminds me. He's plannin' on expanding his operation south. You boys be interested?"

"Just how far south are we talkin'?"

"Brazil."

"Brazil?" Clarence balked. "You're kidding, right?"

"It's only a matter of time before this place isn't safe anymore. I don't think the FBI is convinced you three drowned. Only logical they'd start checking Mickey's operation in Mexico sooner or later. You don't wanna get caught 'cause you were stupid. And who knows, you two might even find some nice ladies and settle down there. Have a couple of kids."

Note the two pen marks on the horse.

KEN WIDNER

"Sounds like you've been talkin' with James. He told Mickey the same thing just before he bonded out of Alcatraz."

"Tell him we appreciate the offer, but I think we're good for now."

"You sure? You're passing up a big opportunity."

"We're sure," John replied, "unless somethin' happens."

Clarence snapped his fingers. "Oh, I almost forgot something." He took out the leather horse Alfred purchased in Tijuana years before. "Would you mind givin' this to Alfred?"

He handed it to Fred.

"I included a couple of marks he'll understand. He'll know where we are when he gets out."

"Sure. I'll take care of it."

"Thanks."

Fred powered down the runway and disappeared in the blue sky. Just as he had promised, Fred sent the leather horse to Alfred. He immediately recognized where it came from and the message his brothers included.

A few short months later, none of them could have imagined the next tragedy that would touch the Anglin family on a personal level, and the nation as a whole.

THE SECOND DEATH, NOVEMBER 22, 1963

Most newspaper around the world reported the news of JFK's assassination, which hit tens of millions of people hard. For the brothers, they experienced the same sense of shock and loss. He was the president of the United States, and the idea that one man could've cut someone like that down in his prime most people found unthinkable. On the other hand, they were also aware of Mickey's hatred for the Kennedys. Their aggressive attacks against him during the congressional hearings left a deep mark on Cohen, and he wanted nothing more than to get back at them.

The brothers must have wondered more than once if he might somehow have been involved with his death, and then again with Robert Kennedy in 1968. Robert was assassinated at the Ambassador Hotel in Los Angeles, which also happened to be Cohen's base of operations for his illegal gambling enterprises from the 1940s.

When Brizzi read about the police capturing the man responsible—Lee Harvey Oswald—he said to John Kelly, "Well, I was never a fan of Kennedy, ever since he and his brother set Mickey up. But I'm glad they caught the guy who did it."

"Yeah, too bad for Oswald," Kelly replied. "But I'm sure he won't make it out of Dallas."

Fred didn't know what to think of his response. Was it based on his association with powerful men who had their way of dealing with injustice, or did Kelly know more than that?

Months later, Candy Barr testified before the Warren Commission that she had become friends with Jack Ruby in the 1950s while a stripper in Dallas. When Candy was paroled from the Goree women's prison in April 1963 after being sentenced for a drug conviction, she moved in with her father and stepmother at Edna, Texas. During that time, the friendship between Candy and Ruby deepened, which she told the commission:

> Jack Ruby called her and said he wanted to hire her to dance at his Carousel Club. She told Ruby that her parole stipulated that the only job she could hold was to raise animals for profit, so he drove to Edna with a pair of dachshund breeding dogs out of his litter. . . . He was accompanied by a man who stayed in the car. When Ruby got ready to leave, Barr walked to the car with him and asked the man if he wanted a drink of water. He told her no, they had to get on back to Dallas. A few weeks later, she . . . watched Ruby on live TV shoot the man who had been in the car with him in Edna.[5]

Candy later recanted her story about Oswald and said that Ruby came to Edna alone. In 1969 she received a pardon from Governor Connally, who had been in the car with JFK when he was shot.

THE THIRD DEATH, JANUARY 11, 1964

Opened in 1923, Kilby is a 2,500-acre facility located outside Montgomery, Alabama. Many convicted felons given the death penalty ended up there after an electric chair was installed in 1927, known as "Yellow Mama."

It was well known among the prison population that "Yellow Mama" had often been used as an intimidation tool by the prison guards. Inmates were walked past the room and allowed to view it, or strapped in the chair and threatened with electrocution if they didn't confess to a crime or agree to become a snitch or whatever else prison officials wanted from them.

When Alfred arrived at Kilby in September 1963, they designated him as a trusty. Usually, inmates earned that privilege after a certain period of time of good behavior. In the letters he mailed home, Alfred said things like, "I like this place" or "I've never felt more free here."

Kilby Prison
KEN WIDNER

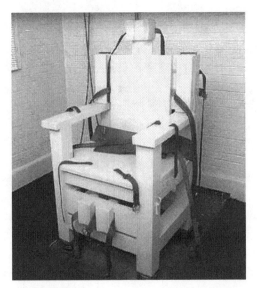

"Yellow Mama"
DEATH ROW (YOUTUBE)

How strange that I, along with my parents, were the last people to see him alive. The following is how my mother remembered our visit on December 21, 1963:

Me and your dad had decided to take Alfred a Christmas dinner. Now that he was closer to us, going to see him was a lot easier. I baked all day that Friday, we had planned to drive over on Saturday during visitation.

A guard directed us out into a big grassy courtyard where several picnic tables were. I thought how odd that they were letting us sit outside, but it was a nice day and almost Christmas, so we figured it was a special day. After a few minutes out comes Alfred from a building behind us. It was so good to see him. The last time I saw him was at the state trial. We all hugged and I cried a bit but it wasn't long before we all set down and let Alfred eat.

While Sue watched you (Ken) play next to us, we talked about what he was doing, how he was doing. He said he never felt better, was going to church at the prison and really liked the place. He had made trusty, which gave him access to more areas and a bit more freedom. Then he told us something that shocked me and your dad.

"I got word from them and I know where they are."

We didn't ask who because a guard was nearby, but me and your dad knew who.

He said, "I'm coming up for a parole hearing the last part of next month. If I get it, and I hope so, I'm heading to where they are."

I told him we'd be praying for him to get it. He never said anything else about it and we never brought it up again during the visit.

When they announced that visitation was ending and we started to walk back, Alfred walked back into the building he came out of. That was the last time I ever saw my brother alive.

The night of January 11, 1964, shook my family to the core. In many ways my mom still hasn't recovered from the terrible news. She remembers the night like it happened yesterday:

It was raining hard, we had already gone to bed, when our next-door neighbor started banging on the door. "Marie, come quick, your brother is on the line. Something has happened to Alfred."

My dad, sister Sue, Alfred holding me, and my mom at Kilby Prison
WIDNER FAMILY

You see, we didn't have a phone then, we were still too poor for that. I ran over not even grabbing my coat. It was my brother, Man, who told me Alfred had been killed at the prison trying to escape. I just couldn't believe what I was hearing, how was it possible? We had just saw him a few days back.

Below is an excerpt of the official FBI report surrounding the death of Alfred.

On January 13, 1964 "Tampa Tribune" newspaper carried article concerning electrocution of ALFRED RAY ANGLIN, brother of ANGLIN subjects. . . . According to the article, ALFRED was killed when he touched high voltage wire lining a window at Kilby Penitentiary, Montgomery, Alabama, when he tried to crawl through window to escape, January 11, 1964.[6]

The FBI report went on to say Alfred and another inmate (his name is redacted) hid in the clothing room on the second floor around 6:30 p.m. At approximately 8:00 p.m. the monitoring system in the prison lobby indicated something had come in contact with the security wires surrounding the compound. When a guard investigated, he encountered the unnamed inmate, who said Alfred had come in contact with the electric wire outside the window. An examination of the window revealed two bars had been sawed at the bottom and bent upward. Outside the window, Alfred's face and body were lying on the roof of the administration offices, his feet still inside.[7]

Soon after, the FBI contacted my family and asked them when we had seen him last and if he had given any indication of escaping from Kilby. That is when we told them about my family's visit two weeks before, where Alfred had discussed his upcoming parole hearing and his hopes of soon being released. The FBI then made us aware of a letter Alfred recently mailed to his sister, in which he indicated he was in good spirits.

White Chapel Funeral Home was given the task of holding Alfred's body until they received the death certificate from Kilby, at which point he would be sent to Ruskin for burial. However, unexpected problems arose that delayed issuing the certificate, which in turn delayed sending his body to the family.

> The family was notified at 11:30 p.m. Saturday night, January 11, 1964, that ALFRED had been accidentally electrocuted at 8:30 p.m. that day while trying to escape from Kilby, and the family paid $283.00 to have the body returned to Ruskin for funeral services, and they stated they were further upset because no death certificate was received with the body, and although several attempts have been made by the funeral director to obtain a death certificate, it has not been forwarded by prison officials.[8]

Not until January 27, two weeks after Alfred's death, did his body finally arrive at the Lewers and Shannon Funeral Home in Ruskin. The funeral director indicated to the family that "the body was in bad shape and had 'stripes' across his back and this caused them to wonder how Alfred died."[9]

The FBI claimed he had been electrocuted during his escape attempt, but the body seemed to have been injured beyond that, which the Ruskin funeral home director discussed with the family.

This then begs the question, why would a trusty with a parole hearing only days away attempt an escape? When we visited Alfred in December, he said was looking forward to his hearing, believing his chances were good they'd approve his parole.

Other parts of the official account also don't add up.

If Alfred and the inmate with him had gotten out of their cell at 8:00 p.m. that night, as the FBI report alleges, how was it no alarms sounded? Also, they had cut and bent two window bars, and yet no one saw or heard anything. Equally mystifying, how did Alfred acquire a hacksaw, pliers, jumper wires, a forged Alabama driver's license, and a watertight pouch filled with photos and documents, but they somehow escaped everyone's attention? The guards checked inmates. The guards searched cells. Then there's the watertight pouch—why need that? Kilby is nowhere near lakes or rivers.

Lastly, the picnic table where we sat with him. Could it have been bugged? Did they hear Alfred say he knew where his brothers were? Seizing upon this opportunity, is it so difficult to believe they used "Yellow Mama" to get him to talk but went too far? This would then account for why the death certificate took so long to get issued and the body sent back to Ruskin—time needed to clean up the mess. Perhaps the state prosecutor was more right than he knew when he said back in 1958, "You will never leave Alabama alive!"

Fred and Kelly were given the job of telling John and Clarence the bad news.

The look on Fred's face after he stepped out of the plane told John everything. "What's wrong? Somethin' happen back home?"

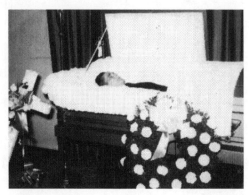

Alfred Anglin's funeral
KEN WIDNER

"You boys should sit down for this."

John did his best to pull himself together after hearing the news. "Do you know what happened?"

"All I know is what Man told me. They said he was tryin' to escape and got caught up in an electrical line. The family's takin' it pretty hard."

Clarence took out a cigarette and struggled lighting it. "That just don't make no sense. All that time in Atlanta and he never once tried to bust out. He thought the law would set things right. And then he tries to escape?"

"Man also told me he said Alfred got word from you about where you were hiding and you three were planning to meet up when he got out."

John's head dropped. "We sent him the leather horse. Do you think the feds found out?"

"There's been some stories that Alfred may have been interrogated by them before he died. They have that electric chair at Kilby, which has been used to get prisoners to talk."

John and Clarence looked at one another.

"That makes a whole lot more sense to me than Alfred doin' somethin' stupid like that."

Clarence took a long drag from his cigarette. "If he did talk, the feds might know where we are. They might have even followed you here."

The air around them stilled and everyone fell silent at the realization the FBI could show up at any moment.

"If that's what happened," Kelly concluded, "then this place isn't safe anymore. We need to get you out of here, now."

Frank let out a slow breath. "Don't fancy leavin' this place, but if it means getting caught if we stay, then I say we go."

After a moment Fred declared, "You know how we talked about Brazil a couple of months back? I don't think you have a choice anymore."

"Brazil, huh?" John looked at Clarence, then at Frank. "Well?"

Clarence flicked his cigarette to the ground. "Brazil it is."

Brazil

"IN ORDER TO SURVIVE," JAMES BULGER WROTE IN A LETTER ABOUT HIS sixteen years on the run,

> I understood the importance of breaking all contact with loved ones and holding to that level of discipline. It was tough to break those ties, but necessary for my own survival and their protection. We all knew the penalty that would fall on the innocents we cared for. You have to factor that into as to why they were never seen or heard from again. Freedom came at such a big price, but it was still better than the long and lonely years spent in prison.[1]

Map of Brazil
PAULA PAULINHA, PIXABAY.COM

When Fred told John, Clarence, and Frank about Alfred's death and his possible confession regarding their whereabouts, they faced a difficult decision. Both brothers had already accepted the idea of cutting all ties with the family, but that choice meant never seeing them again. What the two didn't expect was the emotional and psychological toll it would take on them. Despite years apart during frequent incarcerations, the family had maintained close bonds with John and Clarence, but the brothers also clung to the hope they'd reunite again one day. The decision likewise had a direct impact on John's relationship with Helen. The two had intended to marry, but if the family couldn't be told where they were living, neither could she, and so John had no choice but to cut off all ties with his future bride even before the escape. But now with the FBI bearing down on them, John and Clarence had two options: surrender to the authorities or keep running.

At the time, despite the aggressive interrogation techniques inflicted on Alfred by the FBI, he never revealed his brothers' hiding place. However, the authorities had determined the escapees had gone somewhere deep in Mexico and started to close in on them. Alfred did tell his cellmate at Atlanta he knew his brothers were alive. On February 28, 1964, a month after his death, FBI agents arrived at the penitentiary and spoke with his former cellmate.

He told the agents he had met the escapees fifteen years before when they did time together at Raiford and Georgia State Prisons. Because of his previous relationship with the brothers, Alfred believed him to be trustworthy and shared some of what Man revealed during his visits. After the three broke out, Man let Alfred know they had survived the escape, which he shared with his cellmate on several occasions. Even though Alfred never specifically mentioned where the three lived in Mexico, the cellmate still figured this out on his own.

[Name redacted] advised that if he was to start looking for the Subjects, he would start looking in the vicinity of Guadalajara, Mexico, in that the Subject MORRIS, who speaks fluent Spanish, spent a great deal of time in that area from 1953 to 1957. He stated Morris has a lot of contacts in that area. . . . He explained that the Subjects were all excellent woodsmen and would think nothing of "holing up" in the Guadalajara Mountain Range for years.[2]

Alfred's cellmate also somehow knew Morris spoke Spanish, which is corroborated in the FBI report. The cellmate felt certain the three had left the country and hid themselves in the area of Guadalajara, Mexico, which is only three hundred miles from Mexico City. The authorities would have treated this as credible information and pursued the lead, which had previously been indicated when the FBI interviewed the inmates at Alcatraz after the escape.

But this is not the only source of information that connects Mexico with the escapees. One of the inmates at Alcatraz told the FBI he had heard through the "prisoner grapevine" that John, Clarence, and Frank arrived safely in Mexico, and that another inmate reportedly saw a postcard from Mexico in Warden Blackwell's possession he had received from the three, which he confirmed to a group of newsmen who visited Alcatraz soon after it shut down in 1963.[3]

Clearly, word had gotten around the prison that the three had not only survived but made it safely to Mexico. But how did the prison population become aware of that information unless someone told them? The three likely sources are James Bulger, Mickey Cohen, and Allen West. Or perhaps another inmate overheard them talking in the dining hall or in the exercise yard during the planning phase. Once known, one inmate told another, who told another, until it became common knowledge around the prison. The inmates' belief about the escapees' destination was further strengthened when one of the prisoners saw a postcard Warden Blackwell had received from Mexico not long after the escape, allegedly sent by the three. Though Blackwell didn't say anything about this at the time, he did confirm the truth to the press covering the prison's closure on March 21, 1963.

The compilation of this information gave the FBI the escapees' possible whereabouts. But Mexico is also a very large country. Not until Alfred's cellmate gave them a specific destination in February 1964 did agents search for them there. And with Cohen's drug activities also closely monitored by the FBI, a good chance existed they'd discover the farm he owned outside of Mexico City sooner or later and catch them before they escaped once again. Though nothing could make up for the loss of their brother, word from Fred Brizzi right after Alfred's death gave them the head start they needed. For John, Clarence, and Frank, however, escaping once more, this time to Brazil, meant they'd most likely never see their loved ones again.

The Federative Republic of Brazil is the largest country in South America. At 3.2 million square miles and over 214 million people, Brazil is the world's fifth-largest country by area and the sixth most populous. Its capital is Brasília, the most populous city being São Paulo, with 22 million residents. The federation is composed of twenty-six states and the Federal District. It is the only country in the Americas with Portuguese as the official language. Brazil is also one of the most multicultural and ethnically diverse nations due to more than a century of immigration from around the world, as well as the most populous Roman Catholic country.[4]

Fred and Kelly flew John, Clarence, and Frank down to Congonhas–São Paulo Airport, which first opened in 1936. They then drove them to a remote town in the highlands where rich soil and local rivers made farming ideal. Known for its cotton and coffee, the area seemed good to the brothers for growing marijuana.

First introduced in Brazil by Portuguese colonists in the early 1800s, cannabis steadily increased in use over the years. In the mid-1950s, organized crime leaders like Mickey Cohen recognized the fortune they could make through the illicit drug trade and set up shop in Central and South America. In a poor country like Brazil, bribing local officials to look the other way was commonplace, and so the flow of illegal drugs thrived. Fred Brizzi said as much when he met with my family: "You got to understand something about Brazil. Brazil controls only the cities. The rest of the country is just like the ones here one hundred and fifty years ago. But when you leave Rio de Janeiro, you only got what you got on your hip. That's it, nothing else."

The American gringos, who were likely seen as something of a curiosity by the townspeople, were in all probability accepted into the community over time. John and Clarence were sociable people by nature, and it's not beyond the realm of possibility they became friends with the locals and participated in their festivals and celebrations. With the protection of local magistrates on their payroll, the three operated their marijuana farm out in the open without fear of arrest or reprisal.

With that said, the attacks launched against Cohen by the Kennedys in the 1950s also taught them an important lesson. An ambitious prosecutor hoping to make a name for himself or rival gang eyeing their territory could make things difficult, so they most likely hired locals as security. The three also garnered the goodwill of the community with the implementation of various social programs, such as school and church repairs, upgrading the electrical grid, and giveaways of toys, food, and clothing to the poor. And with the flow of money and services strengthening the local economy, the brothers' marriage prospects rose.

In the late 1960s, which Fred Brizzi later recounted to the family, John and Clarence found wives for themselves. Children soon followed. It is not known if Morris ever married, but the three had carved out a life for themselves despite being fugitives on the run.

Every few months, Fred flew in and picked up the latest harvest. When he did, the four sat together and discussed news from home. They also shared old times, laughed together, and looked forward to a prosperous future. On occasion, when he thought it safe to do so, Man also flew down with Fred.

Then, in 1973, everything changed.

The brothers received a call from Man, who never would contact them in this way unless it was an emergency.

Something sounded off to John. He heard it in Man's voice, his usual jovial tone replaced with a deadly earnest. "I don't know how to tell you, so I'll just say it. Mom died last night."

John and Clarence heard the words but couldn't believe them.

"Mama and Daddy went to church last night like they always did. Daddy said she went to the altar to pray at the end of the service. When she got up she told the pastor that the Lord had given her peace about you boys, and she also said she felt as light as air. She then went back to her seat, fell over, and died right there. Daddy said she didn't feel no pain or nothin'. Just went to be with the Lord."

"Has Daddy said when they're gonna have the funeral?" John asked.

"Not yet. He still has to make the arrangements."

"When you find out you let me know. Clarence and me are gonna be there."

A week later, family, friends, and a large number of people from town met at the Fellowship Primitive Baptist Church Cemetery in Lithia, Florida, not far from Ruskin. It was a hot July day, humid, which wilted the flowers by the grave site. The pastor spoke eloquently about Rachel, who had been a faithful churchgoer her entire life. He also praised her sacrificial spirit, how she raised fourteen children in a two-bedroom house, and how she made sure they were always well fed and made their clothes, a never-ending job for a farmer's wife. Despite having lost a son

Rachel Anglin's headstone
SUMMER SEELY (WIKITREE)

at Kilby, and two others presumed dead, she never lost her faith. And at this moment, she had finished her work on earth and now enjoyed the reward of eternal peace in the loving arms of Jesus.

George, never one for sharing his emotions, sat stone-faced, his gaze cast forward. What most didn't notice a little farther back, two large women dressed in black stood by a tree, their faces obscured by veils. No one had ever seen them before, but they seemed just as touched by the pastor's words. When the service ended, they were gone.

Several days later, John, Clarence, and Frank sat at the dining room table after the others had gone to bed, each with a beer in his hand. During the day, the sounds of children playing and laughing filled the house, their mothers scolding them if things got out of hand. The brothers didn't mind so much. Growing up in a family as large as theirs, noise in the house was a constant, and they missed it when the farm grew too quiet.

Unlike Ruskin, the highlands were not as warm in the summer months and rained far less. But tonight, the air felt thick, heavy.

John took a drink. "I've been doin' some thinking since Mama's funeral, and I say it's time we got out of the drug business. I know it hurt her terrible what we done all these years. Might have even shortened her life some."

"I can't say I blame you," Frank said with a hint of sympathy in his voice. "My mother died years ago, and though I didn't see her much growing up, I still feel her loss at times."

"You know, I've been thinkin' the same thing. Might help Mama rest a little easier knowin' we was livin' honest."

John took out a wad of money from his pocket and set it on the table. "We've made a lot these past years and I've been eyeing a piece of property a couple of valleys over. Big enough to farm and raise some cattle."

Clarence thought a moment. "Sounds about right to me. I'll give ya whatever I've got."

Frank didn't respond. He just sat in his chair, a faraway look in his eyes.

"What do ya say, Frank?" Clarence asked. "You in?"

He finished off his beer. "Seems all three of us have been doing a lot of thinking lately."

"What do ya mean?"

"I've given it my all with you these last ten years, but I think you know by now I'm not a farmer. Never have been."

"What are you sayin'?" John asked

"I've thought about leaving for a while, maybe start a business or something in São Paulo."

"Are you crazy? Someone will spot you there for sure. The feds will swoop in and catch you before you knew they was even there."

Frank laughed. "More than eight million people live in the city. I'd be invisible."

"If they get you, then there's a good chance they'll find us. You wanna take that risk?"

"You know I'd never rat you out."

"Don't have to. Just bein' caught lets them know we're around."

Clarence leaned close. "You can't do it, Frank. We got families to think about. You wanna put them through all that if we got caught?"

Frank chewed on his words before responding. "No. Not fair to them since they haven't done anything wrong."

"Just give it some time," John suggested. "See what the new place is like. If it's not for you, then you can go. What do ya say?"

He grinned. "You know, you boys have done nothing but steer me wrong since the first day we met. How are you gonna live on the straight and narrow without me around?"

For the next few years the brothers and their families, along with Frank Morris, devoted themselves to the new farm. Even before the bank robbery in 1958, John and Clarence had wanted a place of their own, the reason they did the job in the first place.

The Paraiba do Sul River winding through their property gave them all the water they needed for their crops and cattle. And with a moderate climate all year round, citrus and plum trees grew in abundance. Their children, seven in all between John and Clarence, attended a local school, and they made sure they had the best of everything. No one would ever make fun of them because they were poor.

With the money both brothers earned from their stint in the marijuana business and the subsequent sale of beef, fruits, and vegetables at the local market, both brothers built a life for themselves they never thought possible growing up.

In the meantime, Fred Brizzi continued ferrying drugs from Central and South America. With the rise of the Colombian cartels in the 1970s, he soon started transporting drugs from there as well. When he did fly that far south, Fred sometimes paid the brothers a visit. On one particular trip in 1975, he brought Man with him. They both knew the brothers had bought a farm of their own with Morris. Since neither of them had seen the place yet, and with the FBI still no closer to finding the escapees despite a diligent search the past thirteen years, the two figured visiting them together should be relatively safe.

What the two didn't realize at the time was that the FBI had picked up a lead on Clarence and Frank in Brazil. In 1965 they had received word someone had spotted the two in Rio de Janeiro.

As expected, agents were immediately dispatched. The U.S. Department of Justice oversaw offices known as Legal Attachés (Legats) in forty-six locations around the world. Special agents assigned to these offices obtained information for the FBI on crimes and criminals who might be a threat to U.S. citizens or its interests.[5]

Though the document in the report refers to a bail jumper apprehended by the FBI in Rio after being on the run for five years, it is in the context of a Clarence sighting (Frank had also been noted in another FBI document) in the same city. The Legat office had the authority to return this man to the United States after they caught him in Rio, and would do the same with Clarence, John, and Frank should they also be apprehended. However, despite a thorough search, nothing substantive was found and the agents returned to the United States.

Both families gave Man and Fred a warm welcome every time they visited. As is the custom in Brazil, the families served a large meal in their home in a party-like atmosphere, courtesy of John's and Clarence's wives. Music on the radio played in the background as everyone sat around the table and ate traditional foods, such as feijoada, *moqueca*, *akara*, and *picanha* steak, topped off with generous amounts of caipirinha, which the men drank to excess. Laughter filled the house as the families shared one humorous story after another.

At the end of dinner John stood and raised his glass. "Thank you for coming and celebrating our good fortune with us, but I'd like to take a moment and remember those who . . ." John's emotions got the better of him and he paused a moment. "To Alfred and my mother. Para aqueles que perdemos."

"To those we've lost," Frank repeated in English.

Every adult at the table toasted them in unison and finished off their drinks.

Somewhere along the way, Morris left the brothers and disappeared from history.

At the behest of Robert in 1992, Fred Brizzi met with my family and shared with them for the first time that he had been in contact with John and Clarence in Brazil. Though this had been happening since their

Fred Brizzi meets with my family
KEN WIDNER

escape in 1962, he only admitted to "accidentally bumping into them" in Rio de Janeiro in 1975, then visiting their farm.

Fred's health had been in decline in recent years, and Man felt this might be the only opportunity the family would have to hear the truth from someone they trusted. Fred told them in no uncertain terms, "You know, well, nobody positively, absolutely knows they're alive really, but me." When asked where they were living, Fred declared, "Brazil." He met with my family again soon after that, agreeing to be recorded this time. The following are summaries of that recording:

- They bought the farm from an Englishman whose wife died of spider bite or a snakebite.
- The brothers drove Fred and Man around the farm. They noted the dozens of large termite mounds on the property.
- Fifteen or twenty locals worked for the brothers on the farm.
- The farm was a large one. According to Fred, about two hundred thousand acres (though that is most likely an exaggeration or misstatement).
- On a more somber note, the brothers had also shared with Brizzi about the deaths of their parents, Rachel in 1973 and George in 1989. Though the family hadn't been told this at the time, Man kept his brothers apprised of everything important that happened in Ruskin during his visits. At this point, his ongoing relationship with them hadn't yet been revealed.

As proof of Fred's trip to Brazil, he and Man took pictures of the property, which he gave to my mother.

Perhaps the most compelling evidence Fred provided is this photo of John and Clarence on their farm. If verified, this all but closes the case on the escape. Though they had both gained weight over the years and let their hair and sideburns grow, even a cursory examination of the photo reveals features that are unique to John and Clarence.

For example, compare these three photographs of Clarence. The first two were taken before his incarceration in 1958, the other in 1975. Notice

The back of the brothers' farmhouse seen from the road
KEN WIDNER

The Paraiba do Sul River flowing through the property.
KEN WIDNER

The brothers in 1975
KEN WIDNER

how he stands. Clarence is slightly stooped forward, his hands at his side hanging open. Also, the middle and right photos clearly show the rectangle shape of a cigarette pack in his shirt pocket.

For John, how he wore watch is very telling and quite unusual. Rather than having it on the wrist like most people, he placed his on the left forearm above the wrist.

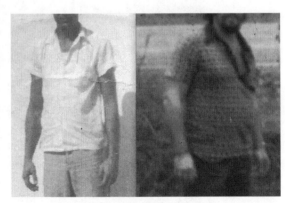

Photos of Clarence through the years, with the same pose
KEN WIDNER

For additional proof, Fred told the truth about my uncles. He described on the tape how John, Clarence, and Frank tied their raft to the transport boat and were towed into the bay the night of the escape, as they had done years before as boys on the Little Manatee River. Remember, this in 1992. At the time, most people believed they tried to paddle their way to Angel Island against powerful tides or swam for it. No one touted the theory the three tied their raft to the transport, until Fred recounted, "We got a rope to tie around the motorboat . . . we didn't swim." This was ten years before the FBI released the official report to the public, which states the exact same thing. How would Brizzi have known this important detail unless he had been told by the brothers? After Fred

Note the location of the watch in the 1975 photo and John wearing one in the 1950s.
KEN WIDNER

had taken the photograph of the brothers, they met with John's wife in town. Man took the photo below of the two.

Fred said this about their meeting, "The picture that I took, well Jerry took it. I was standing by the telephone booth talking to a woman . . . that's their place." (Only known to me and my mother at that time, Robert's other nickname growing up was Jerry.)

Man and Fred also had the opportunity to meet with Frank in town and a blonde woman he was seeing at the time, though she kept to herself and never really interacted with them. "There was another American woman down there with them that was never introduced to me. Might have been the other man's wife, or girlfriend, or whatever. I don't know."

Years later, the authorities questioned a woman named Vickie Lyons in regard to her relationship with Frank Morris. Lyons was one of the aliases used by Morris, as noted in the FBI report. It is highly probable she could've been the same woman Fred and Man met in Brazil.

Fred with John's wife
KEN WIDNER

Helen and Robert (Man) at taping with Fred
KEN WIDNER

If that were not proof enough, John's old girlfriend, Helen, was also with my family when Fred made the 1992 recording. During the course of the conversation, a woman in the room said this regarding Helen: "JW has called her many times." John's full name is John William Anglin, and was known as JW growing up. The woman then added, "She [Helen] said she calls JW. He just don't say anything." Helen also admitted to my mother that she had talked with John on the phone after the escape.

After speaking with my family for a little over an hour, Fred summarized his thoughts about the encounter this way: "Just knowing they're alive, that's a miracle to me."

In 1979, after searching for the three escapees for seventeen years, pursuing thousands of leads, and encountering one dead end after another, the FBI concluded John, Clarence, and Frank most likely drowned the night of June 11, 1962, and their bodies were washed out to the ocean. They officially closed the case on July 23 and transferred all their files and records to the U.S. Marshals Office on December 31, 1979. Their case will remain open until the brothers turn ninety-nine.[6]

In a story twist befitting a Hollywood movie, the film *Escape from Alcatraz*, starring Clint Eastwood, premiered on June 22, 1979, one month before the FBI ended their search.

343

```
FM DIRECTOR, FBI (76-26295)
TO ALL FBI FIELD OFFICES  ROUTINE
ALL LEGAL ATTACHES  ROUTINE
BT
UNCLAS E F T O
FRANK LEE MORRIS - FUGITIVE (A) IO 3584, WF 307; JOHN WILLIAM
ANGLIN - FUGITIVE (A) IO 3583, WF 306; CLARENCE ANGLIN -
FUGITIVE (A) IO 3582, WF 305, EFP; CONSPIRACY; 00; SAN FRANCISCO
    RE BUREAU AIRTEL TO ALL SACS CAPTIONED "INVESTIGATIVE
OPERATIONS, FUGITIVE PROGRAM", DATED AUGUST 8, 1979.
        DISCONTINUE ANY FURTHER EFFORTS TO LOCATE ABOVE CAPTIONED
SUBJECTS.  IN ACCORDANCE WITH INSTRUCTIONS FROM THE DEPARTMENT
OF JUSTICE DATED JULY 23, 1979.  THESE CASES WERE TRANSFERRED
TO THE U.S. MARSHAL'S SERVICE ON DECEMBER 31, 1979.
```

FBI field offices ordered to discontinue the search for the escapees
FBI FILES

Living with the Escape

*When you leave, you have to cut ties with all family members. Not
doing so will expose them to harassment by the authorities.*

—JAMES "WHITEY" BULGER

BORN IN ORLANDO, FLORIDA, TO FRANK AND MARIE ANGLIN WIDNER,
my story began on January 27, 1961. My father had moved the family
from Ruskin to Orlando in search of work, and it was there that my
mother first heard the news about the escape—the day that changed our
family's lives forever. My mother told me the story many times:

> I was ironing some clothes, earning some extra money. You were a
> little older than a year. I had the radio on, listening to music while I
> ironed. When the news broke in, all I heard was that a prison break
> had occurred at Alcatraz. I knew in my heart right then who it was. I
> grabbed you and ran out the door to our neighbor's house. They had
> a TV and I wanted to see what they were saying about it. I couldn't
> hardly stand when I saw pictures of my two brothers flashing up on
> the screen.

Most of the stories I heard over the years about John, Clarence, and Alfred
came from my mother. What really stood out to me was what happened
to the family days, months, and years after that. On one occasion, my
mom and Uncle Man told me about how FBI agents surrounded our

house hours after the escape. At the time, Man and his wife, Billy, lived with my grandparents. The FBI entered the house and told everyone to stay put. Uncle Man didn't feel like he needed to stay anywhere and said to them, "We didn't escape from anywhere."

When he tried to leave, one of the FBI guys grabbed his arm and ordered him back on the couch. "No one's leaving this place until you've answered all our questions!" the agent yelled. I wonder how the agents would have reacted if they discovered the one person who actually did know where my uncles were sat in front of them the whole time. The family had no idea this was just the beginning of the government harassment we'd experience for years.

In an ironic twist of fate, one of my earliest memories happens to be visiting my Uncle Alfred with my parents and sister at Kilby in December 1963. Of course, none of us knew then we would be the last family members to see him alive.

Even before Alfred's death, the weight of the Alcatraz escape hit my family much harder than previous prison breaks over the years. Those incidents only brought the local authorities to my family's house in Ruskin. Alcatraz had the whole federal government after them. Unannounced visits by the FBI became commonplace, as did searching our mail, listening in on our phone calls, and following us around, until they closed the case in 1979. The U.S. Marshals Service, however, picked up right where the FBI left off.

Uncle Man, of course, let John and Clarence know what my family endured, but as much as it pained both brothers they remained in hiding, just like James Bulger had told them: "Leave the country, cut all ties with family members." The one exception—Alfred. The three had previously agreed to reunite at their earliest opportunity, and with Alfred's parole hearing approaching, John and Clarence let him know where they were through Man. None of them, however, could have imagined how this decision cost Alfred his life. As a result of this unfortunate consequence, the brothers decided against any direct contact with the family from then on and opted for indirect forms of communications, which fell on Man's shoulders. For the time being, no one in the family could know the truth about John's and Clarence's whereabouts or if they were still alive.

Perhaps one day the brothers might risk direct contact with their siblings. Until then, the brothers decided to let the world believe they drowned.

In 1963, my family moved once again, this time to Albany, Georgia, so my father could find work. We'd visit my grandparents in Ruskin several times a year, which was always a fun trip. With my mom coming from a big family, there were always lots of cousins to play with. Our trips usually brought the whole family together for a cookout of some sort. The kids hung out with each other, and the adults sat around and talked. Even as children, we all knew their conversations would eventually come around to John and Clarence. Years later, when I was more a part of that circle, I started to notice that one member of the family always changed the subject after a few minutes. It wasn't until the FBI released their seventeen-volume report in 2002 regarding the escape that I began to understand why that same family member, Uncle Man, had been polygraphed by both the FBI and U.S. Marshals. Clearly, they believed he knew something, and to be completely honest, members of my family suspected the same. But with the information now in my possession, I can understand why he never shared anything with my family. He feared the authorities would come after them like they had come after him. But if the secret remained with just one person, himself, then no chance existed of it getting out. And he wasn't talking.

I can remember two times when the FBI stopped by our house in Albany. On the second occasion, my mom was raking the yard while my younger brother and I played nearby. A car stopped in front of the house and out came a young man dressed in a nice coat and tie. Being the curious type, I ran over to him, only to have the man show his ID, followed by, "I'm special agent so-and-so (I don't remember his name), and I'd like to ask you a few questions about John William and Clarence Anglin."

Once again, the agent accused my family of knowing my uncles' whereabouts. In their minds, we were guilty of harboring fugitives from justice, and they threatened to send the guilty parties to prison. Over time, however, the systematic intimidation wrought against my family had the opposite effect. Most of them either stopped believing the threats or just didn't care anymore. I say that because my mom said to an agent one time, "I don't know where they are, and if I did I sure as heck wouldn't tell you!"

In time, the surprise visits by the FBI ended, though the family still believed they were being surveilled. I later found out our suspicions turned out to be true from a U.S. Marshal I became friends with who worked the Alcatraz case for twenty-five years.

Over the years, the escape took on a life of its own. What started as three convicts who broke out of prison became a story of celebrity of a sort as the years passed, with John, Clarence, and Frank made famous by the movie *Escape from Alcatraz*, numerous books, television shows, and documentaries. Even the Escape from Alcatraz Triathlon that I participated in in 2016 is based on this celebrated event. When author Don Denevi, who later published *Riddle of the Rock*, said he wanted to write a book about the escape back in 1990, we thought this was our chance to tell the real story about my uncles. However, I found out in 2014 that he was actually working with the U.S. Marshals, who hoped Denevi could pry the whereabouts of John and Clarence from Uncle Man. To be honest, I was quite surprised my uncle agreed to participate in the book. In the end, my family was paid only a few hundred dollars for their assistance. And what did the U.S. Marshals get? Nothing. Uncle Man might have been tricked, but he wasn't stupid. He'd never reveal their hiding place.

This then added to my shock when Man invited my uncles' childhood friend, Fred Brizzi, to meet with the family. Fortunately for those interested in the Alcatraz story, my mother recorded the meeting, at which Fred gave her the now famous photo of John and Clarence in Brazil. Though he never specified the location where they lived, Brizzi wanted the family to know the two were okay and not to worry about them.

When the FBI released their official report in 2002, I finally began to understand why the U.S. Marshals suspected Man knew more about John and Clarence than he had claimed. Of all the family members the authorities talked with over the years, he was the only one they ever hooked up to a polygraph. Somehow, he beat the test. Yet, despite his denials, Man could never explain to the authorities the account given by Alfred's cellmate back in 1964: "Following the escape, when the newspapers were reporting the Subjects were presumed dead, ANGLIN was very morose and gloomy, but shortly thereafter, he received a visit from another brother, known as MAN and from that point on ANGLIN was his normal, cheery self again."[1]

It's little wonder the FBI believed my uncle knew more than he admitted. The final confirmation came from Man himself in 2009 shortly before he died. He shared these words with my mom and sister: "Your brothers are fine and I have been in constant touch with them for over twenty-five years." I would not find out about his confession until the fiftieth anniversary of the escape in 2012.

Before I had been contacted by the National Park Service about this important event, I received a phone call out of the blue from someone name Michael Dykes, who identified himself as a U.S. Marshal located in San Francisco. He told me he had been assigned the Alcatraz case and wanted to ask me a favor. After all this time, I found it hard to believe the Marshals Service was still involved in the search, yet he needed my help. Dykes proceeded to tell me how he uncovered an FBI document about some bones found at a beach north of San Francisco six months after the escape. With no DNA tests available back then, the bones were buried at a local cemetery. Dykes believed they belonged to one of the escapees and wanted my help getting a DNA sample from my mother, Marie. She and her younger sister, Mearl Taylor, were my uncles' only surviving siblings. I assumed he believed I'd have a better chance at talking my mom into doing this than him. Dykes had previously tracked down a distant relative of Frank Morris, but the results came back negative. This left the Anglin brothers as a possible match.

I agreed to ask her but promised nothing. After speaking with my mom, we both decided not to help. After the years of mutual distrust between us and the FBI, then the Marshals, what would prevent Dykes from taking our DNA and saying it was a match, even if it really wasn't, and finally closing the case? He accepted the family decision, and I thought that was the end of that.

A couple of days later Dykes called again and asked if I'd go behind my family's back and give him a sample from me. I responded the same as before, and that ended that, or so I thought a second time. The National

Park Service had planned a fiftieth-anniversary celebration of the escape and wanted to know if I'd be interested in coming out for the event, which included being interviewed by the press. I was intrigued but hesitant. For years, so-called experts talked about my uncles as though they knew them, but most didn't know the two at all. A big media op like this would give me the opportunity to set the record straight, so I told them I was interested in coming, but only if my mother and aunt flew out with me. I contacted my mom and got the ball rolling.

After coordinating the dates with the park rangers, I worked on securing the hotel rooms and flights. I hadn't been off the phone for more than a few minutes when Marshal Dykes called. He said he heard me and my family had agreed to participate in the event and wanted to meet with us. He even offered to bring some of the escape evidence as a way of garnering our cooperation. Despite his pleasant demeanor, something didn't feel right. How in the world did he know I just booked the travel arrangements? I can tell you the whole family was on high alert the whole time we stayed in San Francisco. We even thought that Dykes might try and steal some DNA from us.

The day we arrived we didn't allow him in our hotel rooms as a precaution. Instead, we met at a McDonald's not far from the hotel. The conversation started out cordial at first, until Dykes tried to persuade my mother and aunt into giving him samples of their DNA. He even brought a copy of the last letter my grandmother wrote to Clarence as leverage. She happened to mail it on June 11, 1962, the day of the escape. Of course, my mother and her sister still said no.

Later that day, the park rangers rolled out the red carpet when we arrived on the island. The head ranger drove the family around and allowed us to go places the public didn't normally see. I have to say that everyone really enjoyed themselves. I think for the first time since the escape government officials treated my family with respect instead of as adversaries.

The rangers set up a table for us so we could answer questions from the press. News organizations from all over the world had shown up, including a reporter from China, which let me know just how big of a story this really is. What amused me about the setup was that on one

Meeting with Marshal Dykes
KEN WIDNER

Reporters asking questions at Alcatraz prison.
KEN WIDNER

side of the table sat my brother David, me, my mother, and Aunt Mearl, who all believed John, Clarence, and Frank survived the escape. And on the other side of the table were Marshal Dykes and Jolene Babyak, both of whom didn't believe my uncles made it. Babyak is the daughter of the associate warden at the time of the escape and has gone on to write books about her experiences there. When these two made disparaging comments about John and Clarence during the Q&A, I found myself getting quite angry, which birthed in me a desire to know everything about my uncles—their lives growing up, the dreams that drove them, the kind of people they really were, and, of course, the events that led their freedom the night of June 11. Little did I know at that time I would soon come into contact with someone who not only knew my uncles quite well but would also help me better understand the escape from an insider's point of view.

Before we left the island, researcher and Alcatraz expert Michael Esslinger gave my mother a letter written by Whitey Bulger. I scarcely knew who he was at that time, but he somehow knew about our visit to the island for the fiftieth anniversary and wanted to reach out to her. We read the letter when we returned home. Whitey introduced himself and told my mother how much he respected my uncles. I believe it was his way of paying homage to their memories. He didn't see them as poorly educated men who were nothing more than Morris's followers, but intelligent and capable individuals who did what no one thought possible.

His timing couldn't have been more appropriate. Still angry about what transpired during the anniversary, I decided to start my search in earnest and looked everywhere I could think of that might shed any information on John and Clarence, such as Alcatraz websites, newspaper accounts, the 2002 FBI Alcatraz report, family members and friends who knew my uncles, and copies of their arrest records and court reports. In short, as the years passed, I knew as much as about Alcatraz and the escape as any person alive, perhaps more so since I had connections to stories, photos, and information unknown outside the family.

Over time, the truth about my uncles slowly materialized—transformed from simple dirt farmers into highly intelligent men who initiated a plan of escape no one thought possible. And it was this pursuit that brought me to the attention of David Karabinas.

David is the CEO of Texas Crew Productions, headquartered in Austin, Texas. Created in 1996, his production company specializes in developing documentaries for networks like CBS, HBO, NBC, Fox Sports, VH1, and the History Channel. Some of the notable shows they've produced are *Sell This House*, *Ironman Triathlon World Championship*, *Ripley's Believe It or Not!*, and *Alcatraz: Search for the Truth*, the latter of which had a profound impact on my life.

As someone who's always on the hunt for a good idea he can sell to a network, David came across the fiftieth anniversary interviews we gave in 2012, along with the 1993 John Leroy Kelly deathbed confession he had recently discovered.

According to the confession written down by Kelly's nurse before he died, he claimed to have been on the boat when the three were pulled from the water the night of the escape and took them to a safehouse in Washington. A sum of fifty thousand dollars had been provided by the Morris and Anglin families so the three could start new lives for themselves in Canada. As they drove north, Kelly and his partner, Robert Michael Kyle, pulled over in a rural area, shot and killed the three, and buried their bodies. They left markers behind as a way of finding them again if necessary, though subsequent searches over the years have turned up nothing.

David thought combining these two stories would make for a compelling show.

Working with retired U.S. Marshal Art Roderick, along with Alcatraz historian Michael Esslinger, they planned on searching the woods outside of Seattle for the bodies of John, Clarence, and Frank.

Though an interesting theory, I knew they didn't end up there since Fred Brizzi had told the family years before the three went south not north. But the show sounded fun, plus it was a way of keeping their story alive.

I made it a point to bring the 1,700-page FBI report with me to the shoot, which I read through during our off-hours. One night, I came across a passage that changed everything. In volume two of the file, in the section that describes my uncles' physical features, I realized they reminded me of the two men in the photo Fred Brizzi had given my mom back in 1992. When I looked at the photo and compared the two, a light bulb went off in my head.

John William Anglin:	Clarence Anglin:
Height—5'10"	Height—5'11"
Weight—140 pounds	Weight—160–168 pounds
Eyes—blue	Eyes—hazel-blue
Hair—blond	Hair—dark brown[2]

I became convinced those two men in the photo were indeed John and Clarence.

As strange as this may sound, when Fred gave the photos to my mother, he never specifically identified that particular one as a picture of my uncles. They were simply snapshots taken in Brazil he wanted my mother to have. Since she is a pack rat by nature, she stuck them in a box where they sat for years. But why would Fred give my mother a photo of unnamed men unless another reason prompted him? With the FBI and U.S. Marshals harassing my family for years, it stands to reason if this new information became known to them, he figured a good chance existed they just might put enough pieces together and track them down.

I immediately let David Karabinas know about my discovery, whereupon he contacted the main office. Production shut down that day, and we all returned home. Several days later, David called me. Texas Crew Productions had scrapped the documentary they had planned and changed it into an examination of the photo and hunt for my uncles. Knowing that it takes months of evidence gathering and endless production meetings before any story gets approved, having them reverse course in a couple of days let me know I was onto something, and that something was big. Not long after, *Alcatraz: Search for the Truth* was green-lit.

Filming started up again in Ruskin in early 2015 at the Primitive Baptist Church Cemetery, where my family is buried. There, we met

Art Roderick, me (Ken), David, and Michael Esslinger at Alcatraz
KEN WIDNER

with Art, who had been assigned the case while an active U.S. Marshal. During his tenure as a marshal, he had extensive experience tracking down criminals in some of the highest-profile cases in U.S. history, including Ruby Ridge and the DC sniper. He has also appeared on CNN as a law enforcement analyst. This was the kind of person the show needed in order to lend credibility in the audience's mind regarding the search. For me, I had my suspicions about Art. He had previously stated he didn't believe they survived the escape, which cast doubt in my mind about his commitment to the truth. But the show brought him onto the team, so David and I had no choice but to work with him.

What I showed Art during filming literally blew him away. As he stated in the episode, the Marshals hadn't received a promising lead since the escape. Essentially, it had become a cold case. But when I showed him the photo, I saw in his eyes that the game had just changed.

For the first time ever, my family agreed to provide the information needed to find my uncles, but on one condition. We had wanted Alfred

David and I present our evidence to Art
HISTORY CHANNEL (YOUTUBE)

exhumed for years so my mother and aunt would finally have their answer about how he really died. In exchange, we'd provide the Marshals with Alfred's DNA and compare it with the bones found in March 1963.

Art took the photo and gave it to Michael Streed, a facial imaging expert based in Los Angeles. Comparing the picture with known photos of John and Clarence, he noted a number of facial details, such as positions of foreheads, eyebrows, ear placement, and jawlines. In the end, Streed concluded with a high level of confidence the two individuals in the photograph were indeed my uncles. As he said to Art after his analysis, "If it was me, I would round up the posse."

At the end of the episode, Art met with me, David, and my mother at her home in Georgia and showed us what he had found during his investigation. He first gave us the results of Alfred's autopsy. Despite our belief he had died at the hands of the FBI during an aggressive interrogation, his body didn't show any signs of bruising or trauma. Alfred may not have been physically beaten, but that didn't mean he hadn't been strapped into the electric chair during questioning and his heart stopped when too much electricity had been applied. Sadly, we will never know.

Next, Art provided us with Alfred's DNA results. As we had hoped, they didn't match the bones found nine months after the escape. The air in the kitchen escaped all at once when he gave us the news. This corroborated what we already knew, that my uncles hadn't drowned the night of June 11, 1962.

For myself, this stoked my determination to tell the world the truth about them, and the only way that would ever happen is if I sat down and wrote their story, which came in the form of a screenplay about their lives growing up in Ruskin.

When *Search for the Truth* aired in October 2015, the number of viewers exceeded everyone's expectations. The network had hoped for one million people. In the end, three million watched the documentary that night. For reasons I still don't understand, the CEO pulled the plug on a planned follow-up episode despite overwhelming interest in the subject.

Though disappointed, I had spent countless hours doing research and talking with people about the escape. No way would I let the History Channel stop the story there, especially after I had made my important discovery. So I decided to push on and see where my search took me.

Along the way, I discovered an interview Uncle Man did with Frank Ahearn in 2016, someone who called himself a skip tracer. A skip tracer is a person who locates missing people. After asking other family members about John and Clarence, Man agreed to talk with him about my uncles, though no one ever knew why he did this.

After interviewing my uncle, Ahearn published the article, "How to Disappear . . . Alcatraz Style," on September 28, 2007. The following are excerpts from the piece:

I wanted to know about the brothers, how they found themselves in a place like Alcatraz. . . . Man told me that Clarence and JW were thick as thieves, and since childhood they had a unique way of communicating between each other, secret destinations to meet up at, phone calls with certain amount of hang-ups determined locations. JW received such a message and met up with Clarence when he escaped the Florida road gang.

June 11, 1962, . . . JW, Clarence and Frank Lee Morris escaped into the dark waters supposedly never to be seen again.

After the escape, Man told me that he was visiting Alfred at Kilby penitentiary and in the prison bathroom Alfred said he received a message from Clarence and that he knew where the brothers were holed up and he was going to meet up with the pair. Alfred attempted to escape prison only to be killed by electrocution.

Long after the Alcatraz escape, there have been several sightings and assumed correspondence from JW and Clarence. The smoking gun by Hollywood standards would be a postcard that arrived one day from Brazil, written in Clarence's writing. . . . I asked to see the postcard from Brazil, however, a week later Man told me the card is gone no one can find it.

The FBI file is an interesting piece of work, the attitude is summed up that most likely the trio drowned in the bay. . . . The secret of Clarence and JW still hides behind the kind smile of a gentle man named Man.[3]

Whitey Bulger had told John, Clarence, and Frank about the necessity of cutting off all ties with the family, lest they risk recapture. No matter how difficult that might have been for them, they heeded his council, and no direct contact was ever made. However, their escape from Alcatraz necessitated Robert's assistance, someone they knew they could trust with their lives. And that trust was well placed. Decades later, despite people's efforts to draw out any clues from my uncle, he never betrayed the three. They had no choice but to disappear in order to remain free, but that freedom came at a price: years of harassment by government agents and a world that thought we had been lying for years. For Robert, the cost came even higher—making sure both sides of the family never saw each other again.

Despite my disappointment with the History Channel, little did I realize at the time how much of an impact that documentary would have on my life.

CHAPTER 28

False Starts

Hurry up and wait.

—MILITARY EXPRESSION

As I DISCUSSED IN THE PREVIOUS CHAPTER, MY SEARCH FOR JOHN AND Clarence began in June 2012, the fiftieth anniversary of the escape. When my brother David, mother, Marie, Aunt Mearl, along with U.S. Marshal Michael Dyke, former guard George DeVincenzi, and Jolene Babyak talked with reporters and answered a myriad of questions about my uncles, I was struck by how many people have a general understanding about the escape, such as the creation of dummy heads and the raft made from raincoats, but most are also equally misinformed about many other important details, undoubtedly based on the many inaccuracies portrayed in the 1979 film *Escape from Alcatraz*.

That experience created within me a desire to know my uncles in a very real sense, and to look for ways of sharing what I found with the world. The result of that decision eventually led to my participation in the 2015 History Channel documentary *Alcatraz: Search for the Truth*.

The audience numbers were better than we had hoped, which let me know interest in my uncles' story remained just as strong as ever. I also noted how television people and mystery sleuths came out of the woodwork after the documentary aired. They saw the merits of my family's claim and wanted to write a book or do a follow-up show on another network, and so reached out to me via emails and texts. To their disappointment, I didn't have much interest in doing another documentary; rather, I focused my attention on my script, which had expanded into three planned films: my uncles' lives before Alcatraz, during Alcatraz, and after.

Someone named Mike Lynch reached out to me as well. I had no idea who he was, but he claimed to be a screenwriter from California who saw the documentary and wanted to talk about cowriting a screenplay with me regarding the escape and my uncles' flight to South America. Normally, I would have ignored such a tweet, but something about his interest in the story intrigued me, so I emailed him. We set up a zoom call, and the two of us talked.

Mike shared with me his fascination with the Alcatraz escape and about the need for telling the rest of the story, as he put it, and hoped I'd be interested in partnering with him. His interest sounded genuine, but years of tangling with the FBI and U.S. Marshals doesn't go away so easily. For all I knew, he could've been an agent posing as a screenwriter, hoping to extract information from me. It had happened before.

I let him know how much I appreciated talking with him, but I declined his offer. I said I was working on a script of my own and things were moving along fine. He asked me if I had ever done something like that before and that it should be edited by a professional. He added I'd only have one shot at pitching it to a perspective producer, and if the script showed the signs of an amateur, they would most definitely pass. He even offered to look at it and let me know what he thought of the story. I told him that at the advice of my lawyer I shouldn't share any part of the script until it had sold. He didn't know at the time I had no lawyer. This was my firm but polite my way of saying no thank you.

The call ended, and I moved forward with the script. A few months later, however, Mike emailed me again, asking if I had made any progress with interested producers. I sent him a brief reply, basically saying I started shopping the script to people who might be interested in the story. Several months later, he emailed again, likewise asking how things were going. He wasn't pushy about it, but I started to get the feeling he didn't let go so easily.

My hopes for having my script produced were buoyed when I got it into Clint Eastwood's hands. He seemed the logical choice for obvious reasons. Though I felt he had gotten a lot wrong in his Alcatraz movie, with my guidance, he'd get it right this time.

Though he liked the story, Eastwood ultimately passed. Everyone I reached out to also said no, just like Mike had predicted. That got me thinking. He said he was a screenwriter. Perhaps he'd agree to read through the script and fix the problems that obviously existed. Maybe even share it with the people he knew in the industry. At this point, I had nothing to lose, so we talked.

I sent him the script and received an email with his comments not long after. He basically said the reason everyone passed was because I had given them the wrong story. People weren't much interested in my uncles prior to arriving at Alcatraz, and no studio would commit itself to a three-movie deal to tell their life stories. He said the only way I'd have a chance of getting a studio interested in doing the movie was if we started at the escape and followed them down to Brazil. What he said made sense, and so I decided to take a chance and tell him everything.

As I shared the details of my research, Mike concluded a feature-length film wouldn't work. Too short. The only way of telling their amazing story was if we aimed for a miniseries. This had never occurred to me before but sounded reasonable. Six episodes, two hours each, gave us twelve hours of screen time, more than enough to tell my uncle's story in a way that would do them justice. So we both rolled up our sleeves and got to work.

The two of us spent the next several months honing the pilot episode, along with the creation of a twenty-minute pitch (a comprehensive document that includes a logline, character biographies, and a rough outline of the series).

By 2017, we felt the pilot had been honed into an engaging, well-crafted story, and so we started pitching production companies. Naturally, I started with Texas Crew Productions, who said they'd take a look at it. As we waited, we pitched other companies, including Scott Hunter at Karga7. Thinking we had a winner on our hands, we figured someone would show an interest in the project sooner or later, but the only positive response we received came from Casey Brumels in April

2018, co-owner of Ping Pong Productions. They asked Mike and me to fly to Los Angeles and tell them more about the story, then they could decide whether or not they'd move forward with the project. Since the two of us were wading into unchartered waters, never having pitched our own show before, we thought it wise to hire an entertainment lawyer who understood how the industry worked.

She told us in no uncertain terms that we shouldn't meet with them in Los Angeles before signing a deal. If we did, they could use anything we talked about and put it in the show without our approval. Even worse, they didn't have to pay us or give us credit. Naturally, this was the last thing we wanted, and so our lawyer asked Casey about signing an agreement before the meeting.

They obliged, and the negotiations began. Our lawyer looked at the offer and suggested changes. After several weeks, Mike began to notice a shift in their correspondence. The company's lawyer reached out to me more and more and less to Mike. Then they said outright they'd prefer only to talk with me and that I could pass everything on to Mike. When that happened, he and I had a frank talk. Mike saw himself as one of the writers for the miniseries, but Ping Pong didn't feel comfortable having him on the show in that capacity since he had no television writing credits. Since this would be a union job, they could only offer script assignments to those in the Writers Guild of America.

Now with no real role for him in the miniseries, he saw the writing on the wall, which he shared with me. He also said if I held out for him there'd be no show. I disagreed with Mike. We started as partners and would remain that way.

In May 2018, his prediction came true. Ping Pong wanted to drop him and hire me as the show's consultant. When I told Mike, he graciously stepped aside and wished me luck on the show. I didn't like the way this turned out since I felt he was being treated unfairly, but I also understood this is a tough business, and they held all the cards.

Not long after, the agreement had been hammered out, and I flew to Los Angeles. What should have been a two-hour meeting turned into one that lasted all day. The more I told Casey about my uncles and the escape, the more excited he became. He even brought different people into the meeting and had me repeat a certain part of the story, and they'd get just as excited.

Casey felt so confident about the show that he said it was a matter of "when" and not "if" they sold it to a network. This also buoyed my hopes of finally being able to tell my uncles' story in an honoring way.

I flew back to Georgia feeling confident about the show starting up soon. I even told my wife we should start looking for a place to live in California since the shoot would take several months. But the weeks passed and I heard nothing. I didn't think much of it at the time. After all, as Casey said, starting a TV show constitutes hiring a small army, not to mention scouting film locations, pitching networks, hiring actors, creating scripts, and the like. But more weeks passed and still nothing. I decided to reach out to Casey and ask if he had heard from anyone. He assured me the show was still moving forward as planned, and even said they recently hired a producer who would not only bring top talent onto the team but also had strong connections with different networks. I felt confident about our chances again and figured things should be starting soon.

During this waiting time, Mike contacted me on occasion and inquired about the show. I told him we were still moving forward, though no follow-up meetings had been scheduled, nor had I returned to California. This left me a little concerned but still hopeful.

More months passed and still nothing. Every time I reached out to Casey, he assured me this was how television worked and that shows always take longer than expected getting a green light. Despite his assurances, I started having my doubts about Ping Pong. Casey had been so certain about our prospects in the beginning, only to follow with months of silence.

Then, in November 2018, Scott Hunter at Karga7 reached out to Mike about the Alcatraz project. Even though they passed on it the year before, the story stuck with him, and he thought maybe we'd be interested in working with him. Mike told Scott I had signed an agreement with Casey but also felt frustrated by the lack of progress. Mike then contacted me about Karga's interest in creating a miniseries of their own and asked for a meeting with us. I figured it couldn't hurt to talk with him, my deal with Ping Pong in effect until November 2019, so we set up a conference call and discussed his ideas. Since we couldn't really do anything with Karga until my contract with Ping Pong expired, we agreed to talk on occasion and check on the show's status.

Shortly before the agreement's termination date, Casey convinced me to extend it to February 2020, which I did since he felt sure about getting a deal soon. In the end, the show never happened with Ping Pong, so Mike and I signed an agreement with Karga7 in May 2020.

Scott immediately got to work setting up a production team. Their first order of business: create a sizzle reel. A month later, they sent it to us. What we saw blew Mike and I away. They created an exciting pitch that covered the main elements of the show, paramount of which was the escape, along with some tantalizing clues about the brothers hiding out in Brazil. Who wouldn't want to buy this show? Karga7 then went about pitching the miniseries to different networks, such as Netflix, History Channel, the Travel Channel, and Hulu. As the months passed, however, so did they, until only History Channel remained. Despite the bad experience I had with History before, I was willing to give them a second chance. We had been told how enthusiastic the company president had been about the show, and so we thought our chances of getting green-lit were good, though at this time Scott left Karga for another production company, replaced with a new producer, Jason Wolf. Scott assured us we'd be in good hands with him and should stay on board as we waited for a decision.

Rather than sign a deal for another year before the agreement expired, the two of us decided to extend our contract with Karga for only three months to August 2021. Not long after, History Channel let us know they were also passing. Mike and I felt both disappointed and mystified. As Scott and Jason had said, never had they seen such support for an idea, yet, for reasons unknown, none of them acted on it. For us, three years had come and gone, and John and Clarence were no closer to being found than when we started.

During the waiting period with Karga7 and the networks, Mike suggested we should start on the book about my uncles we had discussed off and on the previous couple of years. We certainly had the desire, but we held back because of the show, or potential show in our case. We both knew collecting all the evidence and documentation and honing it into an exciting story over a period of months or longer would be something of an undertaking. We didn't want to start a project that big only to have the show green-lit, which we expected would drastically cut down on our writing time. However, as the months came and went and the networks dropped out one by one, we realized the two of us had all the time we needed for such an endeavor.

Despite feeling good about the material, the one nagging feeling we had was the story's ending. Neither Mike nor I had ever been to Brazil, and we both found the idea of going there alone daunting to say the least. We didn't speak the language, and we'd also need someone who could help us with the search. What records still existed from that time, and how might we find those people who knew John, Clarence, and Frank? Based on what Brizzi told my family, we knew John and Clarence had purchased a farm there, but under whose name, theirs or aliases?

What we needed was a production company to assist us in our hunt. They'd pay for our expenses, hire the film crew, and work with locals who'd help speed up the search. But with our contract at Karga7 about the expire and our network prospects exhausted, there seemed little hope of that. Until I received an email.

Brandon Fibbs at Plumbline Pictures had first heard about the Alcatraz miniseries when I met with Casey Brumels back in 2018. He never lost interest in the project, and so he reached out to me and asked about the show's status. His timing couldn't have been more perfect.

I told Mike about Brandon, whose interest in the story wasn't a miniseries like we had hoped but an episode on a TV show whose host went around the world solving mysteries and looking for lost treasure. That meant scaling back the parameters of our search. Mike figured we had nothing to lose at this point. If we didn't like their offer, we didn't have to accept it. So we set up a conference call.

What we didn't know at the time was that Brandon worked on a show called *Expedition Unknown*, hosted by Josh Gates. And what started out as a pleasant conversation on the phone helped lead us to John and Clarence.

Finding John and Clarence

EVEN THOUGH MIKE AND I COULDN'T UNDERSTAND WHY THE NET-
works passed on our proposed miniseries, we had no choice but to let it
go. On the other hand, we felt equally gratified someone in the industry
believed in the merits of our claim and was willing to come along with
us on our search for John and Clarence.

Josh, me, and Mike on location
KEN WIDNER

Rather than get bogged down in negotiations with Plumbline and unnecessarily delay the project for months, Mike and I talked with Brandon right away about signing a nondisclosure agreement, which gave us the ability to share with them our research but at the same time not fear theft of that information. He agreed, and not long after we started sending him a majority of the documents and photos we had accumulated over the years. The more we sent, the more Brandon became convinced the higher-ups would almost certainly green-light the episode for their upcoming tenth season.

But like a bad dream repeating itself, the weeks came and went without a decision. We'd reach out to Brandon and ask him the status of the show, and he'd remind us a final decision only happens after all the story elements have been evaluated. Brandon also let us know that Josh and his team were working on other episodes at that time, some of which took them to different parts of the world. Basically, this was not going to happen as fast as we had hoped.

In the interim, Brandon asked for additional information about Fred Brizzi, and most concerning to me, where we believed the photos had been taken. Except for Mike, I had never revealed that information to anyone outside the family. Brandon made it clear the show would not spend money sending a film crew to Brazil unless we provided evidence of our claim. However, if I did reveal the location, I feared the U.S. Marshals would catch wind of it and send a team to arrest my uncles, assuming they were still alive. I felt torn between the loyalty to my family and getting the episode green-lit and the real story finally told.

By this time, John and Clarence would be in their early nineties, and men in my family don't live that long. With both of them smokers, I figured the two had most likely died by now. Brizzi said they had also married and had children, and possibly grandchildren. Did they know who my uncles really were? What secrets would they reveal if I tracked them down? There was only one way I'd ever find out, and that's if I went, which meant telling Brandon everything.

I let him know about the Chevrolet car plant located in San Jose dos Campos that Fred discussed in the tape, which opened in 1958, and about my uncles owning a farm with cattle and crops, and the Paraiba

Original house photo
KEN WIDNER

Present day
MIKE LYNCH

du Sol River photo taken on their property. Of course, I also gave him the 1975 photo showing my uncles and the termite mound. And perhaps most important, I told Brandon about finding the farmhouse where John and Clarence lived using Google Maps. That location? The small mountain town of Monteiro Lobato.

When Brandon saw the evidence we presented and how well it fit with the 1975 photos and Brizzi tape, he felt sure the company's president, Casey Brumels, would finally green-light the episode. Hearing his name came as a surprise to me. Mike and I thought that Plumbline Pictures produced the show. Turns out, they were a subsidiary of Ping Pong Productions. With Casey calling the shots, I feared we might have a problem. The last time I worked with him, Mike had been pushed out. I let Brandon know things would be different this time around. With our book close to being finished, we were no longer dependent on a TV show to tell my uncles' story. If they dropped Mike again, I would be out as well. Fearing this could jeopardize the deal he had orchestrated, Brandon quickly agreed Mike would stay on the team. He must have made a convincing argument to Casey, who also agreed to my terms.

After a bit of back-and-forth the next couple of months, Ping Pong finally signed off on the Alcatraz-themed episode in January 2022. Contingent on that agreement was hiring a Brazilian investigator and having him check out the places we indicated and do some additional searching for us. This helped us pinpoint promising locations for the shoot and identify people and places with connections to my uncles. They had also brought a retired FBI agent, Stewart Fillmore, onto the team, who had worked with Josh before on an episode about John Dillinger, the notorious gangster from the 1930s. Having been involved in hundreds of criminal investigations, which included fraud, bank robbery, kidnapping, money laundering, and terrorism, Stewart's presence on the show gave our episode a bit more credibility in the audience's eyes.

Filming began on March 3, 2022.

When Mike and I finally met, we seemed to click right away. We also shared our hopes of finding proof my uncles made it to Brazil, though that was largely dependent on Josh and the team.

First stop, Alcatraz. Josh met with Stewart, the "Alcatraz expert," who introduced the Anglin brothers to the audience, along with the prison and important information about the escape. At 3:00 a.m. everyone got up and made their way to a boat waiting for us at the dock. With Alcatraz opening for tourists at 9:30 a.m., the crew had six hours to film, and we'd need every second of it.

The transport boat
MIKE LYNCH

Arriving in the early morning
MIKE LYNCH

John's cell
MIKE LYNCH

Clarence's cell
MIKE LYNCH

The cameramen filmed Josh arriving at the island and meeting with Stewart. After a brief chat, they went to the cellblock and discussed the escape at John's and Clarence's cells. We were actually standing at the spot where this amazing story began.

Stewart told Josh how the brothers, Frank Morris, and Allen West meticulously planned and executed the escape, and all right under the guards' noses. Even after hearing the story countless times in my life, I still cannot help but be impressed by what these men did. It is truly a remarkable story.

Over the next several hours, Josh and the camera crew filmed in front of the cells, in the cells, on top of the cellblock, in the utility corridor behind the cells, outside the cellblock, and along the escape route used by the three, as well as getting shots of seagulls and the bay.

In a quiet moment between filming, Mike and I slipped away and went into the exercise yard. This was my chance to sit where my uncles sat and imagine what their time at Alcatraz must have been like all those years ago.

In the same exercise yard as John, Clarence, Frank, and Whitey
KEN WIDNER

At 9:30 a.m., the crew broke down their equipment and hurried to the pier just as the first tourist boat arrived. Mike and I wondered how the two hundred or so tourists would have reacted if they knew our

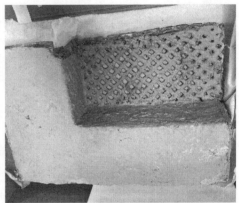

The actual paints, files, paintbrush, and false grille used in the escape
MIKE LYNCH

reason for being there. Of course, with secrecy our primary mandate, we said nothing.

Our next stop was the Park Archives and Records Center in the Presidio of San Francisco. They house a large collection of evidence, photos, and documents related to the Alcatraz escape, which highlights the escapee's resourcefulness, not to mention their drive for freedom.

Josh and Stewart were duly impressed by the ingenuity manifested by the three. For six months, they toiled at night in total silence for a chance to be free again. Josh recognized it would've been out of character for them to methodically plan the escape, only to put their raft in the water and then ask themselves, "Now what do we do?" More likely, they had thought through that part of the plan as well.

The two met Mike and me on camera the next day at a pier across from Alcatraz Island. This is where we made our formal introduction on the show and shared with him our belief that Los Angeles mobster Mickey Cohen had procured a boat for the three, which picked them up after they were towed into the bay by a prison transport. The only question was, could we replicate that?

A raft about the same size used in the escape had been acquired, along with a boat to pull it. Donning wetsuits needed to keep us "escapees" warm in the cold bay waters, we intended to prove John, Clarence, and Frank could indeed have been pulled to freedom rather than paddling their way to Angel Island as West had claimed.

Getting into the bay
MIKE LYNCH

Josh, Stewart, and I prove the escapees could have made it.
MIKE LYNCH

São Paulo
MIKE LYNCH

Under the watchful eye of tourists at Alcatraz, Josh, Stewart, and I slipped the raft into the water and held on for the ride of our lives. As the boat pulled us, we navigated one swell after another, the cold misty water splashing us in the face again and again. Mike stayed on the boat with the crew and commented on what he saw to the cameras, declaring at one point, "If they could survive waves this bad, the three certainly could've made it in much calmer waters."

In the end, we all agreed the theory posited by Mike and myself necessitated additional investigation. Josh had been shown the meticulous planning that went into the escape, how Mickey Cohen assisted them, and the evidence from Fred Brizzi that showed the brothers in Brazil, and the only way of proving our claim was going to South America and continuing the investigation there.

After fifteen hours in the air, the team arrived at São Paulo, Brazil, on March 7. There to meet us was Caio Vilela, the private investigator hired by Ping Pong Productions, who acted as host and guide for us during our stay.

He helped secure a Land Rover for himself, Josh, me, and Mike, and two vans for the film crew. Once these were loaded, we headed north and arrived at our first destination, the city of San Jose dos Campos, about an hour and a half from São Paulo. Based on my research, I believe the 1975 photo of John and Clarence had been taken on their farm in that area.

A field filled with termite mounds
KEN WIDNER

After years of waiting, I finally arrived at Monteiro Lobato.
MIKE LYNCH

Getting out of the rain
MIKE LYNCH

After a bit of searching, we located a field with hundreds of termite mounds stretching into the distance. All of us agreed how closely the photo resembled that location and filmed a scene there.

After we finished our shoot in the valley, we headed for the town of Monteiro Lobato. Since it was still early, the crew did a bit of shooting around town and asked some of the locals if they remembered any Americans living there years before. To a person, no one did.

As I walked around the town, I couldn't help but feel close to my uncles. Were these the same streets they had walked? Might there be family members living there now, long lost cousins who lay just within reach?

Caio told us about a man he met during a scouting trip who had lived there his whole life. He shared with us an amazing story about three Americans hiding out on top of a nearby mountain in 1970 when he was ten years old. The local sheriff investigated and agreed to let them stay, and even brought them food and supplies a couple of times a week. Then one day, the three Americans were gone, and as far as the townspeople knew never returned.

The next day, we all drove up a winding road cut through the jungle. If my uncles wanted to disappear, they chose the perfect spot. When the road ended, we packed up our things and trudged up the mile-long climb. The path was steep, and many of us struggled. To make matters

Our view from the top
KEN WIDNER

The lighter

worse, a huge downpour hit us near the top. The crew scrambled to cover their equipment lest it get ruined. For us, we'd be wearing wet clothes for the rest of the day.

The camera operators filmed a quick scene that highlighted the remoteness of the location as an ideal hiding spot. Josh then broke out the metal detectors the crew had brought. He reasoned if three Americans stayed here for two months, there'd be proof. It didn't take long for me to get a hit. After a bit of digging, Josh unearthed a broken cigarette lighter.

We looked some more but didn't find the top or the igniter, but more important to me was the fact that Clarence had been a smoker all his life. Without any markings, however, we'd have no way of tying it directly to him, though the artifact certainly did point in his direction.

Not long after that, Josh found a small-caliber bullet shell. The bottom read "CBC 380 Auto." A check of that brand revealed this to

Bullet shell

What was a 1951 Lincoln penny doing up there?

be an American company. Like the lighter, we had no way of knowing if it belonged to the three, but it also pointed in their direction. With them being escaped fugitives, it made sense they'd have handguns for protection.

Our last find proved the most compelling—a 1951 Lincoln penny. Our hearts leaped at the sight of it. What was a U.S. coin from the 1950s doing all the way up there? The only possible answer: Americans had been living at that spot sometime in the past.

Celebrating the end of the shoot
KEN WIDNER

The fact that all the found items were buried eight inches deep let us know they had been in the ground for some time, again pointing to the Americans who hid there in 1970.

Unfortunately, the sky was growing dark, so we stopped our search. Everyone donned their headlamps and we headed back down the mountain.

The crew filmed additional shots of us around Monteiro Lobato, but none that revealed anything further about the escapees.

We headed back to São Paulo and finished the shoot at a bar in the downtown area. For Josh, this was his chance to enjoy himself as he danced and mingled with fans after we wrapped.

The crew packed up their equipment, pulled Josh from the crowd, and raced to the airport. Everyone was tired and ready to return home, but all were satisfied we had done a good job.

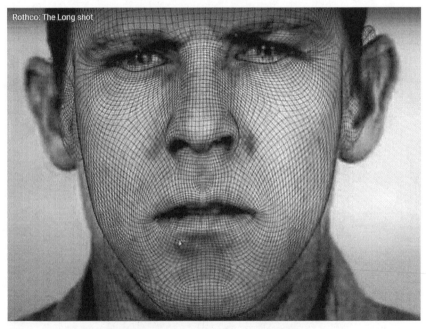

Rothco: The Long shot

Digitized copy of John's face used for analysis
IDENTV

Four months later, the show finally aired. Mike and I couldn't have been happier with the way it turned out. The production team did an excellent job putting the episode together. But what I saw at the end gave me chills. On the show, Stewart had been tasked with having the 1975 photograph of my uncles examined by facial recognition experts. Could we prove these men were indeed John and Clarence? In a Zoom call with Josh, Stewart told him about a company called IDenTV that specializes in facial analysis through the use of automatic content recognition (ACR). Rather than give the results himself, Stewart brought on one of the team members, who could better explain how their process works.

> We . . . feed the algorithm many images of a single person's face along with many images of different people. We repeat this process millions of times and use mathematical models optimized during the training phase to learn how to differentiate one person's face from another.
>
> Once we have a model trained, it provides us with the ability to generate a mathematical fingerprint describing in detail the visual aspects of somebody's face. . . . We can then compare this facial fingerprint to other fingerprints we have in a database to generate a match, similar to how today's police fingerprint matching system works.[1]

At the completion of their analysis, IDenTV determined with 99.7 percent accuracy that the man on the right was indeed John, Clarence on the left about 99 percent. This result is more than amazing. It pretty much closes the case on the escape. For those who have made the accusation that Fred lied about the men in the photo, or that he staged it with other people, the odds of still getting a 99+ percent match for two people is beyond astronomical. And when you consider IDenTV also did a comparison with a thousand random photos from that era and had still gotten a 99 percent match, zero doubt remains. John and Clarence are the two men in the photo.[2]

If you combine this result with the Lincoln penny and lighter found on the mountain near Monteiro Lobato; the handwriting match between letters brothers sent from prison and the Christmas cards the family received after the escape; Fred Brizzi saying he met the brothers in Brazil in 1975; Helen claiming she talked to John on the phone after the escape; Alfred telling his sister, parents, brother, and cellmate John and Clarence were alive and well at an undisclosed location; and Robert's deathbed confession about visiting his brothers over a twenty-five year period, you can only draw one conclusion based on the evidence presented in this book—John, Clarence, and Frank successfully escaped from Alcatraz and eventually arrived in Brazil for what turned out to be their last escape, where they lived for the rest of their lives.

As a last thought, I had hoped to send my mother's DNA to Brazil and see if there's a match in the government database, but their law says testing non-Brazilian citizens is illegal, so there's nothing I can do about that until federal legislators make the necessary changes. However, even without her DNA, I am firmly convinced the vow I made back in 2012 about my uncles is fulfilled, and I can state with complete certainty: John and Clarence Anglin have been found.

Next step, find their families.

POSTSCRIPT

The following recounts what happened with the key people involved in this amazing story.

Jeanette Anglin—The wife of Alfred Anglin. Jeanette was with him when he was arrested in Ohio in January 1958 after the bank robbery. Six years later, she attended his funeral. Jeanette would later tell stories about John calling her, maybe as a way to say he was sorry. She died in 2016. And though she had remarried, Jeanette was always considered a part of the Anglin family.

Candy Barr—After her release from Goree State Farm for women in April 1963, Juanita Dale Slusher (aka Candy Barr) returned to her home-town of Edna, Texas. She became close friends with Dallas nightclub owner Jack Ruby, who killed Lee Harvey Oswald three days after the Kennedy assassination. In 1966, Candy returned to the stripping circuit. She was charged again in 1969 for marijuana possession in Brownwood, Texas, though the case was dismissed for lack of evidence. In 1992, Candy moved from Brownwood back to Edna. Living in quiet retirement with her animals, Candy died from complications from pneumonia in December 2005 at the age of seventy.

Warden Olin Blackwell—At age forty-six, the easygoing Texan became the youngest person to assume a warden position in the federal prison system. While at Alcatraz, many inmates picked up knitting and crocheting, creating colorful pieces that decorated Blackwell's house and office. Considered to have been the least strict warden at Alcatraz, perhaps in part due to him having been a heavy drinker and smoker, he relaxed many of the rules and gave inmates additional privileges.

Blackwell served from 1961 until the prison closed on March 21, 1963. He died on March 7, 1986, in Hart County, Georgia.

Fred Brizzi—Fred continued flying drugs from South and Central America into the United States for many years after the escape. He was caught and sent to prison multiple times during this period. Fred died on April 28, 1998, in Belize and is buried in Salt Lake City, Utah.

James "Whitey" Bulger—After Alcatraz closed in 1963, Whitey was transferred to Leavenworth, then Atlanta. He was paroled in 1965. Whitey started up his criminal activities once again in Boston, which involved extortion, drug trafficking, and murder over the next thirty years. The FBI was poised to arrest him in December 1994, but he was tipped off and became a fugitive. On the run for the next sixteen years, Bulger was finally captured in Santa Monica, California, in June 2011. He was eighty-one-years old at the time. He was convicted of multiple counts of murder and eventually ended up at United States Penitentiary, Hazelton, in West Virginia, where Whitey was found beaten to death in his wheelchair on October 20, 2018.

Mickey Cohen—When Alcatraz closed in March 1963, Mickey was sent to Leavenworth, then Atlanta Federal Penitentiary. There, he was badly injured when inmate Burl McDonald tried to kill him with a lead pipe. This left Cohen permanently disabled. He was released in 1972 and toured the country speaking out against prison abuse. Cohen died of stomach cancer in July 1976. He is interred in the Hillside Memorial Park Cemetery in Culver City, California.

Charles H. German Jr. (aka Herman the German)—He resigned in December 1963 and moved to Carson City, Nevada, with his wife. He later donated his guard's hat and watch to the Presidio Park Archives and Records Center.

Bumpy Johnson—Johnson was paroled from Alcatraz in 1963. In December 1965, he staged a sit-down strike in a police station as a protest against their continued surveillance. He was charged with "refusal to leave a police station" but later acquitted by a judge. Johnson died of congestive heart failure in July 1968 at the age of sixty-two. He is buried in Woodlawn Cemetery in New York City.

Robert Schibline—Sent to Alcatraz in 1958 for bank robbery, Schibline was released from prison in 1965. He married three times and had three daughters. He later opened a successful scuba-diving business. Schibline died in 2021 at the age of eighty-nine.

Helen Taylor—John Anglin called her his queen. The primary motivation for his escapes was his love for Helen and his hope of being reunited with her. The photo she sent him while he was at Alcatraz would aid in his escape as he painted her portrait in his cell, which provided him with the means to paint the dummy heads and false vent covers. Helen would marry again, but John still held a special place in her heart. She died in 2010 but regularly kept in touch with the Anglin family.

Allen West—West was transferred from Alcatraz in February 1963 to McNeil Island, Washington. Over the next four years, he served time in Georgia and Florida and then was released. In 1969, West was given life imprisonment at Florida State Prison for multiple crimes, then in October 1972 he fatally stabbed an inmate over what may have been a racially motivated incident. West died of acute peritonitis in December 1978 at the age of forty-nine.

Marie Widner—The official pack rat of the Anglin family, Marie was the one who preserved the letters, photos, tape recordings, and other items related to John and Clarence used in this book. In 1992, Fred Brizzi entrusted to her the last known photo of the brothers, taken at their Brazil farm in 1975. She has been the voice for John and Clarence Anglin for the last fifty years, which she has passed on to her two sons. Marie is now eighty-eight years old and still holds out hope that one day she will get to meet John and Clarence's children and grandchildren.

Notes

Chapter 1

1. Conor Dever, "This Little Piece of Alcatraz History Was Recently Sold in an Antique Shop in Dublin," *Dublin Journal*, December, 25, 2017, https://www.thejournal.ie/alcatraz-notebook-francis-street-antiques-3752376-Dec2017/.

2. "The Great Escape from Alcatraz," Alcatraz History, 2020, https://www.alcatrazhistory.com/alcesc2.htm.

3. "Alcatraz Escape, Part 7 of 17," FBI Records: The Vault, June 15, 1962, p. 43, https://vault.fbi.gov/Alcatraz%20Escape/Alcatraz%20Escape%20Part%207%20of%2017/view.

4. "Out of Alcatraz—by a Spoon," *San Francisco Chronicle*, June 13, 1962, 9.

5. Eric Braun, *Escape from Alcatraz: The Mystery of the Three Men Who Escaped from the Rock* (North Mankato, MN: Capstone, 2017), 69.

6. "June 1962 Alcatraz Escape Attempt," Wikipedia, https://en.wikipedia.org/wiki/June_1962_Alcatraz_escape_attempt.

7. Ibid.

8. Noyes, "I-Team Exclusive: New Leads in Manhunt for Alcatraz Escapees."

9. "Alcatraz Escape, Part 5 of 17," FBI Records: The Vault, June 22, 1962, p. 44, https://vault.fbi.gov/Alcatraz%20Escape/Alcatraz%20Escape%20Part%205%20of%2017.

Chapter 2

1. Morison Buck, "John Rutland Himes: The Man, the Judge," January 2000, Morison Buck Biographies of Hillsborough County Judges.

Chapter 3

1. "The Seminole Wars," Seminole Nation Museum, 2012, https://seminolenationmuseum.org/history-seminole-nation-the-seminole-wars/.

2. Hillsborough County Planning & Growth Management, "Ruskin," Hillsborough County Historic Resources Survey Report, October 1998, http://www.hillsborough.wateratlas.usf.edu/upload/documents/HILLSBOROUGH_COUNTY_Historic_Resources_Excerpts_Ruskin.pdf.

3. "Ruskin, Florida," Wikipedia, https://en.wikipedia.org/wiki/Ruskin,_Florida.

4. Ibid.

5. "Historic Ruskin Tomato Plant Replaced by Modern Industry in Apollo Beach," *Osprey Observer*, September 13, 2019, https://www.ospreyobserver.com/2019/09/historic-ruskin-tomato-plant-replaced-by-modern-industry-in-apollo-beach/.

6. Kathryn Moschella, "Dickman Family, Ruskin Pioneers, Honored at Annual Chamber Dinner," *Tampa Daily Times*, February 5, 2014, https://www.tampabay.com/news/business/dickman-family-ruskin-pioneers-honored-at-annual-chamber-dinner/2164285/.

CHAPTER 4

1. "Conchas Dam," Wikipedia, https://en.wikipedia.org/wiki/Conchas_Dam.
2. "A Guide to Safety," *Conchas Indian*, February 1939, 10, 16, 18–19.

CHAPTER 5

1. Howard Kahn, "Breach of Probation Gets Boys Two Years," *Tampa Daily Times*, June 6, 1947, 2.
2. Ibid.

CHAPTER 6

1. "Alcatraz Escape, Part 2 of 17," FBI Records: The Vault, June 19, 1962, pp. 46–50, https://vault.fbi.gov/Alcatraz%20Escape/Alcatraz%20Escape%20Part%202%20of%2017/view.
2. "Union Correctional Institution," Wikipedia, https://en.wikipedia.org/wiki/Union_Correctional_Institution.
3. P. Marlin, "Florida State Prison Cemetery in Raiford," *Past Prologue*, January 2019, https://dmarlin.com/pastprologue/blog/florida-state-prison-cemetery/.
4. "Two More State Fugitives Caught," *Tallahassee Democrat*, May 11, 1952, 3.
5. "Two Convicts Are Sentenced," *Tallahassee Democrat*, June 10, 1952, 2.
6. "Limestone," Wikipedia, https://en.wikipedia.org/wiki/Limestone.
7. Frank Ahearn, "How to Disappear . . . Alcatraz Style," OpEdNews.com, September 28, 2007, https://www.opednews.com/articles/life_a_frank_ah_070926_how_to_disappear____.htm.
8. "Alcatraz Escape, Part 13 of 17," FBI Records: The Vault, February 28, 1964, p. 47, https://vault.fbi.gov/Alcatraz%20Escape/Alcatraz%20Escape%20Part%2013%20of%2017/view.

CHAPTER 7

1. James Quinn, "Chuck Landis, Veteran Concert Promoter, Dies at Home at 68," *Los Angeles Times*, March 10, 1986.
2. "Mickey Cohen," Wikipedia, https://en.wikipedia.org/wiki/Mickey_Cohen.
3. "Candy Barr," Wikipedia, https://en.wikipedia.org/wiki/Candy_Barr.
4. Ibid.

CHAPTER 9

1. "McClellan Committee Hearings," Encyclopedia.com, 2019, https://www .encyclopedia.com/history/dictionaries-thesauruses-pictures-and-press-releases/ mcclellan-committee-hearings.

CHAPTER 10

1. Dale Cox, dir., *Alcatraz: Escape to the Wiregrass*, pt. 1, Two Egg TV, 2020, https:// www.youtube.com/watch?v=v4lNtWPvkPc&t=2s.
2. Ibid.
3. Ibid.
4. "Three from Here Arrested for Alabama Bank Robbery," *Tampa Morning Tribune*, January 23, 1958, 5.
5. "6 Held in Columbia Holdup," *Montgomery Advertiser*, January 23, 1958, 1.
6. "3 Hillsborough Brothers Held in Bank Robbery to Stand Trial in Ohio," *Tampa Sunday Tribune*, January 26, 1958, 8.

CHAPTER 11

1. "Tampan, Ruskin Man to Stand Trial in Ohio," *Tampa Daily Times*, January 25, 1958, 2.
2. Jack Bass, "Frank M. Johnson Jr.," *Encyclopedia of Alabama*, http:// encyclopediaofalabama.org/article/h-1253.
3. District Court of the United States for the Middle Division of Alabama Northern Division, formal charges and trial transcript, February 10, 1958.
4. "Anglin Boys Face Second Robbery Trial," *Tampa Daily Times*, March 14, 1958.
5. "Anglins Plead Twin Jeopardy," *Huntsville Times*, March 11, 1958, 7.

CHAPTER 12

1. "United States Penitentiary, Leavenworth," Wikipedia, https://en.wikipedia.org/ wiki/United_States_Penitentiary,_Leavenworth.
2. Pete Early, *The Hot House: Life inside Leavenworth Prison* (New York: Bantam Books, 1993), 4–5.
3. "Prison Documentary—Leavenworth Penitentiary," YouTube.com, October 22, 2017, https://www.youtube.com/watch?v=0f8KYTyxDCU.
4. Kenneth LaMaster, in "U.S. Penitentiary Leavenworth," C-Span broadcast, August 5, 2010, https://www.c-span.org/video/?294929-1/us-penitentiary-leavenworth.
5. "United States Penitentiary, Leavenworth," Wikipedia.
6. Tim Rives and Steve Spence, "Searching Inmate Case Files from the U.S. Penitentiary at Leavenworth, Kansas," *Prologue* 42, no. 2 (Summer 2010), https://www.archives .gov/publications/prologue/2010/summer/leavenworth.html.
7. Scott Paddor, dir., "The Big House," Greystone Communications, 1998, https://www .youtube.com/watch?v=rglDnWdcVF0.
8. "Anglin Tried Leavenworth Escape," *Ottawa Herald*, June 12, 1962, 1.

Chapter 13

1. J. Campbell Bruce, *Escape from Alcatraz: The True Crime Classic* (Emeryville, CA: Ten Speed Press, 2005), 149–53.
2. "Who Was Frank Morris? He Escaped Alcatraz," Ghosts of DC, September 10, 2012, https://ghostsofdc.org/2012/09/10/frank-morris-alcatraz-escape/.
3. Bruce, *Escape from Alcatraz*, 148–49.
4. John M. Cunningham, "Whitey Bulger, American Crime Boss," *Britannica*, August 26, 2020, https://www.britannica.com/biography/Whitey-Bulger.
5. "James 'Whitey' Bulger," Alcatraz History, 2021, https://www.alcatrazhistory.com/bulger.htm.
6. Bruce, *Escape from Alcatraz*, 148.

Chapter 14

1. "Alcatraz Federal Penitentiary," Wikipedia, https://en.wikipedia.org/wiki/Alcatraz_Federal_Penitentiary.
2. "Olin G. Blackwell," Wikipedia, https://en.wikipedia.org/wiki/Olin_G._Blackwell.
3. "Alcatraz Escape, Part 5 of 17," FBI Records: The Vault, June 15, 1962, 71.

Chapter 15

1. "Daily Routine," Alcatraz History, 2021, https://www.alcatrazhistory.com/rock/rock-030.htm.
2. "Minimum Privileges," Alcatraz 101, 2021, http://www.alcatraz101.com/Page9.html.
3. "Alcatraz Federal Penitentiary," Wikipedia.
4. "Alcatraz—Quick Facts," Alcatraz History, 2021, https://www.alcatrazhistory.com/factsnfig.htm.
5. green papaya, "Alcatraz Federal Penitentiary Mess Hall," forum post, Fedora Lounge, August 22, 2017, https://www.thefedoralounge.com/threads/alcatraz-federal-penitentiary-mess-hall-typical-foods-served.91279/.

Chapter 16

1. Ahearn, "How to Disappear."

Chapter 17

1. "Alcatraz Escape, Part 4 of 17," FBI Records: The Vault, June 14, 1962, p. 117, https://vault.fbi.gov/Alcatraz%20Escape/Alcatraz%20Escape%20Part%204%20of%2017/view.
2. "June 1962 Alcatraz Escape Attempt," Wikipedia.
3. "Mickey Cohen," Wikipedia.
4. "Mickey Cohen," Mob Museum, 2021, https://themobmuseum.org/notable_names/mickey-cohen/.

5. "Mickey Cohen FBI Files," Internet Archive, 2014, https://archive.org/stream/MickeyCohen/Cohen%2C%20Meyer%20Harris%2092-HQ-3156%20Part%201%20of%202_djvu.txt.
6. Tere Tereba, "TV Viewers Witnessed Verbal Sparing between Mickey Cohen and Bobby Kennedy," Mob Museum, March 10, 2015, https://themobmuseum.org/blog/tv-viewers-witnessed-verbal-sparring-between-mickey-cohen-and-bobby-kennedy/.
7. Ibid.
8. "Candy Barr," Wikipedia.
9. Paul J. Madigan, "Institution Rules and Regulations," United States Penitentiary, Alcatraz, 1955, 11–12.

CHAPTER 18
1. "Bumpy Johnson," Wikipedia, https://en.wikipedia.org/wiki/Bumpy_Johnson.
2. "Alcatraz Escape, Part 7 of 17," FBI Records: The Vault, June 20, 1962, p. 50.
3. "Earl Warren," Wikipedia, https://en.wikipedia.org/wiki/Earl_Warren.
4. "Alcatraz Escape, Part 7 of 17," FBI Records: The Vault, June 14, 1962, p. 39.
5. "Alcatraz Escape, Part 4 of 17," FBI Records: The Vault, June 14, 1962, p. 119.
6. "Alcatraz Escape, Part 7 of 17," FBI Records: The Vault, June 14, 1962, p. 35.

CHAPTER 19
1. "What Is a Shakedown in Prison?," Quora, https://www.quora.com/What-is-a-shakedown-in-prison.
2. Mr. Lake, "Breaking Rock," *Reflecting through Echoes* blog, https://reflectingthroughechoes.wordpress.com/2011/02/24/breaking-rock/.
3. "Alcatraz Escape, Part 7 of 17," FBI Records: The Vault, June 13, 1962, p. 36.

CHAPTER 20
1. "Alcatraz Escape, Part 7 of 17," FBI Records: The Vault, June 14, 1962, p. 35.
2. "Alcatraz Escape, Part 8 of 17," FBI Records: The Vault, August 8, 1962, p. 91, https://vault.fbi.gov/Alcatraz%20Escape/Alcatraz%20Escape%20Part%208%20of%2017.
3. "New Industries Building," Wikipedia, https://en.wikipedia.org/wiki/New_Industries_Building.
4. "Alcatraz Escape, Part 4 of 17," FBI Records: The Vault, June 14, 1962, p. 120.
5. "Don Eberle Oral History," Presidio Park Archives and Records Center, San Francisco, GOGA 18788, April 29, 1980.
6. "The Great Escape from Alcatraz," Alcatraz History, https://www.alcatrazhistory.com/alcesc2.htm.
7. "Alcatraz Escape, Part 4 of 17," FBI Records: The Vault, June 13, 1962, p. 120.
8. Ibid., p. 121.
9. "Alcatraz Escape, Part 7 of 17," FBI Records: The Vault, June 20, 1962, p. 49.

CHAPTER 21

1. *Meyer Harris Cohen, aka Michael "Mickey" Cohen, Appellant, v. United States of America, Appellee*, 297 F.2d 760 (9th Cir. 1962), p. 1, https://law.justia.com/cases/federal/appellate-courts/F2/297/760/457217/.

2. Ibid.

3. "Alcatraz Escape, Part 5 of 17," FBI Records: The Vault, June 16, 1962, p. 109, https://vault.fbi.gov/Alcatraz%20Escape/Alcatraz%20Escape%20Part%205%20of%2017.

4. Ahearn, "How to Disappear."

5. Ibid.

6. "Alcatraz Escape, Part 13 of 17," FBI Records: The Vault, February 28, 1964, p. 46.

7. "Alcatraz Escape, Part 3 of 17," FBI Records: The Vault, June 21, 1962, pp. 49–50, https://vault.fbi.gov/Alcatraz%20Escape/Alcatraz%20Escape%20Part%203%20of%2017.

8. "Alcatraz Escape, Part 13 of 17," FBI Records: The Vault, February 28, 1964, p. 46.

CHAPTER 22

1. Paul Catala, "Memories of the Rock," *Lakeland Ledger*, June 4, 2019, https://www.theledger.com/news/20190604/florida-man-shared-cellblock-with-famed-alcatraz-escapees.

2. Sheryl McCullom, "'I Told Them You're Gonna Die!': Alcatraz Inmate 1355 Describes the Infamous Prison Escape, Life behind Bars," Crime Online, December 24, 2019, https://www.crimeonline.com/2019/12/24/i-told-them-youre-gonna-die-alcatraz-inmate-1355-describes-the-infamous-prison-escape-life-behind-bars-exclusive/.

3. Ibid.

4. "Alcatraz Escape, Part 7 of 17," FBI Records: The Vault, June 18, 1962, p. 79.

5. "Alcatraz Escape, Part 7 of 17," FBI Records: The Vault, June 14, 1962, p. 42.

6. Ibid., pp. 42–43.

7. Ibid., p. 43.

8. "Alcatraz Escape, Part 7 of 17," FBI Records: The Vault, June 18, 1962, p. 93.

9. Catala, "Memories of the Rock."

10. "Alcatraz Escape, Part 7 of 17," FBI Records: The Vault, June 20, 1962, p. 49.

11. "Alcatraz Escape, Part 7 of 17," FBI Records: The Vault, June 14, 1962, pp. 43–44.

12. Noyes, "I-Team Exclusive: New Leads in Manhunt for Alcatraz Escapees."

13. "Mystery Craft, List of Names Probed by FBI." *Oakland Tribune*, 17 June 1962.

14. Noyes, "I-Team Exclusive: New Leads in Manhunt for Alcatraz Escapees."

15. "Alcatraz Escape, Part 12 of 17," FBI Records: The Vault, July 8, 1963, p. 77, https://vault.fbi.gov/Alcatraz%20Escape/Alcatraz%20Escape%20Part%2012%20of%2017.

CHAPTER 23

1. Michael Esslinger, "Anglin Brothers Escape from Alcatraz Prison," Alcatraz Cruises, October 10, 2022, 2018, https://www.alcatrazcruises.com/blog/2018/06/08/anglin-brothers-escape/.

2. "Alcatraz Escape, Part 6 of 17," FBI Records: The Vault, June 19, 1962, p. 115, https: //vault.fbi.gov/Alcatraz%20Escape/Alcatraz%20Escape%20Part%206%20of%2017.
3. Susan Sloate, *Mysteries Unwrapped: The Secrets of Alcatraz* (New York: Sterling, 2008), 54.
4. Ibid.
5. "Escapes from Alcatraz," SFgeneology, 2021, https://www.sfgenealogy.org/sf/history /sfoealcd.htm#n121.
6. "Alcatraz Escape, Part 1 of 17," FBI Records: The Vault, June 12, 1962, p. 32, https:// vault.fbi.gov/Alcatraz%20Escape/Alcatraz%20Escape%20Part%201%20of%2017.
7. "Alcatraz Escape, Part 5 of 17," FBI Records: The Vault, June 22, 1962, p. 44.
8. Ibid., pp. 44–45.
9. Allan Stein, "NC Man Recalls His Days Guarding Alcatraz Prisoners," *Nevada City (California) Union*, October 15, 1998.
10. "Alcatraz Escape, Part 3 of 17," FBI Records: The Vault, June 22, 1962, p. 76.
11. 11."Alcatraz Escape, Part 8 of 17," FBI Records: The Vault, August 8, 1962, p. 88.
12 "Alcatraz Escape, Part 5 of 17," FBI Records: The Vault, June 22, 1962, pp. 44–45.
13. "Alcatraz Escape, Part 7 of 17," FBI Records: The Vault, June 18, 1962, pp. 27–31.

CHAPTER 24
1. "Alcatraz Escape, Part 12 of 17," FBI Records: The Vault, June 13, 1962, pp. 113–14.
2. McCullom, "'I Told Them You're Gonna Die!'"
3. The entire song can be heard on YouTube: "Sonny James—A Mile and a Quarter," https://www.youtube.com/watch?v=NJcRSn9yVoI.
4. "Alcatraz Escape, Part 11 of 17," FBI Records: The Vault, April 23, 1963, pp. 103–7, https://vault.fbi.gov/Alcatraz%20Escape/Alcatraz%20Escape%20Part%2011%20of %2017.
5. "Alcatraz Escape, Part 11 of 17," FBI Records: The Vault, November 23, 1962, p. 79.
6. "Alcatraz Escape, Part 13 of 17," FBI Records: The Vault, February 28, 1964, p. 46.
7. Ibid.

CHAPTER 25
1. "The Rock: Prison Closure," Federal Bureau of Prisons Historical Information, https: //www.bop.gov/about/history/alcatraz.jsp.
2. "American Civil Liberties Union," Wikipedia, https://en.wikipedia.org/wiki/ American_Civil_Liberties_Union.
3. "*Abbate v. United States*," Wikipedia, https://en.wikipedia.org/wiki/Abbate_v. _United_States.
4. "Mickey Cohen at Alcatraz," Alcatraz History, 2020, https://www.alcatrazhistory .com/cohen-3.htm.
5. Joe Holley, "Know Juanita Slusher? No? Think Candy Barr," *Houston Chronicle*, August 2, 2014, https://www.houstonchronicle.com/news/columnists/native-texan/ article/Know-Juanita-Slusher-No-Think-Candy-Barr-5664914.php.
6. "Alcatraz Escape, Part 13 of 17," FBI Records: The Vault, January 31, 1964, p. 25.

7. "Alcatraz Escape, Part 13 of 17," FBI Records: The Vault, March 31, 1964, p. 37.

8. "Alcatraz Escape, Part 13 of 17," FBI Records: The Vault, January 31, 1964, p. 26.

9. Ibid., p. 27.

CHAPTER 26

1. "James 'Whitey' Bulger Was No Ordinary Criminal," City Experiences, 2021. https://www.cityexperiences.com/blog/james-whitey-bulger-was-no-ordinary-criminal/.

2. "Alcatraz Escape, Part 13 of 17," FBI Records: The Vault, February 28, 1964, p. 46.

3. "Alcatraz Escape, Part 15 of 17," FBI Records: The Vault, January 19, 1979, p. 78, https://vault.fbi.gov/Alcatraz%20Escape/Alcatraz%20Escape%20Part%2015%20of%2017.

4. "Brazil," Wikipedia, https://en.wikipedia.org/wiki/Brazil.

5. "Alcatraz Escape, Part 13 of 17," FBI Records: The Vault, January 20, 1965, p. 77.

6. "Alcatraz Escape, Part 15 of 17," FBI Records: The Vault, January 10, 1980, p. 87.

CHAPTER 27

1. "Alcatraz Escape, Part 13 of 17," FBI Records: The Vault, February 28, 1964, p. 46.

2. "Alcatraz Escape, Part 1 of 17," FBI Records: The Vault, June 21, 1962, pp. 57, 61.

3. Ahearn, "How to Disappear."

CHAPTER 29

1. "Rothco and IDenTV Collaborate to Solve 57-Year-Old Alcatraz Mystery with Cutting-Edge AI," *Creative News*, January 20, 2020, https://www.lbbonline.com/news/rothco-and-identv-collaborate-to-solve-57-year-old-alcatraz-mystery-with-cutting-edge-ai.

2. See the results of their analysis on a short YouTube video at https://www.youtube.com/watch?v=Eg3mi79INO8.